PENGUIN CLASS[ICS]
THE THREE THEBA[N PLAYS]
ANTIGONE, OEDIPUS [THE KING]
OEDIPUS AT COL[ONUS]

SOPHOCLES was born at Colonus, just outside Athens, in 496 B.C. and lived ninety years. His long life spanned the rise and decline of the Athenian Empire, he was a friend of Pericles, and though not an active politician, he held several public offices, both military and civil. The leader of a literary circle and friend of Herodotus, Sophocles was interested in poetic theory as well as practice, and he wrote a prose treatise, *On the Chorus*. He seems to have been content to spend all his life at Athens and is said to have refused several invitations to royal courts. Sophocles first won a prize for tragic drama in 468, defeating the veteran Aeschylus. He wrote over a hundred plays for the Athenian theater and is said to have won the first prize at the City Dionysia eighteen times. Only seven of his tragedies are now extant. Fragments of other plays remain, showing that he drew on a wide range of themes; he also introduced the innovation of a third actor in his tragedies. He died in 406–5 B.C.

ROBERT FAGLES is Arthur W. Marks '19 Professor of Comparative Literature, Emeritus, at Princeton University. He is the recipient of the 1997 PEN/Ralph Manheim Medal for Translation and a 1996 Academy Award in Literature from the American Academy of Arts and Letters. Fagles has been elected to the Academy, the American Academy of Arts and Sciences, and the American Philosophical Society. He has translated the poems of Bacchylides. His translations of Sophocles' *Three Theban Plays*, Aeschylus' *Oresteia* (nominated for a National Book Award), and Homer's *Iliad* (winner of the 1991 Harold Morton Landon Translation Award by The Academy of American Poets, an award from the Translation Center of Columbia University, and the New Jersey Humanities Book Award) are published in Penguin Classics. His original poetry and his translations have appeared in many journals and reviews as well as in his book of poems, *I, Vincent: Poems from the Pictures of Van Gogh*. Mr. Fagles was one of the associate editors of Maynard Mack's Twickenham Edition of Alexander Pope's *Iliad* and *Odyssey*, and, with George Steiner, edited *Homer: A Collection of Critical Essays*. Mr. Fagles' most recent work is a translation of Homer's *Odyssey*, available from Penguin.

BERNARD KNOX is Director Emeritus of Harvard's Center for Hellenic Studies in Washington, D.C. His essays and reviews have appeared in numerous publications and in 1978 he won the George Jean Nathan Award for Dramatic Criticism. His works include *Oedipus at Thebes: Sophocles' Tragic Hero and His Time*; *The Heroic Temper: Studies in Sophoclean Tragedy*; *World and Action: Essays on the Ancient Theatre*; *Essays Ancient and Modern* (awarded the 1989 PEN/Spielvogel-Diamonstein Award); *The Oldest Dead White European Males and Other Reflections on the Classics*; and *Backing into the Future: The Classical Tradition and its Renewal*. He is the editor of *The Norton Book of Classical Literature* and has collaborated with Robert Fagles on the *Iliad* and the *Odyssey*.

SOPHOCLES
THE THREE THEBAN PLAYS

ANTIGONE · OEDIPUS THE KING
OEDIPUS AT COLONUS

TRANSLATED BY
ROBERT FAGLES

INTRODUCTIONS AND
NOTES BY
BERNARD KNOX

PENGUIN BOOKS

PENGUIN BOOKS
Published by the Penguin Group
Penguin Group (USA) Inc., 375 Hudson Street, New York, New York 10014, U.S.A.
Penguin Books Ltd, 80 Strand, London WC2R 0RL, England
Penguin Books Australia Ltd, 250 Camberwell Road, Camberwell, Victoria 3124, Australia
Penguin Books Canada Ltd, 10 Alcorn Avenue, Toronto, Ontario, Canada M4V 3B2
Penguin Books India (P) Ltd, 11 Community Centre, Panchsheel Park, New Delhi – 110 017, India
Penguin Books (N.Z.) Ltd, Cnr Rosedale and Airborne Roads, Albany, Auckland, New Zealand
Penguin Books (South Africa) (Pty) Ltd, 24 Sturdee Avenue,
Rosebank, Johannesburg 2196, South Africa

Penguin Books Ltd, Registered Offices: 80 Strand, London WC2R 0RL, England

First published in the United States of America by
Viking Penguin Inc. 1982
First published in Great Britain by Allen Lane 1982
Published in Penguin Classics 1984
Reprinted with revisions in 1984

40

Copyright © Robert Fagles, 1982, 1984
Introductions and annotations copyright © Bernard Knox, 1982
Oedipus the King copyright © Robert Fagles, 1977, 1979
Oedipus at Colonus copyright © Robert Fagles, 1979, 1980
All rights reserved

ISBN 0 14 044.425 4
Library of Congress Catalog Card
Number 83-13053 (CIP data available)

Printed in the United States of America
Set in Bembo

Portions of this new version of *Oedipus the King* appeared originally in *The Kenyon Review* and *TriQuarterly*. Bernard Knox's Introduction to *Oedipus the King* originally appeared, in abridged form, in *The New Republic*.

These plays in their printed form are designed for the reading public only. All dramatic rights in them are fully protected by copyrights, and no public or private performances—professional or amateur—and no public readings for profit may be given without the written permission of the author and the payment of a royalty. Anyone disregarding the author's rights renders himself liable to prosecution. Communications should be addressed to the author's representative, Georges Borchardt, Inc., 136 East 57th Street, New York, New York 10022, U.S.A.

Except in the United States of America, this book is sold subject to the condition that it shall not, by way of trade or otherwise, be lent, re-sold, hired out, or otherwise circulated without the publisher's prior consent in any form of binding or cover other than that in which it is published and without a similar condition including this condition being imposed on the subsequent purchaser.

FOR KATYA, FOR NINA
tois philois d' orthôs philê

CONTENTS

ACKNOWLEDGMENTS	9
TRANSLATOR'S PREFACE	11
GREECE AND THE THEATER	13

SOPHOCLES: THE THREE THEBAN PLAYS

INTRODUCTION TO ANTIGONE	33
ANTIGONE	55
INTRODUCTION TO OEDIPUS THE KING	129
OEDIPUS THE KING	155
INTRODUCTION TO OEDIPUS AT COLONUS	253
OEDIPUS AT COLONUS	279
A NOTE ON THE TEXT OF SOPHOCLES	389
TEXTUAL VARIANTS	393
NOTES ON THE TRANSLATION	395
ANTIGONE	395
OEDIPUS THE KING	405
OEDIPUS AT COLONUS	414
SELECT BIBLIOGRAPHY	421
THE GENEALOGY OF OEDIPUS	425
GLOSSARY	427

ACKNOWLEDGMENTS

GRATEFUL acknowledgment is made to the following for permission to reprint copyrighted material.

Basic Books, Inc., and George Allen & Unwin: A selection from *The Interpretation of Dreams* by Sigmund Freud, translated and edited by James Strachey. Published in the United States by Basic Books, Inc., by arrangement with George Allen & Unwin and the Hogarth Press, Ltd.

New Directions Publishing Corp. and Faber and Faber Ltd: Two lines from "Ite" from *Personae* by Ezra Pound. Copyright 1926 by Ezra Pound.

University of Chicago Press: A selection from *The Iliad* by Homer, translated with an Introduction by Richmond Lattimore. Copyright 1951 by The University of Chicago.

The illustrations throughout the book were redrawn by Ann Gold from photographs of Mycenaean ornaments and seals from *Crete and Mycenae* by Spyridon Marinatos, published by Harry N. Abrams, Inc., New York, New York. The motif of the crown is from a gold funerary diadem for a woman, discovered in Schliemann's grave circle; the procession is from a gold signet ring from the lower town at Tiryns.

TRANSLATOR'S PREFACE

I HOPE the translation will speak for itself, but not before I say a word of thanks to many people for their help. First among them is Bernard Knox. In addition to writing the introductions and the notes, he determined the Greek text that we have used and tried to hold me closely to its meaning—tried, too, to make my English equal to the task. With countless comments on my work, as the work went through more versions than we can remember, he encouraged me to follow Pound's advice: "Seek ever to stand in the hard Sophoclean light / And take your wounds from it gladly."

Others have helped as well. Robert Fitzgerald spoke for himself and Dudley Fitts and generously left the gates of Thebes ajar. Francis Fergusson shared his conversation and his counsel, as well as a telling stage direction for *Oedipus the King*. Several friends saw my drafts and offered me criticism or assent or a welcome blend of both: Nadia Benabid, Helen Bacon, Sandra Bermann, Toni Burbank, Rebecca Bushnell, Patricia Chappell, Robert Connor, Reginald Gibbons, Michael Goldman, Rachel Hadas, Katherine Hughes, Edmund Keeley, Nita Krevans, Jeffrey Perl, Richard Reid, Susan So, Theodore Weiss, Shira Wolosky and James Zetzel. Mrs. Robert Packer, my administrative aide, and Carol Szymanski lifted many burdens from my shoulders. Princeton University provided the leaves of absence that allowed me to finish the translation and, more important, the seminars in which I studied tragedy with my students.

From the outset, Alan Williams, my editor at The Viking Press, gave me his essential support. Elisabeth Sifton fortified my morale, Nanette Kritzalis, Anne Bass, Charles Verrill and Melissa Browne sped the production of the book, and many others—Juliet Annan, Nancy Gallt, Jean Griffin, Victoria

Meyer and Constance Sayre—treated it with energy and warmth.

As the book appears in Penguin Classics now, my thanks should go to several who are instrumental in the series. Betty Radice, the general editor, carefully read the plays in manuscript and sent me her valuable suggestions. Kathryn Court, my editor and mainstay for the new edition, Marcia Burch, Dan Farley, Edward Iwanicki, Linda Rosenberg, Serena Kahn, and Neil Stuart—all were partisans of the translation in New York. With her fine style, Ann Gold designed *The Three Theban Plays* to be a companion volume to my translation of Aeschylus' *Oresteia*. My English editor, Donald McFarlan, Peter Carson and Lorraine Cooper were gracious hosts at Allen Lane and Penguin Books in London.

Joined by Richard Simon, my agent Georges Borchardt used his skills and steady, heartening trust to find the book its home and help it on its way.

But the last word of thanks should go to Lynne—*tôi gar an kai meizoni / lexaim' an ê soi dia tychês toiasd' iôn?*

R.F.

Princeton, N.J.
1983

GREECE AND THE THEATER

IN THE sixth and fifth centuries before the birth of Christ an ancient civilization reached such heights of intellectual and artistic achievement that every succeeding period of Western culture, from the Roman Empire to the twentieth century, has been heavily in its debt, whether acknowledged or not. Those momentous years saw the beginnings of history and political theory (as well as political democracy) and the development of philosophical thought. In those years architects designed the temples which have dominated our concept of civic building ever since, and sculptors imposed on us an ideal vision of the human form which remains the point of reference even for those artists who turn against it. Not least among the achievements of this great age was the invention and perfection of an artistic medium which we take so unthinkingly for granted that we cannot imagine civilized life without it—the theater.

This outburst of creative energy in every field of endeavor took place in the eastern Mediterranean—Greece, the islands of the Aegean Sea and the Greek cities of the coast of Asia Minor. Earlier civilizations in this area—Babylon to the east and Egypt to the south, for example—had fertile river-valleys for an economic base, but Greece was (and still is) a poor country. "Greece and Poverty," said the historian Herodotus, "have always been bedfellows"; the land, as Odysseus says of Ithaca, his island home, is "a rugged place." From the air, as most travelers first see it now and as the vultures that circle over Apollo's shrine at Delphi always have, it is a forbidding sight. The bare mountain spines and ribs cross-hatch a disjointed grid from sea to sea, the armature of some gigantic statue that was never fleshed out. On the ground this first impression, modified in some details, holds good in the main: one entire third of the surface of Greece is naked rock on which nothing can grow or graze. The stark outlines of these mountains—peaks, range and valleys harshly clear from far away in the inexorable dry sunlight, softened only by the violet tone the twilight gives them for a few exquisite moments—these outlines are the frame and background of everything the Greeks saw. The mountains must have given them that sense of form, of the depth and solidity of natural shapes, which made them a race of sculptors and monumental builders, and it was in the mountains that they found the raw materials, limestone and marble, from which with chisel, hammer and drill they cut the stone images of their gods and columns for temples to house them. The mountains hemmed them in and cut them off from each other; as hard to cross in the winter snows as in the scorching heat of summer, they ringed the Greek horizon and made each lowland settlement a separate world.

Below the naked rock of the peaks, the trees, but there are not many left. Even in Plato's time, in the fourth century B.C., they were growing scarcer and, in fact, in his dialogue the *Critias* (the one which gave the world the myth of Atlantis) he has the Athenian aristocrat after whom the dialogue is named draw a nostalgic contrast between present and past. "What now remains compared with what existed then," he says, "is like the skeleton of a sick man, all the fat and soft earth wasted away and only the bare framework of the land left." He speaks longingly of a time when "the country was unspoiled: its mountains were arable highlands and what is now stony fields was once good soil. And the earth was enriched by the annual rains, which were not lost, as now, by flowing from the bare land into the sea . . . but the deep soil received and stored the water . . ." Since Plato's day things have got much worse; through the years the goats, the charcoalburners and the occupying armies have stripped most of the slopes. On those slopes, in the thickets of prickly shrub and among the rocks which burst into astonishing flower for a short spring season, roam the goats and, lower down, the sheep, herded by fierce dogs and fierce-looking shepherds. This is the no-man's-land of Greece, where unwanted children, like Oedipus, were left to die (but were saved by shepherds); where, not only in story but in grim reality, hunted men found refuge; where brigands and Klefts of the rebellions against the Turks, exiles and the Andartes of the Resistance and the Civil War, have all through Greece's bloody history escaped pursuit, reunited their scattered gangs and then descended like avenging furies on the plains below.

The plains are small, ringed by the mountains, or by mountains and sea, cut off from easy contact with one another; each one is a world apart, with, in ancient times, its own customs, dialect and separate government—the city-state. In the earlier civilizations of the Middle East the easy communications afforded by the rivers had made it possible, and the demands of irrigation, engineering and maintenance had made it necessary, to centralize control. These huge kingdoms, ruled from Babylon or Thebes, imposed uniform laws, taxes and worship over huge expanses of territory. But Greece was split up into separate small worlds: the plains, each with its own customs, laws, political institutions and traditions. They were such separate worlds that an ancient Greek joke book tells the story of a fool who saw the moon and asked his father: "Do they have a moon like that in other cities?"

These city-states were, as often as not, at war with their neighbors—over grazing land, borderlines or cattle raids. The Greeks, who gave us history, philosophy and political science, never managed to solve the problems posed by their political disunity; even the ideal states of their philosophers—the Republic of Plato, the perfect city of Aristotle—make provision for universal military training and active defense against external threats. This permanent insecurity in interstate relations reinforced the bond between citizen and citizen and at the same time directed their energies inward, to feed the competitive spirit that was so marked a feature of Greek life: competition in sports, in art, in politics.

Sometimes the competition was fiercer—for the means of subsistence, for life itself. The land of the plains, though fertile, never grew enough grain, the basic Greek staple, to feed a growing population. There was always a struggle between haves and have-nots; there were always men who had to leave home, either as exiles, to brood on their wrongs and plot for the day of return, or as colonists in search of a new site across the sea, to plow the land for grain and plant the other two basic crops, the olive and the vine. The olive trees, spaced out in regular patterns among the furrows, produced the rich green oil that was and still is an indispensable ingredient of every Greek dish. But the olive gave more than food; the inferior oil from the second or third pressings served as a sort of soap, rubbed into the pores and scraped off with a bronze tool, and as fuel for the small clay lamps which were the ancient Greek's only resource against the darkness. The vine, though the Greek variety seems a frail and puny plant compared with that of Burgundy, produced the wine without which no Greek could live content. Though they drank it sparingly—mixed one to three with water—it was essential to their communal and religious life.

Lowest and last, the sea. Almost tideless, it laps peacefully at the edges of the plains. It provided not only fish to supplement a diet in which meat was a rare luxury but also an easy way of communication with the outside world. Travel by land meant rough hill-tracks, and over those tracks heavy transport was difficult when not impossible; by sea, however, man and freight moved easily. When the Greek mercenaries of Xenophon's *Anabasis*, after months of marching and fighting in the mountains of Turkey, finally reached the Black Sea, one of them said, thankfully, "Now I can go home like Odysseus, flat on my back." And all around this inland sea, the Mediterranean, from Spain to Turkey—at Marseilles, Naples, Syracuse, to name only a few of their cities—the Greeks in search of a new home found everywhere the same climate, could grow the same crops. The sea was the true center of the Greek world: "we live round the sea," says Plato's Socrates, "like frogs . . . around a pond."

One of the frogs around the pond was the city of Athens, huddled beneath a rocky acropolis ten kilometers from the sea. It was the center of Greek intellectual and artistic life for most of the fifth century; it was also, for most of that time, the imperial ruler of the islands and coastal cities of the Aegean. In the early years of the century Athens had played a leading role in the defeat of an invading army from Persia, a huge empire which, based on what is now Iran, controlled the whole land mass from the Aegean coast to the border of India. When the Persian forces advanced south by land and sea against Athens, the inhabitants evacuated their city and took to their ships; the Persians burnt Athens, but the Athenian fleet (and its commander, Themistocles) played a major role in the decisive naval battle of Salamis (480 B.C.). A fifteen-year-old Sophocles, we are told, led the singers in the hymns of celebration and thanksgiving for the victory.

The Persian retreat from Europe was followed by a Greek counter-offensive, its aim the liberation of the Greeks of the islands and Asia Minor coasts. Sparta, the land power of the Greek alliance, withdrew from the enterprise, leaving Athens in effective command of the naval league against Persia. A series of stunning Athenian victories put an end to the Persian naval presence in the Aegean, but the newly liberated Greek cities soon found that they had merely exchanged one master for another. The contributions in ships and money, which had once been voluntary and intended for mutual defense, now became compulsory and were appropriated for Athenian use; cities that tried to leave the league were treated as rebels and subdued. The tribute money paid by the "allies" kept the Athenian fleet in being; it also helped defray the cost of the building program that, by the end of the century, made the Athenian acropolis one of the world's most famous architectural complexes. All this helped to provide employment for the Athenian people, whose well-being was not a matter to be neglected by their political leaders, since Athens was a democracy—by the end of the century a remarkably direct and radical democracy. The revenues of empire and profits from commercial operations promoted and protected by naval power also made possible that lavish expenditure on public festivals which Pericles, in his Funeral Speech, counted as one of the glories of Athenian democracy.

Among these festivals the most famous and popular was the

Dionysia, the celebration of the god Dionysus, which took place every spring, at the end of March or beginning of April. The god was honored by performances, in the theater, of dithyrambs (lyric hymns sung and danced by a chorus of fifty), tragedies and comedies. Dionysus was a god whose territory was originally not in the city at all. He was a god of the country but not of the level plain that surrounds and feeds the city; he and his Maenads, ecstatic women who followed in his train, belonged to the wild—on the vases where we see them painted they range through the pine forests of the high slopes. The mythic accounts of his coming to Greece all tell the same story: his rites disrupted the normal pattern of city-state life, and the authorities acted against him, only to be subdued by the god's irresistible power.

Whether or not these myths preserve some memory of actual events we have no means of telling, but in fifth-century Athens Dionysus was at home in the city; his statue was brought out from the temple in the theater precinct to watch the plays. Seats of honor were reserved for his priests (they are still there—"Reserved for the priest of Dionysus" carved on the marble). The four days of performance were a city festival, open to foreigners as well as citizens, a time when business was suspended, when even prisoners were let out on bail so that they could attend.

Dionysus is the life-spirit of all green vegetation—ivy, pine tree and especially the vine; he is, in Dylan Thomas' phrase, "the force that through the green fuse drives the flower." The drama as we know it in the fifth century must have evolved or been adapted from some kind of performance connected with his worship. We do not know the details but there are some clear connections. For one thing Dionysus is a popular rather than an aristocratic religious figure, a late-comer to the Olympian pantheon immortalized in Homeric epic. His worship in Athens seems to have been given official status under the anti-aristocratic dictatorship of Pisistratus, the sixth-century prelude to the establishment of democracy, and the theater, his true ceremonial, came to full growth under the democratic regime. For another, Dionysus is often portrayed in contemporary vase painting as masked or even as a mask; the actors in the theater played in masks. And lastly Dionysus is a god whose worship can produce states of ecstatic possession, a loss of individual identity in the communal dance, and so perhaps may serve as a divine model for the actor's assumption of an alien personality as well as the audience's temporary identification with the masked figures onstage. In any case the important fact is not so much that the theater was the purlieu of a particular god as that it was from the beginning a sacramental area, a place where divine forces were invoked and put to work, where the performance was, for actors and audience alike, an act of worship.

The audience was, by our standards, immense; the theater building of the late fifth century, to judge from its ruins, could seat between fourteen and fifteen thousand spectators. They sat in rows that rise one above the other on the rocky southeastern slope of the Acropolis and border, for half of its circumference, a circular dancing floor behind which stood a wooden stage building. This was the actors' changing room, where they could change masks as well as costumes, to assume a different role; through its door (which for the audience was the door of the royal palace of Thebes or, with scenic modifications, the entry to the wood of the Erinyes) the actors made their exits and their entrances, though they could also go behind the stage building and approach the acting area from the side, as visitors from the city or abroad. The masks (which made it possible for the male actors to play female parts as well as to play more than one character) were not the grotesque caricatures we know from modern theater decorations; contemporary vase paintings show that they were naturalistic representations of types—bearded king, old man, young girl and so on. The play of facial expression we expect from our actors was in any case ruled out in an open-air theater where the top row of spectators was over fifty-five yards away from the stage area; individuality of character had to be created by the poet's word and the actor's delivery and gesture. By the end of the century the parts were played by professional actors, three for each tragedy, assigned to the dramatists by the magistrate in charge of the festival. Aeschylus, the first great dramatist (who had fought in the ships at Salamis), acted in his own plays; Sophocles followed his example but then, we are told, abandoned the stage because his voice was not strong enough. His younger contemporary and competitor, Euripides (born in the year Salamis was fought) never, as far as we know, appeared on stage.

In addition to actors and spectators, there was a third element of the performance, one older than either of these two. It was the chorus—a Greek word that means "dance"; the chorus of Greek tragedies sang, but it was also and had been in origin a group of dancers. The way Greek theaters are built shows how central to the performance the chorus was; the rows of stone benches one below the other all the way down the hillside focus the spectators' vision not on the stage area but on the circular dancing floor. Choral performances in Greece are much older than the drama; from time immemorial dancers had worshiped the gods, celebrated athletic (and military) victories, mourned the dead and danced on the circular threshing floors which are still to be found on Greek hillsides and which are probably the original of the circular dancing floor in the theater. Drama as we know it was created when an Athenian named Thespis added to the dance and song of the chorus the speech of an actor. With the addition of a second actor, the performers could develop from a sort of dramatic narrative—actor to chorus—to a dramatic relationship—actor to actor—or even a dramatic conflict—actor against actor. This second actor was introduced by Aeschylus, and it is this innovation that entitles him to be called, as he often has been, the creator of tragedy. When Sophocles later added a third actor, the complicated play of relationships between the actors came to dominate the scene, reducing the role of the chorus to that of commentator, where before it had been active participant. But the chorus was always there, and it has an important function: it is an emotional bridge between spectators and actors. An anonymous crowd with only a group identity—Theban citizens, inhabitants of Colonus or whatever—it functioned on stage as if the audience itself were part of the action; all the more so because, unlike the professional actors, the chorus consisted of citizen amateurs, representing their tribal group in the dramatic competition.

For, like almost all Greek institutions, the festival of Dionysus was a contest. Three dramatists on three successive days presented their plays and at the end were awarded first, second or third prize. What these prizes were we do not know; they may have been monetary but they cannot have been substantial enough for anyone to expect to make a living by producing plays. (Sophocles' father seems to have been the wealthy owner of some kind of factory, and his son was educated by the most famous teachers of the day.) The real reward of a first prize was the glory and the admiration of one's fellow-citizens; Sophocles had his full share of such rewards, for we have evidence that he won the first prize at the Dionysia eighteen times, and it is recorded that he never won the third prize. The glory of a first prize was shared by the poet with the chorus, the actors and the *chorêgos,* a private citizen who had paid out of his own pocket for the rich costumes, the training of the chorus and a host of other expenses. He was not, however, as he would be today, the "producer," an entrepreneur who puts the package together for profit. In fact he was a rich citizen, designated by the city authorities for this function; his part in the proceedings was, in effect, a form of enlightened taxation.

The theater was not only a religious festival, it was also an aspect of the city's political life. Athens in the fifth century was a democracy, an increasingly inclusive and participatory one as the century advanced. This radically democratic system was reflected in the organization of the dramatic festival. The prizes were awarded at the end by ten judges, elected on the opening day by lot and sworn to impartiality. Feelings often ran high, and these judges must have been under considerable pressure from the audience. In 468 B.C., the year in which Sophocles first entered the contest, competing against Aeschylus, the tension was such that the magistrate appointed as judges the ten elected generals for that year, among them Cimon, the hero of the naval crusade against Persia. (They gave Sophocles the first prize.) The whole festival reflected not only the organization but also the pride and achievement of the city of Athens. When, later in the century, the league against Persia had become an Athenian maritime empire, the tribute money of the subject cities was brought to Athens at the time of the dramatic festival and displayed in the theater before the plays were performed. The orphaned children of those Athenians who had fallen in battle were cared for and educated by the city; once they had reached young manhood, they were paraded in the theater in full armor, to receive the blessings of the people. Honors and distinctions decreed for foreign heads of state and individuals were conferred in the theater at the festival.

The dramatist who composed and produced the new plays for such an occasion was in a situation unique in the history of the theater. An audience of some fourteen thousand citizens, conscious of the religious solemnity of the occasion and the glory it reflected on the city and the individuals responsible, packed the benches of the theater to hear, as the sun rose, the first lines of the play. A modern reader might expect that a theater such as this would produce drama that was, to use a cant phrase, "relevant, living theater," based on contemporary themes, current issues. At the end of a day's performance in Athens, when the comic poet came on stage, the audience did in fact enjoy a ribald, frank, hard-hitting treatment of contemporary themes—with no holds barred—in which prominent statesmen and individual citizens were held up to ridicule in a style that few modern states would permit. But the first three plays of the day's performance were tragedy, and here, with very few exceptions, the figures who walked the stage, far from being contemporary, were men, women and gods from the far-off past, from the dim beginnings of the youth of the race—an age of heroes and heroines, the legends of the beginnings of the Greek world. The stuff from which the tragic poet made his plays was not contemporary reality but myth. And yet it did reflect contemporary reality, did so perhaps in terms more authoritative because they were not colored by the partisan emotions of the time, terms which were in fact so authoritative that they remain meaningful even for us today.

This is not as paradoxical as it sounds. The dramatist who had one of his characters define the role of the theater as "to hold . . . the mirror up to nature, to show . . . the very age and body of the time his form and pressure," and the actors as "the abstract and brief chronicles of the time," did not set even one of his plays in the Elizabethan England he lived in; his scenes are set in the far past—ancient Rome, medieval England—or in far-off places—Illyria, Bohemia or that magic island of *The Tempest.* Shakespeare used for his plots printed sources—Italian novels, English chronicles, translations of ancient biographies—but the sources of the Greek dramatists were, for the most part, oral; they were the myths, the stories that were told about the past and which, since everyone told the stories differently, offered infinite variety to the playwright.

But this material offered more than variety of dramatic incident. These myths were the only national memory of the remote past, of a time before the Greeks invented the alphabet, so that, shifting and changing though they might be, they had the authority, for the audience, of what we call history. The masked actors on stage were the great figures of the audience's past, their ancestors. Since the myths, retold from generation to generation, were shaped by the selective emphasis of an oral tradition that preserved and created images of universal significance, the masked actors presented to the audience not only historical figures from their past but also poetic symbols of their life and death, their ambitions, fears and hopes. But the myths also had the authority of religion; these stories are the sacred tales of religious cult and recall (or rather create) a time when men and gods were closer than they have been ever since. It so happens that in the three plays presented in this volume the gods do not appear on stage (though they do in other Sophoclean tragedies), but the audience is never allowed to forget them. The characters of the plays appeal to them constantly, and the action raises questions about their role: *Antigone,* no less than the two Oedipus plays, explores the mystery of the divine purposes. The masked actors offered the audience not only a vision of its past, not only great historic figures molded by the oral tradition into shapes symbolic of all human hopes and fears, but also, invoked at every turn if not actually present on stage, those gods whose dispensation of good and evil to mankind seemed to pass all understanding.

Though the details of these traditional stories varied considerably from one teller of the tale to another (and especially from one city to another), and though the dramatist could (and often did) invent new variations, the main outlines of the best-known stories were fairly stable—Oedipus always kills his father and marries his mother, Eteocles and Polynices must kill each other. The dramatist who used this material derived a double benefit from the audience's knowledge of the stories: he could either lull them into expecting the familiar—and so increase the shock effect of some radical innovation in the story—or, renouncing surprise, he could pose the ignorant pronouncements of his characters against the audience's knowledge of their future and so produce dramatic irony. Sophocles was a master of this technique, and *Oedipus the King* the supreme example of its effective use; almost every statement made by Oedipus has a second, sinister meaning for the audience, which knows, as he does not, his past and his future. These grim reverberations are especially powerful in tragedies concerned, as these three plays are from start to finish, with destiny, divine dispensation and the human situation. The audience, with its knowledge of the past and the future, is on the level of the gods; they see the ambition, passion and actions of the characters against the larger pattern of their lives and deaths. The spectator is involved emotionally in the heroic struggles of the protagonist, a man like himself, and at the same time can view his heroic action from the standpoint of superior knowledge, the knowledge possessed by those gods whose prophecies of the future play so large a role in Sophoclean tragedy. These plays gave their audience an image of human life as they saw and lived it, precarious and unpredictable, but also as it must appear to the all-seeing eye of divine omniscience.

The Athenian dramatists found this age-old and powerful material ready to hand; what they did was to add another dimension to it. The stories came from a time when the city was not the full context of men's lives; the myths recall the days of migrations, of the chaotic years of conquest and eventual settlement—a time when great heroic individuals imposed their wills, when tribal, family relationships were infinitely stronger than the bond between citizens, a time in fact before the city made its laws and established its primacy. But the Attic tragedians, in play after play, set these heroes, in their actions and suffering, against the background of the city. The ancient myths (and the epic tradition that first gave them literary form) were concerned with the fate of the hero; the drama is concerned also with the fate of the city which he defends, attacks, rules or represents. And the chorus, which is a representation on stage of the community, constantly calls attention by its very presence as well as its song to this larger dimension.

The fifth-century Athenian prided himself on the fact that he was a fully responsible and active citizen; "each individual," said Pericles in his panegyric of Athenian democracy, the Funeral Speech, "is interested not only in his own affairs but in the affairs of the city as well . . . we Athenians in our own persons take our decisions on policy or submit them to proper discussion." Sophocles was no exception; in fact he was deeply involved in public affairs throughout his long career. He served, for example, as one of the treasurers of the league against Persia in 443 B.C. and as one of the ten generals in command of the fleet charged with suppressing the revolt of Samos some years later. These were the years of Athens' unchallenged greatness; under the leadership of Pericles she steadily built up her influence abroad as well as her economic resources at home. In 431 B.C. those cities of the Peloponnese which had been Athens' allies against Persia, alarmed by the dynamic growth of Athens' power and evident ambition to become the dominant Greek state, provoked a war that lasted twenty-seven years and ended in Athenian defeat.

Pericles died in the third year of this war, but Sophocles lived on almost to the end. In 411 B.C., after Athens suffered a catastrophic defeat in Sicily (the end of a megalomaniac attempt to conquer that rich but distant island), Sophocles was called in to serve on a special board of commissioners to deal with the political and military crisis. In 406 B.C., as the news reached Athens that Euripides had died in Macedonia, Sophocles brought on his chorus dressed in mourning as a tribute to his younger rival. A few months later he himself died at the age of ninety. In the winter after his death the comic poet Aristophanes paid a lighthearted compliment to the memory not so much of the poet as of the man the Athenians mourned and had loved. In his play *The Frogs* the god Dionysus, disgusted with the pitiful productions of the younger dramatists, goes down to Hades to bring Euripides back to life. Asked why he doesn't bring Sophocles instead, he says first that he wants to see how Iophon, Sophocles' son and fellow-tragedian, will do without his father's help, and then adds: "Besides, Euripides, who is a scoundrel, will be more than ready to break out and run off with me. But Sophocles was an easy-going man up here–and will be down there too."

This estimate fits perfectly into the only detailed account of him we have from the pen of a contemporary. Ion of Chios, himself a tragic poet, gives us a specimen of Sophocles' brilliant literary conversation at a banquet held in his honor as he was on his way to Samos to serve as a general under Pericles. He also describes the skillful maneuver that enabled the poet to snatch a kiss from the handsome boy who was serving the wine. As the company applauded, Sophocles said: "I am practicing strategy, gentlemen—since Pericles says that I know how to make poems but not how to be a general. Don't you think my stratagem was successful?" Ion adds that this was typical "of his wit in word and action when the wine was served. But in public life," he goes on, "his conduct was not that of an expert or an activist, it was like that of any well-bred Athenian." One other contemporary source gives the same impression of this remarkable personality, whose long, successful life and universal popularity seem an unlikely source for the tragic world he created on the Attic stage. Phrynichus, another comic poet, wrote an epitaph for him (almost certainly in the play that competed with Aristophanes' *Frogs*): "Blessed Sophocles, who lived a long life, a happy man and a clever one. He composed many fine tragedies and died well, without enduring any misfortune." One great misfortune he escaped by his death: he did not live to see his beloved Athens starved into surrender in 405-4 B.C., the Spartan fleet in the Piraeus, the Long Walls demolished, the end of Athens' great age.

Of the 123 plays our ancient sources credit him with, only seven have survived intact. Three of them, *Antigone*, *Oedipus the King* and *Oedipus at Colonus*, are based on the saga of Thebes, the city of seven gates. We do not know the precise dates for the production of these three plays, but our meager evidence suggests that *Antigone* came first (perhaps in 442 B.C.), *Oedipus the King* next (some time soon after 430 B.C.), and *Oedipus at Colonus* last (in fact it was produced after Sophocles' death). The plays appear in this volume in that order, the chronological order of composition.

This does not correspond to the order of the mythical events in the Theban saga. The story was told in many different ways; Sophocles' version (some of it is undoubtedly his own invention) ran roughly as follows. Laius and Jocasta, king and queen of Thebes, told by Apollo at Delphi that any son they had would kill its father, sent their infant out, its feet pierced with metal pins, to die on the mountainside. But the shepherd who was supposed to abandon it gave it instead to a fellow-shepherd, who came from the other side of Cithaeron, the mountain range between Thebes and Corinth. This shepherd took the child to Polybus and Merope, king and queen of Corinth; they adopted it, for they were childless. They named the child Oedipus (the name suggests, in Greek, "swell-foot"). When he was a grown man, a drunken guest told him that he was not the true son of the royal house; his foster-parents tried to reassure him, but he went to Delphi to ask Apollo. There he was told he would kill his father and marry his mother. He resolved never to return to Corinth; instead of going home, southeast by boat, he went east on foot through the defiles of Mount Parnassus and, at a narrow place where three roads met, quarreled over the right of way with an old man in a wagon. Attacked, he defended himself, killing the old man and (so he thought) all his retainers. The old man was his father, Laius.

Oedipus came down to the plain where the citizens of Thebes were oppressed by a monster, the Sphinx a winged lion with a human, female face. She would leave them alone only when she got an answer to her riddle; many had tried to guess it, failed and been killed. The Thebans promised a great reward to anyone who could free them from the Sphinx: the throne of Thebes and the hand of Jocasta, the widowed queen. Oedipus answered the riddle. "What is it that goes on four feet, three feet and two feet . . . and is most feeble when it walks on four?" His answer was "man—on all fours as a baby, on two feet at maturity, on three as an old man with a stick." The Sphinx threw herself to death off the rocks, and Oedipus entered the city to claim his reward.

For many years he was the successful and beloved ruler of Thebes; he was also the father of two sons, Eteocles and Polynices, and two daughters, Antigone and Ismene. Suddenly a plague struck the city, and the Delphic oracle declared it would cease only when the murderer of Laius was found, to be exiled or executed. Oedipus, after pronouncing a solemn curse on the unknown murderer, proceeded, by persistent questioning and stubborn pursuit of the investigation, to find him. In the process he also discovered his own true identity and recognized that the prophecy made to him long ago at Delphi had been fulfilled. Jocasta hanged herself, and Oedipus, taking the long pins from her robe, put out his eyes. Creon, Jocasta's brother, assumed power in Thebes, ruling together with the two sons of Oedipus. They offended their father and, after pronouncing a curse on them (that they should die by each other's hand), he left Thebes, with Antigone as his guide, to become a wandering beggar on the highways of Greece.

At Thebes the two sons of Oedipus quarreled over their right to the throne; Eteocles prevailed and Polynices left to find allies abroad. At Argos he raised an army, led by seven champions (the Seven against Thebes). Meanwhile the Delphic oracle announced that Oedipus' grave would be the site of victory for the city in whose territory it lay: the blind beggar became a prize to be won. While Creon, acting for Eteocles, and Polynices, acting on his own behalf, set out to find him, the old man had arrived at the hamlet of Colonus just outside Athens. Learning that the wood where he had taken shelter was sacred to the Eumenides, he realized that he had come to his last resting place. Apollo had prophesied this years ago and also told him that by his choice of burial place he could reward his friends and punish his enemies. He decided to confer this gift of victory on Athens, which, in the person of Theseus its king, welcomed him generously and made him a citizen. Attempts to win him for Thebes by Creon and by Polynices for Argos met with failure; Oedipus, summoned by the gods, went to a mysterious death at Colonus, to become a protector, in his grave, of Athenian soil.

Polynices went back to Argos and led his troops against Thebes; the attack was beaten off, and Oedipus' prophetic curse was fulfilled—brother killed brother. Creon, now sole ruler, denied burial to the corpse of Polynices; the penalty for disobedience to this decree was death. It was defied by Antigone, who, captured and brought before Creon, defended her action so resolutely and uncompromisingly that he ordered her imprisoned in an underground tomb, where she would starve to death. He rejected the plea of his son Haemon, who was betrothed to her, and the warning of the prophet Tiresias, who told him that his refusal of burial to the corpse offended the gods. But second thoughts prevailed; he buried Polynices and went to release Antigone. He came too late; she had hanged herself, and Haemon, who had found her body, killed himself in her tomb. Creon's wife, hearing the news, killed herself, cursing her husband for the loss of her son. Creon was left alone to face a second attack on Thebes, a successful one this time, by the *Epigonoi*, the sons of the seven champions who had fallen at the seven gates.

The three Sophoclean plays, arranged according to their place in the saga, would produce the sequence *Oedipus the King, Oedipus at Colonus, Antigone,* and the plays are usually, in translation, presented in that order. Such a sequence however misleads unwary readers into thinking of the plays as a "trilogy" (or a "cycle")—a dramatic unit like the three plays of the *Oresteia* of Aeschylus or of O'Neill's *Mourning Becomes Electra*. Though there are many indications in the texts that Sophocles in the final Oedipus play had the earlier one firmly in mind, each play is a completely independent unit and in fact, though a character may appear in all three (Creon, for example), the point of view from which he is seen differs from one play to another. And in all three plays the mythical antecedents are slightly different; in *Antigone*, to cite just one instance, the heroine refers to the death of Oedipus in terms ("hated, / his reputation in ruins," lines 61–62 of the translation) that are incompatible with *Oedipus at Colonus*. It seemed best therefore to present the reader with the three plays as Sophocles wrote them and the Athenian audience saw them: *Antigone* first, before the outbreak of the disastrous war; *Oedipus the King* next, during the early years of the war and after the Athenian plague of 429 B.C.; and lastly *Oedipus at Colonus*, an old man's play about an old man, written in the desperate final days of the war and produced in 401 B.C. after the poet's death.

But there is also a positive reason for setting the plays in chronological order: they represent successive stages in Sophocles' development as a dramatist and tragic poet. This is not a development that can be plotted in detail; we have only a pitiful remnant of his life's work—seven plays out of 123—and attempts to assess such changes in dramatic method as well as intellectual content are notoriously subjective. Nevertheless it seems safe to say that *Oedipus at Colonus*, written in the poet's last years, expresses a different tragic vision from that which lies behind *Antigone*, written over thirty years earlier, and that *Oedipus the King*, though it deals with themes common to all three plays, is still another modification of the basic tragic view. The plays read in their order of composition suggest a changing concept of the fundamental problems posed in Sophoclean tragedy; those problems and the poet's attitude toward them are the focus of the introductory essays that follow.

SOPHOCLES:
THE THREE THEBAN PLAYS

ANTIGONE

INTRODUCTION

THIS PLAY, it is generally agreed, was produced before and fairly close to the year 441 B.C. Sophocles, as we know from a reliable contemporary source, was one of the nine generals elected, with Pericles, for a campaign against the revolt of Samos in that year. The ancient introduction to the play, found in most of the manuscripts, records a tradition that Sophocles owed his election to office to the popularity of *Antigone*. True or false, this story could only have been based on a widely accepted belief that the play was produced before the year 441.

The story also, by setting *Antigone* in a political context, draws attention to the political content of the play, its concern with the problems of the *polis,* the city-state. *Antigone* resurfaces in a highly political context once again in the fourth century, some sixty years after Sophocles' death; it had by that time become a classic. The orator and statesman Demosthenes had the clerk of the court read out Creon's speech on the proper loyalties of a citizen (lines 194–214 of the translation) as a lesson in patriotism to his political opponent Aeschines (who had once been a professional actor and had played the part of Creon). And in that same century Aristotle quoted the play repeatedly in his treatise the *Politics*.

To the modern world, particularly the world of Victorian England, with its comfortable belief in progress and its confidence that such barbaric acts as exposure of an enemy's corpse were a thing of a distant past, the subject matter of the play seemed academic. Matthew Arnold wrote in 1853 that it was "no longer possible that we should feel a deep interest in the *Antigone* of Sophocles." The twentieth century has lost any such illusions. Two modern adaptations of the play, both of them alive with political urgency, are highlights in the history of the modern theater. In February 1944, in a Paris occupied by the German army, four months before the Allied landings in Normandy, Jean Anouilh produced his *Antigone,* a play in which Antigone is unmistakably identified with the French resistance movement. This is clear from the frequent threats of torture leveled at the heroine (not to be found in Sophocles but characteristic of Gestapo interrogations); the fact, well known to everyone in the audience, that the German Nazi military police often exposed the corpses of executed resistance fighters as a deterrent; and finally from the brilliant characterization of Creon's guards, whose low social origins, vulgar language and callous brutality accurately recall the contemporary *miliciens,* the French fascist terror squads, which were more feared and hated than the Gestapo itself. The reason the German authorities allowed the production of the play is its treatment of Creon. Anouilh presents him as a practical man whose assumption of power faces him with a tragic dilemma: his desire to rule firmly but fairly, to restore and maintain order in a chaotic situation, is frustrated by a determined, fanatical, apparently irrational resistance. These are exactly the terms in which the German military authorities would have described their own position in occupied France. At the first performance the play was greeted with applause from both the French and Germans in the audience.

The other modern adaptation, Bertolt Brecht's radical revision of Hölderlin's translation, staged at Chur in Switzerland in 1948, was less ambivalent. The prologue is a scene in a Berlin air-raid shelter, March 1945, and it is all too clear what Creon is meant to suggest to the audience: he has launched Thebes on an aggressive war against Argos, and Polynices (conscripted by Creon in Brecht's violent reworking of the legend) has been killed for deserting the battle line when he saw his brother Eteocles fall. At the end of the play the tide turns against Thebes as Argos counterattacks; Creon takes Thebes down with him to destruction rather than surrender. Against this Hitlerian black, Antigone is all white; she is the image of what Brecht longed to see—the rising of the German people against Hitler, a resistance that in fact never came to birth. The poem Brecht wrote for the program of the production, an address to Antigone—

Come out of the twilight
and walk before us a while,
friendly, with the light step
of one whose mind is fully made up . . .

—reminds us that Brecht was a lyric poet as well as a dramatist, but it is a dream poem, a lament, a regret for that rising of a whole people against fascism, which Brecht's political creed urgently demanded but which never came "out of the twilight."

Of these two modern adaptations, Anouilh's, which presents the conflict between the protagonists as a real dilemma, is closer to the spirit of the Sophoclean play than Brecht's passionate advocacy of one side against the other. For in the opening scenes of the Sophoclean play Creon is presented in a light that the original audience was certain to regard as favorable: he is the defender of the city, the eloquent champion of its overriding claim on the loyalty of its citizens in time of danger. His opening speech, a declaration of principles, contains echoes of Pericles' Funeral Speech; since that speech was delivered in the winter of 431–30 B.C., long after the first performance of *Antigone,* it seems likely that these phrases come from the common stock of democratic patriotic oratory. The particular action that Creon tries to justify by this general appeal, the exposure of Polynices' corpse, may have caused the audience some uneasiness, but on his main point, that loyalty to the city takes precedence over any private loyalty, to friend or family, they would have agreed with him.

As the chorus obviously does. They express sympathy for Antigone only in the scene where she is led off to her death, and even then in such grudging terms that she takes their declaration as derision. Only when they hear from Tiresias the verdict of the gods and realize from his prophecy of wars to come that Creon's action threatens the city with disaster, do they advise him to countermand his edict. For them the interests of the city are paramount. In the magnificent ode that they sing after the sentry comes to tell Creon that his orders have already been defied, they celebrate the progress of the human race from savagery to civilization: its culmination is the creation of the city.

Man has become master of the sea and land, caught the birds of the air and tamed the beasts of the wild and taught himself speech and "the mood and mind for law that rules the city" (396). They end the song with a caution that man's ingenuity and resourcefulness may lead him to disaster unless he "weaves in / the laws of the land, and the justice of the gods" and they repudiate the man of "reckless daring" (409–10, 415). By the end of the play the audience, if they remember these words, will think of Creon, but at this point the chorus is clearly thinking of the unidentified rebel who has defied the city's ruler and thrown a symbolic handful of dust on the corpse of the city's bitter enemy who was once her friend. They accept, as most of the audience did, Creon's manifesto: "our country *is* our safety. / Only while she voyages true on course / can we establish friendships . . ." (211–13).

This is not to say that Creon is right to order the exposure of the corpse; in fact, by the end of the play it is made clear that his action is a violation of divine law, and besides he has by then long since abandoned any claim to speak for the citizen body as a whole and in their best interest. "Am I to rule this land for others—or myself?" (823) he asks his son Haemon. There is no doubt about what he thinks is the correct answer to that question. But before he is driven by the consequences of Antigone's defiance to reveal his true and deepest motives, he represents a viewpoint few Greeks would have challenged: that in times of crisis, the supreme loyalty of the citizen is to the state and its duly constituted authorities.

It is important to remember this since the natural instinct of all modern readers and playgoers is to sympathize fully with Antigone, the rebel and martyr. This is of course a correct instinct; in the end the gods, through their spokesman, the prophet Tiresias, uphold her claim that divine law does indeed prescribe burial for all dead men. But though she appeals to this law—"the great unwritten, unshakable traditions" (505)—in her magnificent challenge to Creon, she has other motives too. She proclaims again and again, to her sister Ismene as to her opponent Creon, the duty she owes to her brother, to the family relationship. "If I had

allowed / my own mother's son to rot, an unburied corpse"—
she tells the king, "that would have been an agony!" (520–22).
"He is my brother," she tells her sister Ismene, "and—deny it as
you will— / your brother too" (55–56). Creon's denial of burial
to the corpse of Polynices has assaulted this fierce devotion to
blood relationship at a particularly sensitive point, for the funeral
rites, especially the emotional lament over the dead, were, in an
ancient Greek household, the duty and privilege of the women.
(In the villages of Greece today they still are.) Antigone and
Ismene are the last surviving women of the house of Oedipus;
this is why it seems to Antigone that Creon's decree is aimed
particularly at them—"the martial law our good Creon / lays
down for you and me" (37–38)—and why she takes it for granted
Ismene will help her and turns so contemptuously and harshly
against her when she refuses.

Antigone's dedicated loyalty to the family is, however, more
than a private code of conduct; in the context of fifth-century
Athens her challenge to the authority of the city-state and defense of a blood relationship had strong political overtones.
Athenian democratic institutions were egalitarian beyond anything conceivable in modern societies (many important magistracies, for example, were filled by lot, not election), but Athens
had for centuries before the establishment of democracy been
ruled by the great aristocratic families that traced their descent
from heroic or divine ancestors, and these families were still,
under the democracy, powerful, cohesive, exclusive groups,
which maintained their separate identities through religious cults
and family priesthoods. They were powerful concentrations of
patronage and influence, and they worked, within the democratic institutions, openly or through unseen connections, for
the advancement and interests of their members (a phenomenon
not unknown in modern Greece as well).

The political aspect of Antigone's loyalty is emphasized at
once in Creon's inaugural address: "whoever places a friend [the
Greek word *philos* also means "relative"] / above the good of
his own country, he is nothing" (203–4). And when he realizes
later that this is in fact the issue between him and his niece, he

reconfirms her death sentence with a sarcastic reference to Zeus *Homaimos,* the divinity especially associated with the family worship: "let her cry for mercy, sing her hymns / to Zeus who defends all bonds of kindred blood" (735-36).

Antigone appeals not only to the bond of kindred blood but also to the unwritten law, sanctioned by the gods, that the dead must be given proper burial—a religious principle. But Creon's position is not anti-religious; in fact he believes that he has religion on his side. The gods, for him, are the gods of the city, which contains and protects their shrines, celebrates their festivals and sacrifices, and prays to them for deliverance; Creon finds it unthinkable that these gods should demand the burial of a traitor to the city who came with a foreign army at his back

> to burn their temples ringed with pillars,
> . . . scorch their hallowed earth
> and fling their laws to the winds. (323-25)

Once again, there would have been many in the audience who felt the same way. These vivid phrases would have recalled to them the destruction of Athens and the desecration of its temples by the Persian invaders in 480; they would have had no second thoughts about denying burial to the corpse of any Athenian who had fought on the Persian side. Denial of burial in their homeland to traitors, real or supposed, was not unknown in Greece. Themistocles, for example, the hero of the Persian War, was later driven from Athens by his political enemies, who accused him of pro-Persian conspiratorial activity. Hounded from one Greek city to another he finally took refuge in Persian-controlled territory, where he died. When his relatives wished to bring his bones back to be buried in Athenian soil, permission was refused. Creon's decree of course goes much further and forbids burial altogether, but the Athenian attitude toward Themistocles shows that for Sophocles' audience the decree did not sound as outlandishly barbaric as it does to us. In the play, the opening song of the chorus gives tense expression to the terror inspired in the Theban people by Polynices' treacherous attack, their hatred of the foreign warlords he has marshaled against them, and their joy at their own deliverance and his defeat and death.

The opening scenes show us the conflicting claims and loyalties of the two adversaries, solidly based, in both cases, on opposed political and religious principles. This is of course the basic insight of Hegel's famous analysis of the play: he sees it as "a collision between the two highest moral powers." What is wrong with them, in his view, is that they are both "one-sided." But Hegel goes much further than that. He was writing in the first half of the nineteenth century, a period of fervent German nationalism in which the foundations of the unified German state were laid: his views on loyalty to the state were very much those of Creon. "Creon," he says, "is not a tyrant, he is really a moral power. He is not in the wrong."

However, as the action develops the favorable impression created by Creon's opening speech is quickly dissipated. His announcement of his decision to expose the corpse, the concluding section of his speech, is couched in violent, vindictive terms—"carrion for the birds and dogs to tear" (230)—which stand in shocking contrast to the ethical generalities that precede it. This hint of a cruel disposition underlying the statesmanlike façade is broadened by the threat of torture leveled at the sentry (344–50) and the order to execute Antigone in the presence of Haemon, her betrothed (852–54). And as he meets resistance from a series of opponents—Antigone's contemptuous defiance, the rational, political advice of his son Haemon, the imperious summons to obedience of the gods' spokesman, Tiresias—he swiftly abandons the temperate rhetoric of his inaugural address for increasingly savage invective. Against the two sanctions invoked by Antigone, the demands of blood relationship, the rights and privileges of the gods below, he rages in terms ranging from near-blasphemous defiance to scornful mockery.

> Sister's child or closer in blood
> than all my family clustered at my altar
> worshiping Guardian Zeus—she'll never escape,
> . . . the most barbaric death. (543–46)

He will live to regret this wholesale denial of the family bond, for it is precisely through that family clustered at his altar that his punishment will be administered, in the suicides of his son and his wife, both of whom die cursing him.

And for Antigone's appeals to Hades, the great god of the underworld to whom the dead belong, Creon has nothing but contempt; for him "Hades" is simply a word meaning "death," a sentence he is prepared to pass on anyone who stands in his way. He threatens the sentry with torture as a prelude: "simple death won't be enough for you" (348). When asked if he really intends to deprive Haemon of his bride he answers sarcastically: "Death will do it for me" (648). He expects to see Antigone and Ismene turn coward "once they see Death coming for their lives" (655). With a derisive comment he tells his son to abandon Antigone: "Spit her out, / . . . Let her find a husband down among the dead [in Hades' house]" (728–30). And he dismisses Antigone's reverence for Hades and the rights of the dead with mockery as he condemns her to be buried alive: "There let her pray to the one god she worships: / Death" (875–76). But this Hades is not something to be so lightly referred to, used or mocked. In the great choral ode which celebrated Man's progress and powers this was the one insurmountable obstacle that confronted him:

> ready, resourceful man!
> Never without resources
> never an impasse as he marches on the future—
> only Death, from Death alone he will find no rescue . . . (401–4)

And Creon, in the end, looking at the corpse of his son and hearing the news of his wife's suicide, speaks of Hades for the first time with the fearful respect that is his due, not as an instrument of policy or a subject for sardonic word-play, but as a divine power, a dreadful presence: "harbor of Death, so choked, so hard to cleanse!— / why me? why are you killing me?" (1413–14).

Creon is forced at last to recognize the strength of those social and religious imperatives that Antigone obeys, but long before this happens he has abandoned the principles which he had proclaimed as authority for his own actions. His claim to be representative of the whole community is forgotten as he refuses to accept Haemon's report that the citizens, though they dare not speak out, disapprove of his action; he denies the relevance of such a report even if true—"And is Thebes about to tell me how to rule?" (821)—and finally repudiates his principles in specific terms by an assertion that the city belongs to him—"The city *is* the king's—that's the law!" (825). This autocratic phrase puts the finishing touch to the picture Sophocles is drawing for his audience: Creon has now displayed all the characteristics of the "tyrant," a despotic ruler who seizes power and retains it by intimidation and force. Athens had lived under the rule of a "tyrant" before the democracy was established in 508 B.C., and the name and institution were still regarded with abhorrence. Creon goes on to abandon the gods whose temples crown the city's high places, the gods he once claimed as his own, and his language is even more violent. The blind prophet Tiresias tells him that the birds and dogs are fouling the altars of the city's gods with the carrion flesh of Polynices; he must bury the corpse. His furious reply begins with a characteristic accusation that the prophet has been bribed (the sentry had this same accusation flung at him), but what follows is a hideously blasphemous defiance of those gods Creon once claimed to serve:

> You'll never bury that body in the grave,
> not even if Zeus's eagles rip the corpse
> and wing their rotten pickings off to the throne of god!   (1151–53)

At this high point in his stubborn rage (he will break by the end of the scene and try, too late, to avoid the divine wrath), he is sustained by nothing except his tyrannical insistence on his own will, come what may, and his outraged refusal to be defeated by a woman. "No woman," he says, "is going to lord it over me" (593). "I am not the man, not now: she is the man / if this victory goes to her and she goes free" (541–42).

Antigone, on her side, is just as indifferent to Creon's principles of action as he is to hers. She mentions the city only in her last agonized laments before she is led off to her living death:

> O my city, all your fine rich sons!
> ... springs of the Dirce,
> holy grove of Thebes ... (934-36)

But here she is appealing for sympathy to the city over the heads of the chorus, the city's symbolic representative on stage. In all her arguments with Creon and Ismene she speaks as one wholly unconscious of the rights and duties membership in the city confers and imposes, as if no unit larger than the family existed. It is a position just as extreme as Creon's insistence that the demands of the city take precedence over all others, for the living and the dead alike.

Like Creon, she acts in the name of gods, but they are different gods. There is more than a little truth in Creon's mocking comment that Hades is "the one god she worships" (875). She is from the beginning "much possessed by death"; together with Ismene she is the last survivor of a doomed family, burdened with such sorrow that she finds life hardly worth living. "Who on earth," she says to Creon, "alive in the midst of so much grief as I, / could fail to find his death a rich reward?" (516-18). She has performed the funeral rites for mother, father and her brother Eteocles:

> I washed you with my hands,
> I dressed you all, I poured the sacred cups
> across your tombs. (989-91)

She now sacrifices her life to perform a symbolic burial, a handful of dust sprinkled on the corpse, for Polynices, the brother left to rot on the battlefield. She looks forward to her reunion with her beloved dead in that dark kingdom where Persephone, the bride of Hades, welcomes the ghosts (980-82). It is in the name of Hades, one of the three great gods who rule the universe, that she defends the right of Polynices and of all human beings to proper burial. "Death [Hades] longs for the same rites for all" (584), she tells Creon—for patriot and traitor alike; she rejects Ismene's plea to be allowed to share her fate with an appeal to the same stern authority: "Who did the work? / Let the dead and the god of death bear witness!" (610-11). In

Creon's gods, the city's patrons and defenders, she shows no interest at all. Zeus she mentions twice: once as the source of all the calamities that have fallen and are still to fall on the house of Oedipus (3–5), and once again at the beginning of her famous speech about the unwritten laws. But the context here suggests strongly that she is thinking about Zeus in his special relationship to the underworld, Zeus *Chthonios* (Underworld Zeus). "It wasn't Zeus," she says,

> who made this proclamation. . . .
> Nor did that Justice, dwelling with the gods
> beneath the earth, ordain such laws for men. (499–502)

From first to last her religious devotion and duty are to the divine powers of the world below, the masters of that world where lie her family dead, to which she herself, reluctant but fascinated, is irresistibly drawn.

But, like Creon, she ends by denying the great sanctions she invoked to justify her action. In his case the process was spread out over the course of several scenes, as he reacted to each fresh pressure that was brought to bear on him; Antigone turns her back on the claims of blood relationship and the nether gods in one sentence: three lines in Greek, no more. They are the emotional high point of the speech she makes just before she is led off to her death.

> Never, I tell you,
> if I had been the mother of children
> or if my husband died, exposed and rotting—
> I'd never have taken this ordeal upon myself,
> never defied our people's will. (995–99)

These unexpected words are part of the long speech that concludes a scene of lyric lamentation and is in effect her farewell to the land of the living. They are certainly a total repudiation of her proud claim that she acted as the champion of the unwritten laws and the infernal gods, for, as she herself told Creon, those laws and those gods have no preferences, they long "for the same rites for all" (584). And her assertion that she would not have done for her children what she has done for Polynices is a spectacular betrayal of that fanatical loyalty to blood relationship which she urged on Ismene and defended against Creon, for there is no closer relationship imaginable than that between the mother and the children of her own body. Creon turned his back on his guiding principles step by step, in reaction to opposition based on those principles; Antigone's rejection of her public values is just as complete, but it is the sudden product of a lonely, brooding introspection, a last-minute assessment of her motives, on which the imminence of death confers a merciless clarity. She did it because Polynices was her brother; she would not have done it for husband or child. She goes on to justify this disturbing statement by an argument which is more disturbing still: husband and children, she says, could be replaced by others but, since her parents are dead, she could never have another brother. It so happens that we can identify the source of this strange piece of reasoning; it is a story in the *Histories* of Sophocles' friend Herodotus (a work from which Sophocles borrowed material more than once). Darius the Great King had condemned to death for treason a Persian noble, Intaphrenes, and all the men of his family. The wife of Intaphrenes begged importunately for their lives; offered one, she chose her brother's. When Darius asked her why, she replied in words that are unmistakably the original of Antigone's lines. But what makes sense in the story makes less in the play. The wife of Intaphrenes saves her brother's life, but Polynices is already dead; Antigone's phrase "no brother could ever spring to light again" (1004) would be fully appropriate only if Antigone had managed to save Polynices' life rather than bury his corpse.

For this reason, and also because of some stylistic anomalies in this part of the speech, but most of all because they felt that the words are unworthy of the Antigone who spoke so nobly for the unwritten laws, many great scholars and also a great poet and dramatist, Goethe, have refused to believe that Sophocles wrote them. "I would give a great deal," Goethe told his friend Eckermann in 1827, "if some talented scholar could prove that these lines were interpolated, not genuine." Goethe did not know that the attempt had already been made, six years earlier; many others have tried since—Sir Richard Jebb, the greatest English editor of Sophocles, pronounced against them—and opinion today is still divided. Obviously a decision on this point is of vital significance for the interpretation of the play as a whole: with these lines removed, Antigone goes to her prison-tomb with no flicker of self-doubt, the flawless champion of the family bond and the unwritten laws, "whole as the marble, founded as the rock"—unlike Creon, she is not, in the end, reduced to recognizing that her motive is purely personal.

There is however one objective piece of evidence that speaks volumes for the authenticity of the disputed lines. Aristotle, writing his treatise on rhetoric less than a century after the death of Sophocles, summarizes this part of Antigone's speech and quotes the two lines about the irreplaceability of a brother. He is telling the would-be orator that if, in a law-court speech for the defense, he has to describe an action that seems inappropriate for the character of his client and hard to believe, he must provide an explanation for it "as in the example Sophocles gives, the one from *Antigone*"—the phrasing suggests that the passage was well known to Aristotle's readers. Evidently he does not find the passage as repellent as Goethe and Jebb did; he recognizes that Antigone's initial statement is, in terms of her character, "hard to believe" (*apiston*), but apparently he finds her explanation rhetorically satisfactory. He does not, however, for one moment suspect the authenticity of the lines. And this should make modern critics think twice before they make another attempt to oblige the shade of Goethe. Aristotle was head of a philosophical school which, under his direction, investigated the origins and early history of drama and drew up its chronology, based on official documents; he was himself the author of the most influential critique of the drama ever written, the *Poetics;* he was an acute critic of poetic style, with a keen eye for improprieties of diction and syntax; and, finally, he was perfectly conscious of the possibility of really damaging inconsistency of character, for in the *Poetics* he criticized Euripides' *Iphigenia in Aulis* on precisely that score. His acceptance of Antigone's speech as genuine demands that rather than suppress it we should try to understand it.

This is Antigone's third and last appearance on stage; in the prologue she planned her action, in the confrontation with Creon she defended it, and now, under guard, she is on her way to the prison which is to be her tomb. In lyric meters, the dramatic medium for unbridled emotion, she appeals to the chorus for sympathy and mourns for the marriage hymn she will never hear (this is as close as she ever comes to mentioning Haemon). She gets little comfort from the Theban elders; the only consolation they offer is a reminder that she may be the victim of a family curse—"do you pay for your father's terrible ordeal?" (946)—a suggestion that touches her to the quick and provokes a horror-struck rehearsal of the tormented loves and crimes of the house of Oedipus. There is, as she goes on to say, no one left to mourn her; the lyric lament she sings in this scene is her attempt to provide for herself that funeral dirge which her blood relatives would have wailed over her corpse, if they had not already preceded her into the realm of Hades. This is recognized by Creon, who cuts off the song with a sarcastic comment: "if a man could wail his own dirge *before* he dies, / he'd never finish" (970–71). And he orders the guards to take her away.

Her song cut off, she turns from the lyric medium of emotion to spoken verse, the vehicle of reasoned statement, for her farewell speech. It is not directed at anyone on stage; it resembles a soliloquy, a private meditation. It is an attempt to understand the real reasons for the action that has brought her to the brink of death. After an address to the tomb and prison where she expects to be reunited with her family she speaks to Polynices (Creon is referred to in the third person). It is to Polynices that she is speaking when she says that she would not have given her life for anyone but a brother; it is as if she had already left the world of the living and joined that community of the family dead she speaks of with such love. Now, in the face of death, oblivious of the presence of Creon and the chorus, with no public case to make, no arguments to counter, she can at last identify the driving force behind her action, the private, irrational imperative which was at the root of her championship of the rights of family and the dead against the demands of the state. It is her fanatical devotion to one particular family, her own, the doomed, incestuous, accursed house of Oedipus and especially to its most unfortunate member, the brother whose corpse lay exposed to the birds and dogs. When she tells him that she has done for him what she would not have done for husband or children she is not speaking in wholly hypothetical terms, for in sober fact she has sacrificed, for his sake, her marriage to Haemon and the children that might have issued from it.

And in this moment of self-discovery she realizes that she is absolutely alone, not only rejected by men but also abandoned by gods. "What law of the mighty gods have I transgressed?" (1013) she asks—as well she may, for whatever her motive may have been, her action was a blow struck for the rights of Hades and the dead. Unlike Christians whose master told them not to look for signs from heaven (Matthew 16:4), the ancient Greek expected if not direct intervention at least some manifestation of favor or support from his gods when he believed his cause was just—a flight of eagles, the bird of Zeus, or lightning and thunder, the signs which, in the last play, summon Oedipus to his resting place. But Antigone has to renounce this prospect: "Why look to the heavens any more . . . ?" (1014). She must go to her death as she has lived, alone, without a word of approval or a helping hand from men or gods.

Antigone's discovery that her deepest motives were purely personal has been overinterpreted by those who would suppress the passage on the grounds that, to quote Jebb's eloquent indictment, "she suddenly gives up that which, throughout the drama, has been the immovable basis of her action—the universal and unqualified validity of the divine law." This formulation is too absolute. Before the raw immediacy of death, which, as Doctor Johnson remarked, wonderfully concentrates the mind, she has sounded the depths of her own soul and identified the determinant of those high principles she proclaimed in public.

But that does not mean that they were a pretense, still less that she has now abandoned them. She dies for them. In her very last words, as she calls on the chorus to bear witness to her unjust fate, she claims once more and for the last time that she is the champion of divine law—she suffers "all for reverence, my reverence for the gods!" (1034).

Unlike Creon, who after proclaiming the predominance of the city's interests rides roughshod over them, speaking and acting like a tyrant, who after extolling the city's gods dismisses Tiresias, their spokesman, with a blasphemous insult, Antigone does not betray the loyalties she spoke for. No word of compromise or surrender comes to her lips, no plea for mercy; she has nothing to say to Creon—in fact the last words of her speech are a prayer to the gods for his punishment. "But if these men are wrong"—she does not even name him—

> let them suffer
> nothing worse than they mete out to me—
> these masters of injustice! (1019–21)

The chorus is appalled. "Still the same rough winds, the wild passion / raging through the girl" (1022–23). And Creon, in a fury, repeats his order to the guards to take her away, quickly. And this time there is no delay.

Antigone reaffirms the rightness of her action, despite the open disapproval of the chorus and the silent indifference of the gods; she has not changed—"still the same rough winds, the wild passion . . ." The chorus here restates the judgment it has passed on her earlier in the scene: "Your own blind will, your passion has destroyed you" (962). This is of course the verdict of a chorus that is clearly sympathetic to Creon's political program (and also afraid of his wrath), but it contains an element of truth. This young princess is a formidable being, a combination of cold resolve and fierce intensity. Unlike Anouilh's Antigone she has no tender emotions; except when she speaks to Polynices, she is all hard steel. Once she has made up her mind to act, no persuasion, no threat, not death itself can break her resolution. She will not yield a point or give an inch: "she hasn't learned," says the chorus, "to bend before adversity" (527)—and she never does. Those who oppose her will are met with contempt and defiance; friends who try to dissuade her are treated as enemies. Even when she despairs of the gods to whom she had looked for help, she does not waver; she goes to her death with a last disdainful insult to Creon: "see what I suffer now / at the hands of what breed of men" (1032-33).

This is a pattern of character and behavior which is found in other Sophoclean dramatic figures also; not only in the Oedipus of the other two plays of this volume but also in the protagonists of *Ajax, Electra* and *Philoctetes.* They are of course very different from each other, but they all have in common the same uncompromising determination, the same high sense of their own worth and a consequent quickness to take offense, the readiness to die rather than surrender—a heroic temper. This figure of the tragic hero, though it had a nonhuman predecessor in the Aeschylean Titan Prometheus and its origin in the great Achilles of the Homeric *Iliad,* seems, as far as we can tell from what remains of Attic tragedy, to have been a peculiarly Sophoclean creation. In his plays he explores time and again the destinies of human beings who refuse to recognize the limits imposed on the individual will by men and gods, and go to death or triumph, magnificently defiant to the last.

Antigone is such a heroic figure, and this is another of the ways in which she is different from Creon. Not only does Creon, unlike Antigone, betray in action the principles he claimed to stand for; he also, subjected to pressure that falls far short of the death Antigone is faced with, collapses in abject surrender. He was sure Antigone would give way when force was applied; he has seen "the stiffest stubborn wills / fall the hardest; the toughest iron . . . crack and shatter" (528-31)—but he is wrong. He is the one who is shattered. Tiresias tells him that he will lose a child of his own to death in return for the living being he has imprisoned in the tomb and the corpse he has kept in the sunlight. He hesitates: "I'm shaken, torn. / It's a dreadful thing to yield . . ." (1218-19). But yield he does. "What should I do?" he asks the chorus (1223) and they tell him:

release Antigone, bury Polynices. But he arrives too late; Antigone, independent to the last, has chosen her own way to die—she has hanged herself in the tomb. Creon finds Haemon mourning his betrothed; the son spits in his father's face, tries to run him through with his sword and, failing, kills himself. Creon's wife, Eurydice, hearing the news, kills herself too, her last words a curse on her husband.

Creon, as we learned from his speech to Haemon earlier in the play, had his own idea of what a family should be. "That's what a man prays for: to produce good sons— / a household full of them, dutiful and attentive . . ." (715–16). His savage dismissal of the claims of that blood relationship Antigone stood for has been punished with exquisite appropriateness, in the destruction of his own family, the curses of his son and wife. Tiresias predicted that he would have to repay the gods below with a death—"one born of your own loins" (1184); the payment has been double, son and wife as well. The gods of the city whom he claimed to defend, have, through the medium of the blind seer, denounced his action, and the city he proposed to steer on a firm course is now, as Tiresias told him, threatened by the other cities whose dead were left to rot, like Polynices, outside the walls of Thebes (1201–5). He is revealed as a disastrous failure, both as head of a family and head of state, an offender against heaven and a man without family or friends, without the respect of his fellow-citizens. He may well describe himself as "no one. Nothing" (1446).

Antigone asked the gods to punish Creon if he was wrong, and they have. They have shown to all the world that her action was right. But she did not live to see her vindication. She took her own life and by that action sealed the doom and ensured the punishment of Creon. But the will of the gods remains, as in all three of these plays, mysterious; revealed partially, if at all, through prophets rejected and prophecies misunderstood, it is the insoluble riddle at the heart of Sophocles' tragic vision. The gods told Creon he was wrong, but it is noticeable that Tiresias, their spokesman, does not say Antigone was right, he does not praise her—in fact he does not mention her. Antigone was ready to admit, if the gods did not save her and she suffered death, that she was wrong (1017–18); these words suggest that she hanged herself not just to cut short the lingering agony of starvation and imprisonment but in a sort of existential despair. Why did the gods not save her, since they approved her action? Was it because her motives, even those she openly proclaimed, were too narrow—her total indifference to the city and its rights an offense to heaven? Because, to use Eliot's phrase, she "did the right thing for the wrong reason"? We are not told. Her death, which leads directly to the destruction of Creon's family, is a thread in a tragic web spun by powers who are beyond our comprehension. "Since the gods conceal all things divine," runs a fragment from a lost Sophoclean play, "you will never understand them, not though you go searching to the ends of the earth."

The gods do not praise Antigone, nor does anyone else in the play—except the young man who loves her so passionately that he cannot bear to live without her. Haemon tells his father what the Thebans are saying behind his back, the "murmurs in the dark" (775): that Antigone deserves not death but "a glowing crown of gold!" (782). Whether this is a true report (and the chorus does not praise Antigone even when they have been convinced that she was right) or just his own feelings attributed to others for the sake of his argument, it is a timely reminder of Antigone's heroic status. In the somber world of the play, against the background of so many sudden deaths and the dark mystery of the divine dispensation, her courage and steadfastness are a gleam of light; she is the embodiment of the only consolation tragedy can offer—that in certain heroic natures unmerited suffering and death can be met with a greatness of soul which, because it is purely human, brings honor to us all.

ANTIGONE

CHARACTERS

ANTIGONE
daughter of Oedipus and Jocasta

ISMENE
sister of Antigone

A CHORUS
of old Theban citizens and their **LEADER**

CREON
king of Thebes, uncle of Antigone and Ismene

A SENTRY

HAEMON
son of Creon and Eurydice

TIRESIAS
a blind prophet

A MESSENGER

EURYDICE
wife of Creon

Guards, attendants, and a boy

[Line numbers at the head of each page refer to the Greek text; those in the margin refer to the English translation.]

TIME AND SCENE: *The royal house of Thebes. It is still night, and the invading armies of Argos have just been driven from the city. Fighting on opposite sides, the sons of Oedipus, Eteocles and Polynices, have killed each other in combat. Their uncle,* CREON, *is now king of Thebes.*

Enter ANTIGONE, *slipping through the central doors of the palace. She motions to her sister,* ISMENE, *who follows her cautiously toward an altar at the center of the stage.*

ANTIGONE:
My own flesh and blood—dear sister, dear Ismene,
how many griefs our father Oedipus handed down!
Do you know one, I ask you, one grief
that Zeus will not perfect for the two of us
while we still live and breathe? There's nothing, 5
no pain—our lives are pain—no private shame,
no public disgrace, nothing I haven't seen
in your griefs and mine. And now this:
an emergency decree, they say, the Commander
has just now declared for all of Thebes. 10
What, haven't you heard? Don't you see?
The doom reserved for enemies
marches on the ones we love the most.

ISMENE:
Not I, I haven't heard a word, Antigone.
Nothing of loved ones, 15
no joy or pain has come my way, not since
the two of us were robbed of our two brothers,
both gone in a day, a double blow—
not since the armies of Argos vanished,
just this very night. I know nothing more, 20
whether our luck's improved or ruin's still to come.

ANTIGONE:
I thought so. That's why I brought you out here,
past the gates, so you could hear in private.

ISMENE:
What's the matter? Trouble, clearly . . .
you sound so dark, so grim.   25

ANTIGONE:
Why not? Our own brothers' burial!
Hasn't Creon graced one with all the rites,
disgraced the other? Eteocles, they say,
has been given full military honors,
rightly so—Creon has laid him in the earth   30
and he goes with glory down among the dead.
But the body of Polynices, who died miserably—
why, a city-wide proclamation, rumor has it,
forbids anyone to bury him, even mourn him.
He's to be left unwept, unburied, a lovely treasure   35
for birds that scan the field and feast to their heart's content.

Such, I hear, is the martial law our good Creon
lays down for you and me—yes, me, I tell you—
and he's coming here to alert the uninformed
in no uncertain terms,   40
and he won't treat the matter lightly. Whoever
disobeys in the least will die, his doom is sealed:
stoning to death inside the city walls!

There you have it. You'll soon show what you are,
worth your breeding, Ismene, or a coward—   45
for all your royal blood.

ISMENE:
My poor sister, if things have come to this,
who am I to make or mend them, tell me,
what good am I to you?

ANTIGONE:
                    Decide.
Will you share the labor, share the work?   50

ISMENE:
What work, what's the risk? What do you mean?

ANTIGONE:
                        Raising her hands.
Will you lift up his body with these bare hands
and lower it with me?

ISMENE:
                    What? You'd bury him—
when a law forbids the city?

ANTIGONE:
                    Yes!
He is my brother and—deny it as you will—   55
your brother too.
No one will ever convict me for a traitor.

ISMENE:
So desperate, and Creon has expressly—

ANTIGONE:
                        No,
he has no right to keep me from my own.

ISMENE:
Oh my sister, think—
think how our own father died, hated,
his reputation in ruins, driven on
by the crimes he brought to light himself
to gouge out his eyes with his own hands—
then mother . . . his mother and wife, both in one,
mutilating her life in the twisted noose—
and last, our two brothers dead in a single day,
both shedding their own blood, poor suffering boys,
battling out their common destiny hand-to-hand.

Now look at the two of us, left so alone . . .
think what a death we'll die, the worst of all
if we violate the laws and override
the fixed decree of the throne, its power—
we must be sensible. Remember we are women,
we're not born to contend with men. Then too,
we're underlings, ruled by much stronger hands,
so we must submit in this, and things still worse.

I, for one, I'll beg the dead to forgive me—
I'm forced, I have no choice—I must obey
the ones who stand in power. Why rush to extremes?
It's madness, madness.

ANTIGONE:
>I won't insist,
no, even if you should have a change of heart,
I'd never welcome you in the labor, not with me.
So, do as you like, whatever suits you best—
I will bury him myself.
And even if I die in the act, that death will be a glory.
I will lie with the one I love and loved by him—
an outrage sacred to the gods! I have longer
to please the dead than please the living here:
in the kingdom down below I'll lie forever.
Do as you like, dishonor the laws
the gods hold in honor.

ISMENE:
>I'd do them no dishonor . . .
but defy the city? I have no strength for that.

ANTIGONE:
You have your excuses. I am on my way,
I will raise a mound for him, for my dear brother.

ISMENE:
Oh Antigone, you're so rash—I'm so afraid for you!

ANTIGONE:
Don't fear for me. Set your own life in order.

ISMENE:
Then don't, at least, blurt this out to anyone.
Keep it a secret. I'll join you in that, I promise.

ANTIGONE:
Dear god, shout it from the rooftops. I'll hate you
all the more for silence—tell the world!

ISMENE:
So fiery—and it ought to chill your heart.

ANTIGONE:
I know I please where I must please the most.

ISMENE:
Yes, if you can, but you're in love with impossibility.

ANTIGONE:
Very well then, once my strength gives out
I will be done at last.

ISMENE:
                You're wrong from the start,
you're off on a hopeless quest.

ANTIGONE:
If you say so, you will make me hate you,
and the hatred of the dead, by all rights,
will haunt you night and day.
But leave me to my own absurdity, leave me
to suffer this—dreadful thing. I will suffer
nothing as great as death without glory.

Exit to the side.

ISMENE:
Then go if you must, but rest assured,
wild, irrational as you are, my sister,
you are truly dear to the ones who love you.

Withdrawing to the palace.

Enter a CHORUS, *the old citizens of Thebes, chanting as the sun begins to rise.*

CHORUS:
Glory!—great beam of the sun, brightest of all
that ever rose on the seven gates of Thebes,
   you burn through night at last!
        Great eye of the golden day,
mounting the Dirce's banks you throw him back—
the enemy out of Argos, the white shield, the man of bronze—
he's flying headlong now
        the bridle of fate stampeding him with pain!

    And he had driven against our borders,
    launched by the warring claims of Polynices—
    like an eagle screaming, winging havoc
    over the land, wings of armor
    shielded white as snow,
    a huge army massing,
    crested helmets bristling for assault.

He hovered above our roofs, his vast maw gaping
closing down around our seven gates,
   his spears thirsting for the kill
        but now he's gone, look,
before he could glut his jaws with Theban blood
or the god of fire put our crown of towers to the torch.
He grappled the Dragon none can master—Thebes—
        the clang of our arms like thunder at his back!

    Zeus hates with a vengeance all bravado,
    the mighty boasts of men. He watched them
    coming on in a rising flood, the pride
    of their golden armor ringing shrill—
    and brandishing his lightning
    blasted the fighter just at the goal,
    rushing to shout his triumph from our walls.

Down from the heights he crashed, pounding down on the earth!
And a moment ago, blazing torch in hand—
>   mad for attack, ecstatic
he breathed his rage, the storm 150
> of his fury hurling at our heads!
But now his high hopes have laid him low
and down the enemy ranks the iron god of war
> deals his rewards, his stunning blows—Ares
> rapture of battle, our right arm in the crisis. 155

> Seven captains marshaled at seven gates
> seven against their equals, gave
> their brazen trophies up to Zeus,
> god of the breaking rout of battle,
> all but two: those blood brothers, 160
> one father, one mother—matched in rage,
> spears matched for the twin conquest—
> clashed and won the common prize of death.

But now for Victory! Glorious in the morning,
joy in her eyes to meet our joy 165
> she is winging down to Thebes,
our fleets of chariots wheeling in her wake—
> Now let us win oblivion from the wars,
thronging the temples of the gods
in singing, dancing choirs through the night! 170
>   Lord Dionysus, god of the dance
>   that shakes the land of Thebes, now lead the way!

>> *Enter* CREON *from the palace,*
>> *attended by his guard.*

But look, the king of the realm is coming,
Creon, the new man for the new day,
whatever the gods are sending now . . . 175
what new plan will he launch?
Why this, this special session?
Why this sudden call to the old men
summoned at one command?

CREON:
                              My countrymen,
the ship of state is safe. The gods who rocked her,
after a long, merciless pounding in the storm,
have righted her once more.
                              Out of the whole city
I have called you here alone. Well I know,
first, your undeviating respect
for the throne and royal power of King Laius.
Next, while Oedipus steered the land of Thebes,
and even after he died, your loyalty was unshakable,
you still stood by their children. Now then,
since the two sons are dead—two blows of fate
in the same day, cut down by each other's hands,
both killers, both brothers stained with blood—
as I am next in kin to the dead,
I now possess the throne and all its powers.

Of course you cannot know a man completely,
his character, his principles, sense of judgment,
not till he's shown his colors, ruling the people,
making laws. Experience, there's the test.
As I see it, whoever assumes the task,
the awesome task of setting the city's course,
and refuses to adopt the soundest policies
but fearing someone, keeps his lips locked tight,
he's utterly worthless. So I rate him now,
I always have. And whoever places a friend
above the good of his own country, he is nothing:
I have no use for him. Zeus my witness,
Zeus who sees all things, always—

I could never stand by silent, watching destruction
march against our city, putting safety to rout,
nor could I ever make that man a friend of mine
who menaces our country. Remember this: 210
our country *is* our safety.
Only while she voyages true on course
can we establish friendships, truer than blood itself.
Such are my standards. They make our city great.

Closely akin to them I have proclaimed, 215
just now, the following decree to our people
concerning the two sons of Oedipus.
Eteocles, who died fighting for Thebes,
excelling all in arms: he shall be buried,
crowned with a hero's honors, the cups we pour 220
to soak the earth and reach the famous dead.

But as for his blood brother, Polynices,
who returned from exile, home to his father-city
and the gods of his race, consumed with one desire—
to burn them roof to roots—who thirsted to drink 225
his kinsmen's blood and sell the rest to slavery:
that man—a proclamation has forbidden the city
to dignify him with burial, mourn him at all.
No, he must be left unburied, his corpse
carrion for the birds and dogs to tear, 230
an obscenity for the citizens to behold!

These are my principles. Never at my hands
will the traitor be honored above the patriot.
But whoever proves his loyalty to the state—
I'll prize that man in death as well as life. 235

LEADER:
If this is your pleasure, Creon, treating
our city's enemy and our friend this way....
The power is yours, I suppose, to enforce it
with the laws, both for the dead and all of us,
the living.

CREON:
                Follow my orders closely then,   240
be on your guard.

LEADER:
                We are too old.
Lay that burden on younger shoulders.

CREON:
                            No, no,
I don't mean the body—I've posted guards already.

LEADER:
What commands for us then? What other service?

CREON:
See that you never side with those who break my orders.   245

LEADER:
Never. Only a fool could be in love with death.

CREON:
Death is the price—you're right. But all too often
the mere hope of money has ruined many men.

A SENTRY *enters from the side.*

SENTRY:
                                My lord,
I can't say I'm winded from running, or set out
with any spring in my legs either—no sir, 250
I was lost in thought, and it made me stop, often,
dead in my tracks, wheeling, turning back,
and all the time a voice inside me muttering,
"Idiot, why? You're going straight to your death."
Then muttering, "Stopped again, poor fool? 255
If somebody gets the news to Creon first,
what's to save your neck?"
                                And so,
mulling it over, on I trudged, dragging my feet,
you can make a short road take forever . . .
but at last, look, common sense won out, 260
I'm here, and I'm all yours,
and even though I come empty-handed
I'll tell my story just the same, because
I've come with a good grip on one hope,
what will come will come, whatever fate— 265

CREON:
Come to the point!
What's wrong—why so afraid?

SENTRY:
First, myself, I've got to tell you,
I didn't do it, didn't see who did—
Be fair, don't take it out on me. 270

CREON:
You're playing it safe, soldier,
barricading yourself from any trouble.
It's obvious, you've something strange to tell.

SENTRY:
Dangerous too, and danger makes you delay
for all you're worth.

CREON:
Out with it—then dismiss!

SENTRY:
All right, here it comes. The body—
someone's just buried it, then run off . .
sprinkled some dry dust on the flesh,
given it proper rites.

CREON:
                    What?
What man alive would dare—

SENTRY:
                        I've no idea, I swear it.
There was no mark of a spade, no pickaxe there,
no earth turned up, the ground packed hard and dry,
unbroken, no tracks, no wheelruts, nothing,
the workman left no trace. Just at sunup
the first watch of the day points it out—
it was a wonder! We were stunned . . .
a terrific burden too, for all of us, listen:
you can't see the corpse, not that it's buried,
really, just a light cover of road-dust on it,
as if someone meant to lay the dead to rest
and keep from getting cursed.
Not a sign in sight that dogs or wild beasts
had worried the body, even torn the skin.

But what came next! Rough talk flew thick and fast, 295
guard grilling guard—we'd have come to blows
at last, nothing to stop it; each man for himself
and each the culprit, no one caught red-handed,
all of us pleading ignorance, dodging the charges,
ready to take up red-hot iron in our fists, 300
go through fire, swear oaths to the gods—
"I didn't do it, I had no hand in it either,
not in the plotting, not the work itself!"

Finally, after all this wrangling came to nothing,
one man spoke out and made us stare at the ground, 305
hanging our heads in fear. No way to counter him,
no way to take his advice and come through
safe and sound. Here's what he said:
"Look, we've got to report the facts to Creon,
we can't keep this hidden." Well, that won out, 310
and the lot fell to me, condemned me,
unlucky as ever, I got the prize. So here I am,
against my will and yours too, well I know—
no one wants the man who brings bad news.

LEADER:
                                      My king,
ever since he began I've been debating in my mind, 315
could this possibly be the work of the gods?

CREON:
                                        Stop—
before you make me choke with anger—the gods!
You, you're senile, must you be insane?
You say—why it's intolerable—say the gods
could have the slightest concern for that corpse?   320
Tell me, was it for meritorious service
they proceeded to bury him, prized him so? The hero
who came to burn their temples ringed with pillars,
their golden treasures—scorch their hallowed earth
and fling their laws to the winds.   325
Exactly when did you last see the gods
celebrating traitors? Inconceivable!

No, from the first there were certain citizens
who could hardly stand the spirit of my regime,
grumbling against me in the dark, heads together,   330
tossing wildly, never keeping their necks beneath
the yoke, loyally submitting to their king.
These are the instigators, I'm convinced—
they've perverted my own guard, bribed them
to do their work.
                    Money! Nothing worse   335
in our lives, so current, rampant, so corrupting.
Money—you demolish cities, root men from their homes,
you train and twist good minds and set them on
to the most atrocious schemes. No limit,
you make them adept at every kind of outrage,   340
every godless crime—money!
                              Everyone—
the whole crew bribed to commit this crime,
they've made one thing sure at least:
sooner or later they will pay the price.

Wheeling on the SENTRY.

You—
I swear to Zeus as I still believe in Zeus, 345
if you don't find the man who buried that corpse,
the very man, and produce him before my eyes,
simple death won't be enough for you,
not till we string you up alive
and wring the immorality out of you. 350
Then you can steal the rest of your days,
better informed about where to make a killing.
You'll have learned, at last, it doesn't pay
to itch for rewards from every hand that beckons.
Filthy profits wreck most men, you'll see— 355
they'll never save your life.

SENTRY:
                    Please,
may I say a word or two, or just turn and go?

CREON:
Can't you tell? Everything you say offends me.

SENTRY:
Where does it hurt you, in the ears or in the heart?

CREON:
And who are you to pinpoint my displeasure? 360

SENTRY:
The culprit grates on your feelings,
I just annoy your ears.

CREON:
                    Still talking?
You talk too much! A born nuisance—

SENTRY·
                        Maybe so,
but I never did this thing, so help me!

CREON:
                            Yes you did—
what's more, you squandered your life for silver!   365

SENTRY:
Oh it's terrible when the one who does the judging
judges things all wrong.

CREON:
                    Well now,
you just be clever about your judgments—
if you fail to produce the criminals for me,
you'll swear your dirty money brought you pain.   370

                        *Turning sharply, reentering
                        the palace.*

SENTRY:
I hope he's found. Best thing by far.
But caught or not, that's in the lap of fortune:
I'll never come back, you've seen the last of me.
I'm saved, even now, and I never thought,
I never hoped—   375
dear gods, I owe you all my thanks!

Rushing out.

CHORUS:
                                    Numberless wonders
terrible wonders walk the world but none the match for man—
that great wonder crossing the heaving gray sea,
            driven on by the blasts of winter
on through breakers crashing left and right,   380
   holds his steady course
and the oldest of the gods he wears away—
the Earth, the immortal, the inexhaustible—
as his plows go back and forth, year in, year out
   with the breed of stallions turning up the furrows.   385

And the blithe, lightheaded race of birds he snares,
the tribes of savage beasts, the life that swarms the depths—
                        with one fling of his nets
woven and coiled tight, he takes them all,
   man the skilled, the brilliant!   390
He conquers all, taming with his techniques
the prey that roams the cliffs and wild lairs,
training the stallion, clamping the yoke across
   his shaggy neck, and the tireless mountain bull.

And speech and thought, quick as the wind 395
and the mood and mind for law that rules the city—
   all these he has taught himself
and shelter from the arrows of the frost
when there's rough lodging under the cold clear sky
and the shafts of lashing rain— 400
      ready, resourceful man!
         Never without resources
never an impasse as he marches on the future—
only Death, from Death alone he will find no rescue
but from desperate plagues he has plotted his escapes. 405

Man the master, ingenious past all measure
past all dreams, the skills within his grasp—
   he forges on, now to destruction
now again to greatness. When he weaves in
the laws of the land, and the justice of the gods 410
that binds his oaths together
      he and his city rise high—
         but the city casts out
that man who weds himself to inhumanity
thanks to reckless daring. Never share my hearth 415
never think my thoughts, whoever does such things.

Enter ANTIGONE *from the side,*
accompanied by the SENTRY.

Here is a dark sign from the gods—
what to make of this? I know her,
how can I deny it? That young girl's Antigone!
Wretched, child of a wretched father,   420
Oedipus. Look, is it possible?
They bring you in like a prisoner—
why? did you break the king's laws?
Did they take you in some act of mad defiance?

SENTRY:
She's the one, she did it single-handed—   425
we caught her burying the body. Where's Creon?

Enter CREON *from the palace.*

LEADER:
Back again, just in time when you need him.

CREON:
In time for what? What is it?

SENTRY:
My king,
there's nothing you can swear you'll never do—
second thoughts make liars of us all. 430
I could have sworn I wouldn't hurry back
(what with your threats, the buffeting I just took),
but a stroke of luck beyond our wildest hopes,
what a joy, there's nothing like it. So,
back I've come, breaking my oath, who cares? 435
I'm bringing in our prisoner—this young girl—
we took her giving the dead the last rites.
But no casting lots this time; this is *my* luck,
my prize, no one else's.
Now, my lord,
here she is. Take her, question her, 440
cross-examine her to your heart's content.
But set me free, it's only right—
I'm rid of this dreadful business once for all.

CREON:
Prisoner! Her? You took her—where, doing what?

SENTRY:
Burying the man. That's the whole story.

CREON:
What? 445
You mean what you say, you're telling me the truth?

SENTRY:
She's the one. With my own eyes I saw her
bury the body, just what you've forbidden.
There. Is that plain and clear?

CREON:
What did you see? Did you catch her in the act?   450

SENTRY:
Here's what happened. We went back to our post,
those threats of yours breathing down our necks—
we brushed the corpse clean of the dust that covered it,
stripped it bare . . . it was slimy, going soft,
and we took to high ground, backs to the wind   455
so the stink of him couldn't hit us;
jostling, baiting each other to keep awake,
shouting back and forth—no napping on the job,
not this time. And so the hours dragged by
until the sun stood dead above our heads,   460
a huge white ball in the noon sky, beating,
blazing down, and then it happened—
suddenly, a whirlwind!
Twisting a great dust-storm up from the earth,
a black plague of the heavens, filling the plain,   465
ripping the leaves off every tree in sight,
choking the air and sky. We squinted hard
and took our whipping from the gods.

And after the storm passed—it seemed endless—
there, we saw the girl!   470
And she cried out a sharp, piercing cry,
like a bird come back to an empty nest,
peering into its bed, and all the babies gone . . .
Just so, when she sees the corpse bare
she bursts into a long, shattering wail   475
and calls down withering curses on the heads
of all who did the work. And she scoops up dry dust,
handfuls, quickly, and lifting a fine bronze urn,
lifting it high and pouring, she crowns the dead
with three full libations.

                    Soon as we saw
we rushed her, closed on the kill like hunters,
and she, she didn't flinch. We interrogated her,
charging her with offenses past and present—
she stood up to it all, denied nothing. I tell you,
it made me ache and laugh in the same breath.
It's pure joy to escape the worst yourself,
it hurts a man to bring down his friends.
But all that, I'm afraid, means less to me
than my own skin. That's the way I'm made.

CREON:

Wheeling on ANTIGONE.

                                    You,
with your eyes fixed on the ground—speak up.
Do you deny you did this, yes or no?

ANTIGONE:
I did it. I don't deny a thing.

CREON:

To the SENTRY.

You, get out, wherever you please—
you're clear of a very heavy charge.

He leaves; CREON *turns back to*
ANTIGONE.

You, tell me briefly, no long speeches—
were you aware a decree had forbidden this?

ANTIGONE:
Well aware. How could I avoid it? It was public.

CREON:
And still you had the gall to break this law?

ANTIGONE:
Of course I did. It wasn't Zeus, not in the least,
who made this proclamation—not to me.
Nor did that Justice, dwelling with the gods
beneath the earth, ordain such laws for men.
Nor did I think your edict had such force
that you, a mere mortal, could override the gods,
the great unwritten, unshakable traditions.
They are alive, not just today or yesterday:
they live forever, from the first of time,
and no one knows when they first saw the light.

These laws—I was not about to break them,
not out of fear of some man's wounded pride,
and face the retribution of the gods.
Die I must, I've known it all my life—
how could I keep from knowing?—even without
your death-sentence ringing in my ears.
And if I am to die before my time
I consider that a gain. Who on earth,
alive in the midst of so much grief as I,
could fail to find his death a rich reward?
So for me, at least, to meet this doom of yours
is precious little pain. But if I had allowed
my own mother's son to rot, an unburied corpse—
that would have been an agony! This is nothing.
And if my present actions strike you as foolish,
let's just say I've been accused of folly
by a fool.

LEADER:
           Like father like daughter,
passionate, wild . . .
she hasn't learned to bend before adversity.

CREON:
No? Believe me, the stiffest stubborn wills
fall the hardest; the toughest iron,
tempered strong in the white-hot fire,
you'll see it crack and shatter first of all.
And I've known spirited horses you can break
with a light bit—proud, rebellious horses.
There's no room for pride, not in a slave,
not with the lord and master standing by.

This girl was an old hand at insolence
when she overrode the edicts we made public.
But once she had done it—the insolence,
twice over—to glory in it, laughing,
mocking us to our face with what she'd done.
I am not the man, not now: she is the man
if this victory goes to her and she goes free.

Never! Sister's child or closer in blood
than all my family clustered at my altar
worshiping Guardian Zeus—she'll never escape,
she and her blood sister, the most barbaric death.
Yes, I accuse her sister of an equal part
in scheming this, this burial.

To his attendants.

Bring her here!
I just saw her inside, hysterical, gone to pieces.
It never fails: the mind convicts itself
in advance, when scoundrels are up to no good,
plotting in the dark. Oh but I hate it more
when a traitor, caught red-handed,
tries to glorify his crimes.

ANTIGONE:
Creon, what more do you want
than my arrest and execution?

CREON:
Nothing. Then I have it all.

ANTIGONE:
Then why delay? Your moralizing repels me,
every word you say—pray god it always will.
So naturally all I say repels you too.
                              Enough.   560
Give me glory! What greater glory could I win
than to give my own brother decent burial?
These citizens here would all agree,
                    To the CHORUS.
they would praise me too
if their lips weren't locked in fear.   565

                    Pointing to CREON.

Lucky tyrants—the perquisites of power!
Ruthless power to do and say whatever pleases *them*.

CREON:
You alone, of all the people in Thebes,
see things that way.

ANTIGONE:
                    They see it just that way
but defer to you and keep their tongues in leash.   570

CREON:
And you, aren't you ashamed to differ so from them?
So disloyal!

ANTIGONE:
          Not ashamed for a moment,
not to honor my brother, my own flesh and blood.

CREON:
Wasn't Eteocles a brother too—cut down, facing him?

ANTIGONE:
Brother, yes, by the same mother, the same father.

CREON:
Then how can you render his enemy such honors,
such impieties in his eyes?

ANTIGONE:
He will never testify to that,
Eteocles dead and buried.

CREON:
                He will—
if you honor the traitor just as much as him.

ANTIGONE:
But it was his brother, not some slave that died—

CREON:
Ravaging our country!—
but Eteocles died fighting in our behalf.

ANTIGONE:
No matter—Death longs for the same rites for all.

CREON:
Never the same for the patriot and the traitor.

ANTIGONE:
Who, Creon, who on earth can say the ones below
don't find this pure and uncorrupt?

CREON:
Never. Once an enemy, never a friend,
not even after death.

ANTIGONE:
I was born to join in love, not hate— 590
that is my nature.

CREON:
          Go down below and love,
if love you must—love the dead! While I'm alive,
no woman is going to lord it over me.

> *Enter* ISMENE *from the palace,
> under guard.*

CHORUS:
                    Look,
Ismene's coming, weeping a sister's tears,
loving sister, under a cloud . . .   595
her face is flushed, her cheeks streaming.
Sorrow puts her lovely radiance in the dark.

CREON:
                         You—
in my own house, you viper, slinking undetected,
sucking my life-blood! I never knew
I was breeding twin disasters, the two of you   600
rising up against my throne. Come, tell me,
will you confess your part in the crime or not?
Answer me. Swear to me.

ISMENE:
          I did it, yes—
if only she consents—I share the guilt,
the consequences too.

ANTIGONE:
                    No,   605
Justice will never suffer that—not you,
you were unwilling. I never brought you in.

ISMENE:
But now you face such dangers . . . I'm not ashamed
to sail through trouble with you,
make your troubles mine.

ANTIGONE:
                         Who did the work?   610
Let the dead and the god of death bear witness!
I have no love for a friend who loves in words alone.

ISMENE:
Oh no, my sister, don't reject me, please,
let me die beside you, consecrating
the dead together.

ANTIGONE:
                    Never share my dying,   615
don't lay claim to what you never touched.
My death will be enough.

ISMENE:
What do I care for life, cut off from you?

ANTIGONE:
Ask Creon. Your concern is all for him.

ISMENE:
Why abuse me so? It doesn't help you now.

ANTIGONE:
                                                You're right— 620
if I mock you, I get no pleasure from it,
only pain.

ISMENE:
         Tell me, dear one,
what can I do to help you, even now?

ANTIGONE:
Save yourself. I don't grudge you your survival.

ISMENE:
Oh no, no, denied my portion in your death?   625

ANTIGONE:
You chose to live, I chose to die.

ISMENE:
                    Not, at least,
without every kind of caution I could voice.

ANTIGONE:
Your wisdom appealed to one world—mine, another.

ISMENE:
But look, we're both guilty, both condemned to death.

ANTIGONE:
Courage! Live your life. I gave myself to death,   630
long ago, so I might serve the dead.

CREON:
They're both mad, I tell you, the two of them.
One's just shown it, the other's been that way
since she was born.

ISMENE:
                    True, my king,
the sense we were born with cannot last forever . . . 635
commit cruelty on a person long enough
and the mind begins to go.

CREON:
                    Yours did,
when you chose to commit your crimes with her.

ISMENE:
How can I live alone, without her?

CREON:
                        Her?
Don't even mention her—she no longer exists. 640

ISMENE:
What? You'd kill your own son's bride?

CREON:
                           Absolutely:
there are other fields for him to plow.

ISMENE:
                        Perhaps,
but never as true, as close a bond as theirs.

CREON:
A worthless woman for my son? It repels me.

ISMENE:
Dearest Haemon, your father wrongs you so! 645

CREON:
Enough, enough—you and your talk of marriage!

ISMENE:
Creon—you're really going to rob your son of Antigone?

CREON:
Death will do it for me—break their marriage off.

LEADER:
So, it's settled then? Antigone must die?

CREON:
Settled, yes—we both know that. 650

To the guards.

Stop wasting time. Take them in.
From now on they'll act like women.
Tie them up, no more running loose;
even the bravest will cut and run,
once they see Death coming for their lives. 655

The guards escort ANTIGONE *and*
ISMENE *into the palace.* CREON
*remains while the old citizens form
their* CHORUS.

CHORUS:
Blest, they are the truly blest who all their lives
have never tasted devastation. For others, once
the gods have rocked a house to its foundations
   the ruin will never cease, cresting on and on
from one generation on throughout the race—   660
like a great mounting tide
driven on by savage northern gales,
       surging over the dead black depths
roiling up from the bottom dark heaves of sand
and the headlands, taking the storm's onslaught full-force,   665
roar, and the low moaning
             echoes on and on
                         and now
as in ancient times I see the sorrows of the house,
the living heirs of the old ancestral kings,
piling on the sorrows of the dead
   and one generation cannot free the next—   670
some god will bring them crashing down,
the race finds no release.
And now the light, the hope
       springing up from the late last root
in the house of Oedipus, that hope's cut down in turn   675
by the long, bloody knife swung by the gods of death
by a senseless word
             by fury at the heart.

Zeus,
yours is the power, Zeus, what man on earth
can override it, who can hold it back?
Power that neither Sleep, the all-ensnaring   680
    no, nor the tireless months of heaven
can ever overmaster—young through all time,
mighty lord of power, you hold fast
    the dazzling crystal mansions of Olympus.
And throughout the future, late and soon   685
as through the past, your law prevails:
no towering form of greatness
        enters into the lives of mortals
                    free and clear of ruin.
                              True,
our dreams, our high hopes voyaging far and wide   690
bring sheer delight to many, to many others
    delusion, blithe, mindless lusts
and the fraud steals on one slowly . . . unaware
till he trips and puts his foot into the fire.
    He was a wise old man who coined   695
the famous saying: "Sooner or later
foul is fair, fair is foul
to the man the gods will ruin"—
    He goes his way for a moment only
                    free of blinding ruin.   700

                    Enter HAEMON *from the palace.*

Here's Haemon now, the last of all your sons.
Does he come in tears for his bride,
his doomed bride, Antigone—
bitter at being cheated of their marriage?

CREON:
We'll soon know, better than seers could tell us.

Turning to HAEMON.

Son, you've heard the final verdict on your bride?
Are you coming now, raving against your father?
Or do you love me, no matter what I do?

HAEMON:
Father, I'm your *son* . . . you in your wisdom
set my bearings for me—I obey you.
No marriage could ever mean more to me than you,
whatever good direction you may offer.

CREON:
                       Fine, Haemon.
That's how you ought to feel within your heart,
subordinate to your father's will in every way.
That's what a man prays for: to produce good sons—
a household full of them, dutiful and attentive,
so they can pay his enemy back with interest
and match the respect their father shows his friend.
But the man who rears a brood of useless children,
what has he brought into the world, I ask you?
Nothing but trouble for himself, and mockery
from his enemies laughing in his face.
                       Oh Haemon,
never lose your sense of judgment over a woman.
The warmth, the rush of pleasure, it all goes cold
in your arms, I warn you . . . a worthless woman
in your house, a misery in your bed.
What wound cuts deeper than a loved one
turned against you? Spit her out,
like a mortal enemy—let the girl go.
Let her find a husband down among the dead.

Imagine it: I caught her in naked rebellion,
the traitor, the only one in the whole city.
I'm not about to prove myself a liar,
not to my people, no, I'm going to kill her!
That's right—so let her cry for mercy, sing her hymns   735
to Zeus who defends all bonds of kindred blood.
Why, if I bring up my own kin to be rebels,
think what I'd suffer from the world at large.
Show me the man who rules his household well:
I'll show you someone fit to rule the state.   740
That good man, my son,
I have every confidence he and he alone
can give commands and take them too. Staunch
in the storm of spears he'll stand his ground,
a loyal, unflinching comrade at your side.   745

But whoever steps out of line, violates the laws
or presumes to hand out orders to his superiors,
he'll win no praise from me. But that man
the city places in authority, his orders
must be obeyed, large and small,   750
right and wrong.
                    Anarchy—
show me a greater crime in all the earth!
She, she destroys cities, rips up houses,
breaks the ranks of spearmen into headlong rout.
But the ones who last it out, the great mass of them   755
owe their lives to discipline. Therefore
we must defend the men who live by law,
never let some woman triumph over us.
Better to fall from power, if fall we must,
at the hands of a man—never be rated   760
inferior to a woman, never.

LEADER:
             To us,
unless old age has robbed us of our wits,
you seem to say what you have to say with sense.

HAEMON:
Father, only the gods endow a man with reason,
the finest of all their gifts, a treasure. 765
Far be it from me—I haven't the skill,
and certainly no desire, to tell you when,
if ever, you make a slip in speech . . . though
someone else might have a good suggestion.

Of course it's not for you, 770
in the normal run of things, to watch
whatever men say or do, or find to criticize.
The man in the street, you know, dreads your glance,
he'd never say anything displeasing to your face.
But it's for me to catch the murmurs in the dark, 775
the way the city mourns for this young girl.
"No woman," they say, "ever deserved death less,
and such a brutal death for such a glorious action.
She, with her own dear brother lying in his blood—
she couldn't bear to leave him dead, unburied, 780
food for the wild dogs or wheeling vultures.
Death? She deserves a glowing crown of gold!"
So they say, and the rumor spreads in secret,
darkly . . .
       I rejoice in your success, father—
nothing more precious to me in the world. 785
What medal of honor brighter to his children
than a father's growing glory? Or a child's
to his proud father? Now don't, please,
be quite so single-minded, self-involved,
or assume the world is wrong and you are right. 790
Whoever thinks that he alone possesses intelligence,
the gift of eloquence, he and no one else,
and character too . . . such men, I tell you,
spread them open—you will find them empty.

                            No,
it's no disgrace for a man, even a wise man,   795
to learn many things and not to be too rigid.
You've seen trees by a raging winter torrent,
how many sway with the flood and salvage every twig,
but not the stubborn—they're ripped out, roots and all.
Bend or break. The same when a man is sailing: 800
haul your sheets too taut, never give an inch,
you'll capsize, and go the rest of the voyage
keel up and the rowing-benches under.

Oh give way. Relax your anger—change!
I'm young, I know, but let me offer this: 805
it would be best by far, I admit,
if a man were born infallible, right by nature.
If not—and things don't often go that way,
it's best to learn from those with good advice.

LEADER:
You'd do well, my lord, if he's speaking to the point,   810
to learn from him,

                        Turning to HAEMON.

                and you, my boy, from him.
You both are talking sense.

CREON:
                        So,
men our age, we're to be lectured, are we?—
schooled by a boy his age?

HAEMON:
Only in what is right. But if I seem young,   815
look less to my years and more to what I do

CREON:
Do? Is admiring rebels an achievement?

HAEMON:
I'd never suggest that you admire treason.

CREON:
                                        Oh?—
isn't that just the sickness that's attacked her?

HAEMON:
The whole city of Thebes denies it, to a man.   820

CREON:
And is Thebes about to tell me how to rule?

HAEMON:
Now, you see? Who's talking like a child?

CREON:
Am I to rule this land for others—or myself?

HAEMON:
It's no city at all, owned by one man alone.

CREON:
What? The city *is* the king's—that's the law!   825

HAEMON:
What a splendid king you'd make of a desert island—
you and you alone.

CREON:
                        To the CHORUS.
            This boy, I do believe,
is fighting on her side, the woman's side.

HAEMON:
If you are a woman, yes—
my concern is all for you. 830

CREON:
Why, you degenerate—bandying accusations,
threatening me with justice, your own father!

HAEMON:
I see my father offending justice—wrong.

CREON:
                              Wrong?
To protect my royal rights?

HAEMON:
                        Protect your rights?
When you trample down the honors of the gods? 835

CREON:
You, you soul of corruption, rotten through—
woman's accomplice!

HAEMON:
                  That may be,
but you will never find me accomplice to a criminal.

CREON:
That's what *she* is,
and every word you say is a blatant appeal for her— 840

HAEMON:
And you, and me, and the gods beneath the earth.

CREON:
You will never marry her, not while she's alive.

HAEMON:
Then she will die . . . but her death will kill another.

CREON:
What, brazen threats? You go too far!

HAEMON:
                    What threat?
Combating your empty, mindless judgments with a word?   845

CREON:
You'll suffer for your sermons, you and your empty wisdom!

HAEMON:
If you weren't my father, I'd say you were insane.

CREON:
Don't flatter me with Father—you woman's slave!

HAEMON:
You really expect to fling abuse at me
and not receive the same?

CREON:
                Is that so!   850
Now, by heaven, I promise you, you'll pay—
taunting, insulting me! Bring her out,
that hateful—she'll die now, here,
in front of his eyes, beside her groom!

HAEMON:
No, no, she will never die beside me—   855
don't delude yourself. And you will never
see me, never set eyes on my face again.
Rage your heart out, rage with friends
who can stand the sight of you.
                    Rushing out.

LEADER:
Gone, my king, in a burst of anger. 860
A temper young as his . . . hurt him once,
he may do something violent.

CREON:
                    Let him do—
dream up something desperate, past all human limit!
Good riddance. Rest assured,
he'll never save those two young girls from death. 865

LEADER:
Both of them, you really intend to kill them both?

CREON:
No, not her, the one whose hands are clean—
you're quite right.

LEADER:
            But Antigone—
what sort of death do you have in mind for her?

CREON:
I will take her down some wild, desolate path 870
never trod by men, and wall her up alive
in a rocky vault, and set out short rations,
just the measure piety demands
to keep the entire city free of defilement.
There let her pray to the one god she worships: 875
Death—who knows?—may just reprieve her from death.
Or she may learn at last, better late than never,
what a waste of breath it is to worship Death.

Exit to the palace.

CHORUS:
Love, never conquered in battle
Love the plunderer laying waste the rich! 880
Love standing the night-watch
        guarding a girl's soft cheek,
you range the seas, the shepherds' steadings off in the wilds—
not even the deathless gods can flee your onset,
nothing human born for a day— 885
whoever feels your grip is driven mad.
                Love!—
you wrench the minds of the righteous into outrage,
swerve them to their ruin—you have ignited this,
this kindred strife, father and son at war
        and Love alone the victor— 890
warm glance of the bride triumphant, burning with desire!
Throned in power, side-by-side with the mighty laws!
Irresistible Aphrodite, never conquered—
Love, you mock us for your sport.

                ANTIGONE *is brought from the palace*
                under guard.

    But now, even I would rebel against the king, 895
    I would break all bounds when I see this—
    I fill with tears, I cannot hold them back,
    not any more . . . I see Antigone make her way
    to the bridal vault where all are laid to rest.

ANTIGONE:
Look at me, men of my fatherland,
   setting out on the last road
looking into the last light of day
the last I will ever see . . .
the god of death who puts us all to bed
takes me down to the banks of Acheron alive—
   denied my part in the wedding-songs,
no wedding-song in the dusk has crowned my marriage—
I go to wed the lord of the dark waters.

CHORUS:
   Not crowned with glory or with a dirge,
   you leave for the deep pit of the dead.
   No withering illness laid you low,
   no strokes of the sword—a law to yourself,
   alone, no mortal like you, ever, you go down
   to the halls of Death alive and breathing.

ANTIGONE:
But think of Niobe—well I know her story—
   think what a living death she died,
Tantalus' daughter, stranger queen from the east:
there on the mountain heights, growing stone
binding as ivy, slowly walled her round
and the rains will never cease, the legends say
the snows will never leave her . . .
   wasting away, under her brows the tears
showering down her breasting ridge and slopes—
a rocky death like hers puts me to sleep.

CHORUS:
   But she was a god, born of gods,
   and we are only mortals born to die.
   And yet, of course, it's a great thing
   for a dying girl to hear, even to hear
   she shares a destiny equal to the gods,
   during life and later, once she's dead.

ANTIGONE:

                                          O you mock me!
Why, in the name of all my fathers' gods
why can't you wait till I am gone—
   must you abuse me to my face?
O my city, all your fine rich sons!
And you, you springs of the Dirce,
holy grove of Thebes where the chariots gather,
     you at least, you'll bear me witness, look,
unmourned by friends and forced by such crude laws
I go to my rockbound prison, strange new tomb—
   always a stranger, O dear god,
   I have no home on earth and none below,
     not with the living, not with the breathless dead.

CHORUS:
     You went too far, the last limits of daring—
     smashing against the high throne of Justice!
        Your life's in ruins, child—I wonder . . .
     do you pay for your father's terrible ordeal?

ANTIGONE:
There—at last you've touched it, the worst pain
the worst anguish! Raking up the grief for father
   three times over, for all the doom
that's struck us down, the brilliant house of Laius.
O mother, your marriage-bed
the coiling horrors, the coupling there—
   you with your own son, my father—doomstruck mother!
Such, such were my parents, and I their wretched child.
I go to them now, cursed, unwed, to share their home—
   I am a stranger! O dear brother, doomed
   in your marriage—your marriage murders mine,
     your dying drags me down to death alive!

Enter Creon.

CHORUS:
>Reverence asks some reverence in return—
>but attacks on power never go unchecked, 960
>> not by the man who holds the reins of power.
>Your own blind will, your passion has destroyed you.

ANTIGONE:
>No one to weep for me, my friends,
>no wedding-song—they take me away
>in all my pain . . . the road lies open, waiting. 965
>Never again, the law forbids me to see
>the sacred eye of day. I am agony!
>No tears for the destiny that's mine,
>no loved one mourns my death.

CREON:
>>>>>>>>> Can't you see?
>If a man could wail his own dirge *before* he dies, 970
>he'd never finish.

To the guards.

>>Take her away, quickly!
>Wall her up in the tomb, you have your orders.
>Abandon her there, alone, and let her choose—
>death or a buried life with a good roof for shelter.
>As for myself, my hands are clean. This young girl— 975
>dead or alive, she will be stripped of her rights,
>her stranger's rights, here in the world above.

ANTIGONE:
O tomb, my bridal-bed—my house, my prison
cut in the hollow rock, my everlasting watch!
I'll soon be there, soon embrace my own,   *980*
the great growing family of our dead
Persephone has received among her ghosts.

                  I,
the last of them all, the most reviled by far,
go down before my destined time's run out.
But still I go, cherishing one good hope: *985*
my arrival may be dear to father,
dear to you, my mother,
dear to you, my loving brother, Eteocles—
When you died I washed you with my hands,
I dressed you all, I poured the sacred cups   *990*
across your tombs. But now, Polynices,
because I laid your body out as well,
this, this is my reward. Nevertheless
I honored you—the decent will admit it—
well and wisely too.
                  Never, I tell you,   *995*
if I had been the mother of children
or if my husband died, exposed and rotting—
I'd never have taken this ordeal upon myself,
never defied our people's will. What law,
you ask, do I satisfy with what I say?   *1000*
A husband dead, there might have been another.
A child by another too, if I had lost the first.
But mother and father both lost in the halls of Death,
no brother could ever spring to light again.

For this law alone I held you first in honor. 1005
For this, Creon, the king, judges me a criminal
guilty of dreadful outrage, my dear brother!
And now he leads me off, a captive in his hands,
with no part in the bridal-song, the bridal-bed,
denied all joy of marriage, raising children— 1010
deserted so by loved ones, struck by fate,
I descend alive to the caverns of the dead.

What law of the mighty gods have I transgressed?
Why look to the heavens any more, tormented as I am?
Whom to call, what comrades now? Just think, 1015
my reverence only brands me for irreverence!
Very well: if this is the pleasure of the gods,
once I suffer I will know that I was wrong.
But if these men are wrong, let them suffer
nothing worse than they mete out to me— 1020
these masters of injustice!

LEADER:
Still the same rough winds, the wild passion
raging through the girl.

CREON:

>   *To the guards.*
> Take her away.
You're wasting time—you'll pay for it too.

ANTIGONE:
Oh god, the voice of death. It's come, it's here.   1025

CREON:
True. Not a word of hope—your doom is sealed.

ANTIGONE:
>   Land of Thebes, city of all my fathers—
>   O you gods, the first gods of the race!
>   They drag me away, now, no more delay.
>   Look on me, you noble sons of Thebes—   1030
>   the last of a great line of kings,
>   I alone, see what I suffer now
>   at the hands of what breed of men—
>   all for reverence, my reverence for the gods!

>   *She leaves under guard: the* CHORUS
>   *gathers.*

CHORUS:
>   Danaë, Danaë— 1035
> even she endured a fate like yours,
>   in all her lovely strength she traded
> the light of day for the bolted brazen vault—
> buried within her tomb, her bridal-chamber,
> wed to the yoke and broken. 1040
>   But she was of glorious birth
>   my child, my child
> and treasured the seed of Zeus within her womb,
> the cloudburst streaming gold!
>   The power of fate is a wonder, 1045
>   dark, terrible wonder—
>   neither wealth nor armies
>   towered walls nor ships
>   black hulls lashed by the salt
>   can save us from that force. 1050
>
> The yoke tamed him too
>   young Lycurgus flaming in anger
> king of Edonia, all for his mad taunts
> Dionysus clamped him down, encased
> in the chain-mail of rock 1055
>   and there his rage
>   his terrible flowering rage burst—
> sobbing, dying away . . . at last that madman
> came to know his god—
>   the power he mocked, the power 1060
>   he taunted in all his frenzy
>   trying to stamp out
>   the women strong with the god—
>   the torch, the raving sacred cries— .
>   enraging the Muses who adore the flute. 1065

And far north where the Black Rocks
    cut the sea in half
and murderous straits
split the coast of Thrace
    a forbidding city stands   *1070*
where once, hard by the walls
the savage Ares thrilled to watch
a king's new queen, a Fury rearing in rage
    against his two royal sons—
    her bloody hands, her dagger-shuttle   *1075*
stabbing out their eyes—cursed, blinding wounds—
their eyes blind sockets screaming for revenge!

They wailed in agony, cries echoing cries
    the princes doomed at birth . . .
and their mother doomed to chains,   *1080*
walled up in a tomb of stone—
    but she traced her own birth back
to a proud Athenian line and the high gods
and off in caverns half the world away,
born of the wild North Wind   *1085*
    she sprang on her father's gales,
    racing stallions up the leaping cliffs—
child of the heavens. But even on her the Fates
the gray everlasting Fates rode hard
my child, my child.

Enter TIRESIAS, *the blind prophet, led by a boy.*

TIRESIAS:
                        Lords of Thebes,
I and the boy have come together,
hand in hand. Two see with the eyes of one . . .
so the blind must go, with a guide to lead the way.

CREON:
What is it, old Tiresias? What news now?

TIRESIAS:
I will teach you. And you obey the seer.

CREON:
                                I will,
I've never wavered from your advice before.

TIRESIAS:
And so you kept the city straight on course.

CREON:
I owe you a great deal, I swear to that.

TIRESIAS:
Then reflect, my son: you are poised,
once more, on the razor-edge of fate.

CREON:
What is it? I shudder to hear you.

TIRESIAS:
                    You will learn
when you listen to the warnings of my craft.
As I sat on the ancient seat of augury,
in the sanctuary where every bird I know
will hover at my hands—suddenly I heard it,   1105
a strange voice in the wingbeats, unintelligible,
barbaric, a mad scream! Talons flashing, ripping,
they were killing each other—that much I knew—
the murderous fury whirring in those wings
made that much clear!
                    I was afraid,   1110
I turned quickly, tested the burnt-sacrifice,
ignited the altar at all points—but no fire,
the god in the fire never blazed.
Not from those offerings . . . over the embers
slid a heavy ooze from the long thighbones,   1115
smoking, sputtering out, and the bladder
puffed and burst—spraying gall into the air—
and the fat wrapping the bones slithered off
and left them glistening white. No fire!
The rites failed that might have blazed the future   1120
with a sign. So I learned from the boy here:
he is my guide, as I am guide to others.
                            And it is you—
your high resolve that sets this plague on Thebes.
The public altars and sacred hearths are fouled,
one and all, by the birds and dogs with carrion   1125
torn from the corpse, the doomstruck son of Oedipus!
And so the gods are deaf to our prayers, they spurn
the offerings in our hands, the flame of holy flesh.
No birds cry out an omen clear and true—
they're gorged with the murdered victim's blood and fat.   1130

Take these things to heart, my son, I warn you.
All men make mistakes, it is only human.
But once the wrong is done, a man
can turn his back on folly, misfortune too,
if he tries to make amends, however low he's fallen, 1135
and stops his bullnecked ways. Stubbornness
brands you for stupidity—pride is a crime.
No, yield to the dead!
Never stab the fighter when he's down.
Where's the glory, killing the dead twice over? 1140

I mean you well. I give you sound advice.
It's best to learn from a good adviser
when he speaks for your own good:
it's pure gain.

CREON:
     Old man—all of you! So,
you shoot your arrows at my head like archers at the target—
I even have *him* loosed on me, this fortune-teller.
Oh his ilk has tried to sell me short
and ship me off for years. Well,
drive your bargains, traffic—much as you like—
in the gold of India, silver-gold of Sardis. 1150
You'll never bury that body in the grave,
not even if Zeus's eagles rip the corpse
and wing their rotten pickings off to the throne of god!
Never, not even in fear of such defilement
will I tolerate his burial, that traitor. 1155
Well I know, we can't defile the gods—
no mortal has the power.
     No,
reverend old Tiresias, all men fall,
it's only human, but the wisest fall obscenely
when they glorify obscene advice with rhetoric— 1160
all for their own gain.

TIRESIAS:
Oh god, is there a man alive
who knows, who actually believes . . .

CREON:
                              What now?
What earth-shattering truth are you about to utter?

TIRESIAS:
. . . just how much a sense of judgment, wisdom   1165
is the greatest gift we have?

CREON:
                         Just as much, I'd say,
as a twisted mind is the worst affliction known.

TIRESIAS:
You are the one who's sick, Creon, sick to death.

CREON:
I am in no mood to trade insults with a seer.

TIRESIAS:
You have already, calling my prophecies a lie.

CREON:
                                   Why not?   1170
You and the whole breed of seers are mad for money!

TIRESIAS:
And the whole race of tyrants lusts for filthy gain.

CREON:
This slander of yours—
are you aware you're speaking to the king?

TIRESIAS:
Well aware. Who helped you save the city?

CREON:
                                        You—   1175
you have your skills, old seer, but you lust for injustice!

TIRESIAS:
You will drive me to utter the dreadful secret in my heart.

CREON:
Spit it out! Just don't speak it out for profit.

TIRESIAS:
Profit? No, not a bit of profit, not for you.

CREON:
Know full well, you'll never buy off my resolve.   1180

TIRESIAS:
Then know this too, learn this by heart!
The chariot of the sun will not race through
so many circuits more, before you have surrendered
one born of your own loins, your own flesh and blood,
a corpse for corpses given in return, since you have thrust   1185
to the world below a child sprung for the world above,
ruthlessly lodged a living soul within the grave—
then you've robbed the gods below the earth,
keeping a dead body here in the bright air,
unburied, unsung, unhallowed by the rites.   1190

You, you have no business with the dead,
nor do the gods above—this is violence
you have forced upon the heavens.
And so the avengers, the dark destroyers late
but true to the mark, now lie in wait for you,   1195
the Furies sent by the gods and the god of death
to strike you down with the pains that you perfected!

There. Reflect on that, tell me I've been bribed.
The day comes soon, no long test of time, not now,
when the mourning cries for men and women break   1200
throughout your halls. Great hatred rises against you—
cities in tumult, all whose mutilated sons
the dogs have graced with burial, or the wild beasts
or a wheeling crow that wings the ungodly stench of carrion
back to each city, each warrior's hearth and home.   1205

These arrows for your heart! Since you've raked me
I loose them like an archer in my anger,
arrows deadly true. You'll never escape
their burning, searing force.

Motioning to his escort.

Come, boy, take me home.   1210
So he can vent his rage on younger men,
and learn to keep a gentler tongue in his head
and better sense than what he carries now.

Exit to the side.

LEADER:
The old man's gone, my king—
terrible prophecies. Well I know, 1215
since the hair on this old head went gray,
he's never lied to Thebes.

CREON:
I know it myself—I'm shaken, torn.
It's a dreadful thing to yield . . . but resist now?
Lay my pride bare to the blows of ruin? 1220
That's dreadful too.

LEADER:
              But good advice,
Creon, take it now, you must.

CREON:
What should I do? Tell me . . . I'll obey.

LEADER:
Go! Free the girl from the rocky vault
and raise a mound for the body you exposed. 1225

CREON:
That's your advice? You think I should give in?

LEADER:
Yes, my king, quickly. Disasters sent by the gods
cut short our follies in a flash.

CREON:
                    Oh it's hard,
giving up the heart's desire . . . but I will do it—
no more fighting a losing battle with necessity.

LEADER:
Do it now, go, don't leave it to others.

CREON:
Now—I'm on my way! Come, each of you,
take up axes, make for the high ground,
over there, quickly! I and my better judgment
have come round to this—I shackled her,
I'll set her free myself. I am afraid . . .
it's best to keep the established laws
to the very day we die.

Rushing out, followed by his entourage. The CHORUS *clusters around the altar.*

CHORUS:
God of a hundred names!
                   Great Dionysus—
     Son and glory of Semele! Pride of Thebes—   1240
Child of Zeus whose thunder rocks the clouds—
Lord of the famous lands of evening—
King of the Mysteries!
                   King of Eleusis, Demeter's plain
her breasting hills that welcome in the world—
Great Dionysus!
               Bacchus, living in Thebes   1245
the mother-city of all your frenzied women—
                            Bacchus
  living along the Ismenus' rippling waters
standing over the field sown with the Dragon's teeth!

You—we have seen you through the flaring smoky fires,
   your torches blazing over the twin peaks   1250
where nymphs of the hallowed cave climb onward
               fired with you, your sacred rage—
we have seen you at Castalia's running spring
and down from the heights of Nysa crowned with ivy
the greening shore rioting vines and grapes   1255
   down you come in your storm of wild women
      ecstatic, mystic cries—
                         Dionysus—
down to watch and ward the roads of Thebes!

First of all cities, Thebes you honor first
you and your mother, bride of the lightning—
come, Dionysus! now your people lie
in the iron grip of plague,
come in your racing, healing stride
        down Parnassus' slopes
or across the moaning straits.
                Lord of the dancing—
dance, dance the constellations breathing fire!
Great master of the voices of the night!
Child of Zeus, God's offspring, come, come forth!
Lord, king, dance with your nymphs, swirling, raving
arm-in-arm in frenzy through the night
   they dance you, Iacchus—
              Dance, Dionysus
giver of all good things!

Enter a MESSENGER *from the side.*

MESSENGER:
            Neighbors,
friends of the house of Cadmus and the kings,
there's not a thing in this mortal life of ours
I'd praise or blame as settled once for all.
Fortune lifts and Fortune fells the lucky
and unlucky every day. No prophet on earth
can tell a man his fate. Take Creon:
there was a man to rouse your envy once,
as I see it. He saved the realm from enemies,
taking power, he alone, the lord of the fatherland,
he set us true on course—he flourished like a tree
with the noble line of sons he bred and reared . . .
and now it's lost, all gone.

                    Believe me,
when a man has squandered his true joys,   1285
he's good as dead, I tell you, a living corpse.
Pile up riches in your house, as much as you like—
live like a king with a huge show of pomp,
but if real delight is missing from the lot,
I wouldn't give you a wisp of smoke for it,   1290
not compared with joy.

LEADER:
                    What now?
What new grief do you bring the house of kings?

MESSENGER:
Dead, dead—and the living are guilty of their death!

LEADER:
Who's the murderer? Who is dead? Tell us.

MESSENGER:
Haemon's gone, his blood spilled by the very hand—   1295

LEADER:
His father's or his own?

MESSENGER:
                    His own . . .
raging mad with his father for the death—

LEADER:
                            Oh great seer,
you saw it all, you brought your word to birth!

MESSENGER:
Those are the facts. Deal with them as you will.

> *As he turns to go,* EURYDICE *enters
> from the palace.*

LEADER:
Look, Eurydice. Poor woman, Creon's wife, 1300
so close at hand. By chance perhaps,
unless she's heard the news about her son.

EURYDICE:
                              My countrymen,
all of you—I caught the sound of your words
as I was leaving to do my part,
to appeal to queen Athena with my prayers. 1305
I was just loosing the bolts, opening the doors,
when a voice filled with sorrow, family sorrow,
struck my ears, and I fell back, terrified,
into the women's arms—everything went black.
Tell me the news, again, whatever it is . . . 1310
sorrow and I are hardly strangers.
I can bear the worst.

MESSENGER:
              I—dear lady,
I'll speak as an eye-witness. I was there.
And I won't pass over one word of the truth.
Why should I try to soothe you with a story, 1315
only to prove a liar in a moment?
Truth is always best.
              So,
I escorted your lord, I guided him
to the edge of the plain where the body lay,
Polynices, torn by the dogs and still unmourned. 1320
And saying a prayer to Hecate of the Crossroads,
Pluto too, to hold their anger and be kind,
we washed the dead in a bath of holy water
and plucking some fresh branches, gathering . . .
what was left of him, we burned them all together 1325
and raised a high mound of native earth, and then
we turned and made for that rocky vault of hers,
the hollow, empty bed of the bride of Death.

And far off, one of us heard a voice,
a long wail rising, echoing   1330
out of that unhallowed wedding-chamber,
he ran to alert the master and Creon pressed on,
closer—the strange, inscrutable cry came sharper,
throbbing around him now, and he let loose
a cry of his own, enough to wrench the heart,   1335
"Oh god, am I the prophet now? going down
the darkest road I've ever gone? My son—
it's *his* dear voice, he greets me! Go, men,
closer, quickly! Go through the gap,
the rocks are dragged back—   1340
right to the tomb's very mouth—and look,
see if it's Haemon's voice I think I hear,
or the gods have robbed me of my senses."

The king was shattered. We took his orders,
went and searched, and there in the deepest,   1345
dark recesses of the tomb we found her . . .
hanged by the neck in a fine linen noose,
strangled in her veils—and the boy,
his arms flung around her waist,
clinging to her, wailing for his bride,   1350
dead and down below, for his father's crimes
and the bed of his marriage blighted by misfortune.
When Creon saw him, he gave a deep sob,
he ran in, shouting, crying out to him,
"Oh my child—what have you done? what seized you,   1355
what insanity? what disaster drove you mad?
Come out, my son! I beg you on my knees!"
But the boy gave him a wild burning glance,
spat in his face, not a word in reply,
he drew his sword—his father rushed out,   1360
running as Haemon lunged and missed!—
and then, doomed, desperate with himself,
suddenly leaning his full weight on the blade,
he buried it in his body, halfway to the hilt.

And still in his senses, pouring his arms around her,   1365
he embraced the girl and breathing hard,
released a quick rush of blood,
bright red on her cheek glistening white.
And there he lies, body enfolding body . . .
he has won his bride at last, poor boy,   1370
not here but in the houses of the dead.

Creon shows the world that of all the ills
afflicting men the worst is lack of judgment.

> EURYDICE *turns and reenters the palace.*

LEADER:
What do you make of that? The lady's gone,
without a word, good or bad.

MESSENGER:
                        I'm alarmed too   1375
but here's my hope—faced with her son's death
she finds it unbecoming to mourn in public.
Inside, under her roof, she'll set her women
to the task and wail the sorrow of the house.
She's too discreet. She won't do something rash.   1380

LEADER:
I'm not so sure. To me, at least,
a long heavy silence promises danger,
just as much as a lot of empty outcries.

MESSENGER:
We'll see if she's holding something back,
hiding some passion in her heart.   1385
I'm going in. You may be right—who knows?
Even too much silence has its dangers.

> *Exit to the palace. Enter* CREON
> *from the side, escorted by attendants*
> *carrying* HAEMON's *body on a bier.*

LEADER:
> The king himself! Coming toward us,
> look, holding the boy's head in his hands.
> Clear, damning proof, if it's right to say so— 1390
> proof of his own madness, no one else's,
>> no, his own blind wrongs.

CREON:
>> Ohhh,
> so senseless, so insane . . . my crimes,
> my stubborn, deadly—
> Look at us, the killer, the killed, 1395
> father and son, the same blood—the misery!
> My plans, my mad fanatic heart,
> my son, cut off so young!
> Ai, dead, lost to the world,
> not through your stupidity, no, my own.

LEADER:
>> Too late, 1400
> too late, you see what justice means.

CREON:
>> Oh I've learned
> through blood and tears! Then, it was then,
> when the god came down and struck me—a great weight
> shattering, driving me down that wild savage path,
> ruining, trampling down my joy. Oh the agony, 1405
>> the heartbreaking agonies of our lives.

Enter the MESSENGER *from the palace.*

MESSENGER:
>> Master,
> what a hoard of grief you have, and you'll have more.
> The grief that lies to hand you've brought yourself—

Pointing to HAEMON's *body.*

> the rest, in the house, you'll see it all too soon.

CREON:
What now? What's worse than this?

MESSENGER:
                            The queen is dead.
The mother of this dead boy . . . mother to the end—
poor thing, her wounds are fresh.

CREON:
                    No, no,
    harbor of Death, so choked, so hard to cleanse!—
    why me? why are you killing me?
    Herald of pain, more words, more grief?
    I died once, you kill me again and again!
    What's the report, boy . . . some news for me?
    My wife dead? O dear god!
    Slaughter heaped on slaughter?

                    The doors open; the body of
                    EURYDICE *is brought out on her bier.*

MESSENGER:
                            See for yourself:
now they bring her body from the palace.

CREON:
                                Oh no,
    another, a second loss to break the heart.
    What next, what fate still waits for me?
    I just held my son in my arms and now,
    look, a new corpse rising before my eyes—
        wretched, helpless mother—O my son!

MESSENGER:
She stabbed herself at the altar,
then her eyes went dark, after she'd raised
a cry for the noble fate of Megareus, the hero
killed in the first assault, then for Haemon,
then with her dying breath she called down   1430
torments on your head—you killed her sons.

CREON:
                                    Oh the dread,
   I shudder with dread! Why not kill me too?—
   run me through with a good sharp sword?
   Oh god, the misery, anguish—
   I, I'm churning with it, going under.   1435

MESSENGER:
Yes, and the dead, the woman lying there,
piles the guilt of all their deaths on you.

CREON:
How did she end her life, what bloody stroke?

MESSENGER:
She drove home to the heart with her own hand,
once she learned her son was dead . . . that agony.   1440

CREON:
       And the guilt is all mine—
       can never be fixed on another man,
       no escape for me. I killed you,
       I, god help me, I admit it all!

                        To his attendants.

       Take me away, quickly, out of sight.   1445
       I don't even exist—I'm no one. Nothing.

LEADER:
Good advice, if there's any good in suffering.
Quickest is best when troubles block the way.

CREON:
Kneeling in prayer.
    Come, let it come!—that best of fates for me
    that brings the final day, best fate of all.
    Oh quickly, now—
    so I never have to see another sunrise.

LEADER:
That will come when it comes;
we must deal with all that lies before us.
The future rests with the ones who tend the future.

CREON:
That prayer—I poured my heart into that prayer!

LEADER:
No more prayers now. For mortal men
there is no escape from the doom we must endure.

CREON:
    Take me away, I beg you, out of sight.
    A rash, indiscriminate fool!
    I murdered you, my son, against my will—
    you too, my wife . . .
                   Wailing wreck of a man,
whom to look to? where to lean for support?

Desperately turning from HAEMON *to*
EURYDICE *on their biers.*

Whatever I touch goes wrong—once more
a crushing fate's come down upon my head!

The MESSENGER *and attendants lead*
CREON *into the palace.*

CHORUS:
>   Wisdom is by far the greatest part of joy,
>   and reverence toward the gods must be safeguarded.
>   The mighty words of the proud are paid in full
>   with mighty blows of fate, and at long last
>   those blows will teach us wisdom.   1470

The old citizens exit to the side.

OEDIPUS THE KING

INTRODUCTION

THIS PLAY is universally recognized as the dramatic masterpiece of the Greek theater. Aristotle cites it as the most brilliant example of theatrical plot, the model for all to follow, and all the generations since who have seen it staged—no matter how inadequate the production or how poor the translation—have agreed with his assessment as they found themselves moved to pity and fear by the swift development of its ferociously logical plot. The story of Oedipus, the myth, was of course very old in Sophocles' time and very well known to his audience. It was his use of well-known material that made the play new. He chose to concentrate attention not on the actions of Oedipus which had made his name a byword—his violation of the two most formidable taboos observed by almost every human society—but on the moment of his discovery of the truth. And Sophocles engineered this discovery not by divine agency (as Homer did) and not by chance, but through the persistent, courageous action of Oedipus himself. The hero of the play is thus his own destroyer; he is the detective who tracks down and identifies the criminal—who turns out to be himself.

The play has also been almost universally regarded as the classic example of the "tragedy of fate." To the rationalist critics of the eighteenth century and still more to the firm believers in human progress of the nineteenth, this aspect of the play was a historical curiosity, to be discounted; but our own more anxious age has seen in the situation of Oedipus an image of its own fears. In the very first year of our century Sigmund Freud in his *Interpretation of Dreams* offered a famous and influential interpretation of the destiny of Oedipus the King:

> *Oedipus Rex* is what is known as a tragedy of destiny. Its tragic effect is said to lie in the contrast between the supreme will of the gods and the vain attempts of mankind to escape the evil that threatens them. The lesson which, it is said, the deeply moved spectator should learn from the tragedy is submission to the divine will and realization of his own impotence. Modern dramatists have accordingly tried to achieve a similar tragic effect by weaving the same contrast into a plot invented by themselves. But the spectators have looked on unmoved while a curse or an oracle was fulfilled in spite of all the efforts of some innocent man: later tragedies of destiny have failed in their effect.
>
> If *Oedipus Rex* moves the modern audience no less than it did the contemporary Greek one, the explanation can only be that its effect does not lie in the contrast between destiny and human will, but is to be looked for in the particular nature of the material on which that contrast is exemplified. There must be something which makes a voice within us ready to recognize the compelling force of destiny in the *Oedipus,* while we can dismiss as merely arbitrary such dispositions as are laid down in [Grillparzer's] *Die Ahnfrau* or other modern tragedies of destiny. And a factor of this kind is in fact involved in the story of King Oedipus. His destiny moves us only because it might have been ours—because the oracle laid the same curse upon us before our birth as upon him. It is the fate of all of us, perhaps, to direct our first sexual impulse towards our mother and our first hatred and our first murderous wish against our father. Our dreams convince us that this is so.
>
> (Trans. James Strachey)

This passage is of course a landmark in the history of modern thought, and it is fascinating to observe that this idea, which, valid or not, has had enormous influence, stems from an attempt to answer a literary problem—why does the play have this overpowering effect on modern audiences?—and that this problem is raised by an ancient Greek tragedy. As a piece of literary criticism, however, it leaves much to be desired. If the effect of the play did indeed depend on the "particular nature of the material," then one would expect modern audiences to be just as deeply moved by a performance of Voltaire's *Edipe,* whereas, in fact, the play is rarely produced and then only as a museum piece. At any rate, though the primordial urges and fears that are Freud's concern are perhaps inherent in the myths, they are not exploited in the Sophoclean play. And indeed Freud himself, in a later passage in the same work, admits as much: "the further modification of the legend," he says, "originates . . . in a misconceived secondary revision of the material, which has sought to exploit it for theological purposes." This "further modification" is the Sophoclean play.

Sophocles' play has served modern man and his haunted sense of being caught in a trap not only as a base for a psychoanalytic theory which dooms the male infant to guilt and anxiety from his mother's breast, but also as the model for a modern drama that presents to us, using the ancient figures, our own terror of the unknown future which we fear we cannot control—our deep fear that every step we take forward on what we think is the road of progress may really be a step toward a foreordained rendezvous with disaster. The greatest of these modern versions is undoubtedly Jean Cocteau's *Machine Infernale;* the title alone is, as the French say, a whole program. Cocteau also worked with Stravinsky on an operatic version of the Sophoclean play (the text in liturgical Latin), and for a recording of this work he wrote a prologue that sums up his compelling vision of man's place in a strange and haunted universe. "*Spectateurs,*" says the author in his forceful, rather nasal voice, "*sans le savoir* . . . without knowing it, Oedipus is at grips with the powers that watch us from the other side of death. They have spread for him, since the day of his birth, a trap and you are going to watch it snap shut." This is of course much more explicit (and much more despairing) than the Sophoclean play; it stems, like the beautiful and terrifying second act of the *Machine Infernale,* in which the Sphinx and Anubis play their fiendish game with Oedipus, from a modern vision of a death-haunted universe, from the obsessed imagination that gives us also, in the film *Orphée,* the unforgettable images of Death at work: her black-uniformed motorcyclists, enigmatic radio messages and rubber gloves.

Parallel with this modern adaptation of the Oedipus story, serving new psychologies and mythologies of the irrational, goes a reinterpretation of the Sophoclean play itself by scholars and critics along similar lines. Yeats, who translated the play for production at the Abbey Theatre in Dublin, described his reaction to a rehearsal in the words: "I had but one overwhelming emotion, a sense as of the actual presence in a terrible sacrament of the god." Taking his cue from the work of Frazer and Harrison, who emphasize the religious, tribal, primitive aspects of the Greek tradition, Francis Fergusson, in his brilliant book *The Idea of a Theater,* gives us a vision of the Sophoclean masterpiece as an Athenian mystery play, a solemn rite of sacrifice that purges the community of its collective guilt by punishing a scapegoat, one man who perishes for the good of the people—an emphasis taken up and broadened by René Girard in his *Violence and the Sacred.* Some such interpretation must have been the base for the Tyrone Guthrie film of the play's production at Stratford, Ontario: the actors wear hideous masks, for all the world like Halloween goblins, and the effect of the performance is to suggest some Stone Age ceremony of human sacrifice.

All this is a reaction, predictable and perhaps even necessary, against the nineteenth-century worship of the Greek rational "enlightenment"—a vision of ancient Greece dear to the hearts of optimistic Victorians who found in Greece, as each successive generation in the West has done since the Renaissance, their own image. But the reaction toward the mysterious, the irrational, has gone too far. For Sophocles' play, read without preconceptions of any kind, gives an entirely different impression. There is not one supernatural event in it, no gods (as there are in so many other Greek plays), no monsters (like jackal-headed Anubis in Cocteau's play), nothing that is not, given the mythical situation, inexorably logical and human. So far as the action is concerned, it is the most relentlessly secular of the Sophoclean tragedies. Destiny, fate and the will of the gods do indeed loom ominously behind the human action, but that action, far from suggesting primeval rituals and satanic divinities, reflects, at every point, contemporary realities familiar to the audience that first saw the play.

The voice of destiny in the play is the oracle of Apollo.

Through his priests at Delphi, Apollo told Laius that he would be killed by his own son, and later told Oedipus that he would kill his father and marry his mother. At the beginning of the play Apollo tells Creon that Thebes will be saved from the plague only when the murderer of Laius is found and expelled. This Delphic oracle, which for modern poets—Yeats, for example—can conjure up mystic romantic visions, was, for Sophocles and his audience, a fact of life, an institution as present and solid, as uncompromising (and sometimes infuriating) as the Vatican is for us. States and individuals alike consulted it as a matter of course about important decisions; Sparta asked Apollo if it should declare war on Athens in 431 B.C. (it was told to go ahead and was promised victory), and at the end of the war young Xenophon asked it whether he should join the expedition of Cyrus and go up-country into Asia Minor as a mercenary soldier fighting against the Great King. The oracle maintained contacts with peoples and rulers all over the Greek and barbarian worlds; it promoted revolutions, upheld dynasties, guided the foundation of colonies—its wealth and political influence were immense.

Its power was based on a widespread, indeed in early times universal, belief in the efficacy of divine prophecy. The gods knew everything, including what was going to happen, and so their advice was precious; the most influential dispenser of such advice was Apollo, son of Zeus. His knowledge is celebrated in a famous passage of the Ninth Pythian Ode of Pindar, who wrote in the same century as Sophocles:

> You know the appointed end
> of all things, and all the ways.
> You know how many leaves the earth unfolds in spring,
> how many grains of sand are driven by storm wind and wave
> in the rivers and the sea.
> You see clear the shape of the future
> and what will bring it to pass.   (44–49 in the Greek)

In such a faith, private individuals and official representatives of state had for centuries made the journey by land and sea to Apollo's temple in its magnificent setting on a high plateau below Mount Parnassus; in gratitude for the god's advice kings and cities had lavished gifts on the sanctuary and even built treasuries on the site to house their precious offerings.

When Sophocles was a boy, the Spartan infantry at Plataea, the final battle of the Persian War, had stood motionless under a murderous fire of Persian arrows while their prophets tried (like Tiresias in *Antigone*) to obtain a prediction from their observation of the sacrificial ritual; only when the signs were declared favorable did the soldiers advance against the enemy. The historian Herodotus, who describes this incident in his history of the war, states emphatically in another passage his own belief in the truth of divine prophecy and rejects firmly the arguments of those who deny it. But his protest is the voice of the older generation. In the last half of the fifth century B.C., particularly in Athens, this belief in prophecy and with it belief in the religious tradition as a whole was under attack. Philosophers and sophists (the new professional teachers of rhetoric, political theory and a host of allied subjects) were examining all accepted ideas with a critical eye: the fifth century in Athens was an age of intellectual revolution. Among the younger intellectuals prophecies, especially those peddled by self-appointed professional seers (a class of operator common in ancient Greece but not unknown in modern America), were viewed with skepticism if not scorn; inevitably some of the skepticism spread to embrace the more respectable oracular establishments that claimed to transmit divine instructions. Thucydides, the historian of the Peloponnesian War, dismissed prophecy contemptuously in a couple of cynical sentences, and Euripides attacked it, sometimes lightheartedly, sometimes bitterly, in one play after another. The philosophical attack on it was more radical; the dictum of the sophist Protagoras—"the individual man is the measure of all things, of the existence of what exists and the nonexistence of what does not"—subjected prophecy, and for that matter the gods themselves, to a harsh criterion that found them wanting.

When he chose as the subject of his tragedy a story about a man who tried to avoid the fulfillment of a prophecy of Apollo, believed he had succeeded, and cast scorn on all the oracles, only to find out that he had fulfilled that prophecy long ago, Sophocles was dealing with matters that had urgent contemporary significance; prophecy was one of the great controversial questions of the day. It was in fact the key question, for the rationalist critique of the whole archaic religious tradition had concentrated its fire on this particular sector. Far more than prophecy was involved. For if the case for divine foreknowledge could be successfully demolished, the whole traditional religious edifice went down with it. If the gods did not know the future, they did not know any more than man. These are exactly the issues of the Sophoclean play. When the chorus hears Jocasta dismiss divine prophecy and Oedipus agree with her (948-49), they actually pray to Zeus to fulfill the dreadful prophecies they have just heard Jocasta and Oedipus report. They identify prophecy with the very existence of the gods. Never again, they say, will they go reverent to Delphi or to any oracular shrine of the gods

> unless these prophecies all come true
> for all mankind to point toward in wonder. . . .
> They are dying, the old oracles sent to Laius,
> now our masters strike them off the rolls.
> Nowhere Apollo's golden glory now—
> the gods, the gods go down.   (989-97)

By this emphasis Sophocles gave the age-old story contemporary and controversial significance, and he had other ways besides to make his audience see themselves in the ancient figures he brought to such disturbing life on stage. The play opens, for example, with a group of priests begging a ruler for relief from plague, and the first choral ode, a prayer to the gods, rehearses the harrowing details of the city's suffering—

> children dead in the womb
> and life on life goes down
> you can watch them go
> like seabirds winging west. . . .
> generations strewn on the ground
> unburied . . . the dead spreading death . . .   (198-208)

The Athenians were all too familiar with plague; in the second summer of the war, in a city overcrowded with refugees from the Spartan invasion of Attica, plague had raged in the city, and it had recurred over the next three or four years.

But more important for the play's impact on the audience than this grim setting is the characterization of the play's central figure, Oedipus the King. The poet's language presents him to the audience not as a figure of the mythical past but as one fully contemporary; in fact he is easily recognizable as an epitome of the Athenian character as they themselves conceived it and as their enemies saw it too. One trait after another in the character of Sophocles' Oedipus corresponds to Athenian qualities praised by Pericles in his Funeral Speech or denounced by the Corinthians in their attack on Athenian imperialism at the congress in Sparta before the war.

Oedipus is clearly a man of action, swift and vigorous action, and this is a markedly Athenian characteristic. "Athens," said Pericles, "will be the envy of the man who has a will to action"; the Corinthians, from the opposite point of view, say the same thing—"Their nature not only forbids them to remain inactive but denies the possibility of inaction to the rest of mankind." In the play Oedipus' will to action never falters, and it forces Tiresias, Jocasta and the shepherd, in spite of their reluctance, to play their part in the swift progress toward the discovery of the truth and his own fall. The priest in the opening scene appeals to Oedipus as "the man of experience"; experience is the result of constant action and this too—especially their experience in naval warfare—is a quality celebrated by Athens' orators and feared by her enemies. Oedipus is courageous, and it was characteristic of Athenian courage that it rose to its greatest heights when the situation seemed most desperate. This is exactly what we see in the play—Oedipus' most defiant and optimistic statement comes when Jocasta, knowing the truth, has gone off to hang herself, and the audience waits for the appearance of the shepherd who, under duress, will reluctantly supply the last piece of evidence that identifies Oedipus as the son of Laius and Jocasta.

Oedipus is quick to decide and to act; he anticipates advice and suggestion. When the priest hints that he should send to Delphi for help he has already done so; when the chorus suggests sending for Tiresias, the prophet has already been summoned and is on the way. This swiftness in action is a well-known Athenian quality, one their enemies are well aware of. "They are the only people," say the Corinthians, "who simultaneously hope for and have what they plan, because of their quick fulfillment of decisions." But this action is not rash, it is based on reflection; Oedipus reached the decision to apply to Delphi "groping, laboring over many paths of thought" (79). This too is typically Athenian. "We are unique," says Pericles, "in our combination of the most courageous action and rational discussion of our plans." The Athenians also spoke with pride of the intelligence which informed such discussion: Pericles attributes the Athenian victories over the Persians "not to luck, but to intelligence." And this is the claim of Oedipus, too: "the flight of my own intelligence hit the mark" (453), he says, as he recalls his solution of the riddle of the Sphinx. The riddle has sinister verbal connections with his fate (his name in Greek is *Oidipous* and *dipous* is the Greek word for "two-footed" in the riddle, not to mention the later prophecy of Tiresias that he would leave Thebes as a blind man, "a stick tapping before him step by step," 519), but the answer he proposed to the riddle—"Man"—is appropriate for the optimistic picture of man's achievement and potential that the figure of Oedipus represents.

His solution to the riddle, as he reminds Tiresias, the professional diviner, was a triumph of the amateur; "it cried out for a prophet," he says,

> Where were you? . . .
> No, but I came by, Oedipus the ignorant,
> *I* stopped the Sphinx! (448–52)

So Pericles boasts in the Funeral Speech that the Athenians, though they refuse to regiment their lives for war like the Spartan professionals, can face them confidently in the field. And Oedipus' adaptability to circumstances—he came to Thebes a homeless wanderer and became the admired ruler of a great city—this too is typically Athenian: Pericles claims "that the individual Athenian addresses himself to the most varied types of action with the utmost versatility and grace."

Above all, as we see from the priest's speech in the prologue and the prompt, energetic action Oedipus takes to rescue his subjects from the plague, he is a man dedicated to the interests and the needs of the city. It is this public spirit that drives him on to the discovery of the truth—to reject Creon's hint that the matter should be kept under wraps, to send for Tiresias, to pronounce the curse and sentence of banishment on the murderer of Laius. This spirit was the great civic virtue that Pericles preached—"I would have you fix your eyes every day on the greatness of Athens until you fall in love with her"—and which the enemies of Athens knew they had to reckon with— "In the city's service," say the Corinthians, "they use their bodies as if they did not belong to them."

All this does not necessarily mean that Sophocles' audience drew a conscious parallel between Oedipus and Athens (or even that Sophocles himself did); what is important is that they could have seen in Oedipus a man endowed with the temperament and talents they prized most highly in their own democratic leaders and in their ideal vision of themselves. Oedipus the King is a dramatic embodiment of the creative vigor and intellectual daring of the fifth-century Athenian spirit.

But there is an even greater dimension to this extraordinary dramatic figure. The fifth century in Athens saw the birth of the historical spirit; the human race awakened for the first time to a consciousness of its past and a tentative confidence in its future. The past came to be seen no longer as a golden age from which there had been a decline if not a fall, but as a steady progress from primitive barbarism to the high civilization of the city-state. One of the new teachers, the sophist Protagoras, was particularly associated with this idea; he wrote a book called *The State of Things in the Beginning,* and his outline of human social history is clearly the basis of Plato's re-creation of him in the dialogue entitled *Protagoras*. But much more important, because contemporary, is the clear reflection of his ideas in that chorus of *Antigone* that sings the praise of man the resourceful. "Man the master, ingenious past all measure . . . / he forges on . . ." (406–8). Three of the most important achievements of man celebrated in that ode are his conquest of the earth, the sea and the animals. And Oedipus, in the images of the play, is presented to us as hunter, sailor and plowman. He is the hunter who follows "the trail of the ancient guilt" (124); the sailor who, in the chorus' words, "set our beloved land—storm-tossed, shattered— / straight on course" (765–66), and he is also the plowman—"How," sings the chorus when the truth is out at last,

> how could the furrows your father plowed
> bear you, your agony, harrowing on
> in silence O so long? (1338–40)

These images, recurrent throughout the play, recall the first decisive steps that brought man from nomadic savagery to settled, stable culture, made him master of the land and sea and the creatures inhabiting them. But Oedipus speaks too in terms that connect him with more advanced stages of human progress. Among these—the culmination of the *Antigone* ode—was the creation of the city-state, "the mood and mind for law that rules the city" (396). Oedipus is a ruling statesman; he is a self-made man who has won and kept control of the state, a master of the political art, and he is conscious of his achievement and its value:

> O power—
> wealth and empire, skill outstripping skill
> in the heady rivalries of life

—he bursts out when Tiresias accuses him, "what envy lurks inside you!" (432–35). The words conjure up the feverish activity, the political ferment of Athenian imperial democracy. And, as head of the state, Oedipus is the enforcer of the law. He is, in the play, the investigator, prosecutor and judge of a murderer. In all these aspects he represents the social and intellectual progress that had resulted in the establishment of Athenian democracy and its courts of law, a triumph of human progress celebrated in the last play of Aeschylus' *Oresteia*.

The figure of Oedipus represents not only the techniques of the transition from savagery to civilization and the political achievements of the newly settled society but also the temper and methods of the fifth-century intellectual revolution. His speeches are full of words, phrases and attitudes that link him with the "enlightenment" of Sophocles' own Athens. "I'll bring it all to light," he says (150); he is like some Protagoras or Democritus dispelling the darkness of ignorance and superstition. He is a questioner, a researcher, a discoverer—the Greek words are those of the sophistic vocabulary. Above all Oedipus is presented to the audience as a symbol of two of the greatest scientific achievements of the age—mathematics and medicine. Mathematical language recurs incessantly in the imagery of the play—such terms as "measure" (*metrein*), "equate" (*isoun*), "define" (*diorizein*)—and at one climactic moment Oedipus, seizing on a numerical discrepancy in the evidence against him, dismisses it with a mathematical axiom: "One can't equal many" (934). This obsessive image, Oedipus the calculator, is one more means of investing the mythical figure with the salient characteristics of the fifth-century achievement, but it is also magnificently functional. For, in his search for truth, he is engaged in a great calculation, to determine the measure of man, whom Protagoras called "the measure of all things."

Functional too is the richly developed image of Oedipus as a physician. Hippocrates of Cos and his school of physicians had in this same century founded Western medicine; their treatises and casebooks are still extant, and in them we can see the new methods at work: detailed observations of hundreds of cases, classification of symptoms, plotting of the regular course of individual diseases and then diagnosis, prognosis (these are Greek words, their words). In the play the city suffers from a disease, and Oedipus is the physician to whom all turn for a cure. "After a painful search," he says, "I found one cure: / I acted at once" (80–81). And the metaphor extends throughout the play: the sickness, the cure, and the physician who will find it.

And all these images, like the plot, like the hero, have what Aristotle called their *peripeteia,* their reversal. The hunter catches a dreadful prey, the seaman steers his ship into an unspeakable harbor—"one and the same wide harbor served you / son and father both" (1335-36)—the plowman sows and reaps a fearful harvest, the investigator finds the criminal and the judge convicts him—they are all the same man—the revealer turns into the thing revealed, the finder into the thing found, the calculator finds he is himself the solution of the equation and the physician discovers that he is the disease. The catastrophe of the tragic hero thus becomes the catastrophe of fifth-century man; all his furious energy and intellectual daring drive him on to this terrible discovery of his fundamental ignorance—he is not the measure of all things but the thing measured and found wanting.

The reversal of the tragic hero is singled out for praise by Aristotle because it comes about through recognition, in this case Oedipus' recognition of his own identity. But he recognizes also that the prophecies given to his father and to him by Apollo were true prophecies, that they had been fulfilled long ago, that every step taken to evade them, from the exposure of the child to the decision never to go back to Corinth, was part of the pattern of their fulfillment. "And as I fled I reached that very spot / where the great king . . . met his death" (881-82). And this does pose, for the modern reader as for the ancient spectator, the question of fate and, though those spectators could not have expressed the idea in abstract terms, of free will and human freedom.

This basic theme has often been discounted on the grounds that the opposition of fate and free will, providence and chance, determined and open universe, is not explicitly formulated until much later than Sophocles' time, in the philosophical discussions of the late fourth and third centuries. This is true (though it must not be forgotten that we have lost the writings of the fifth-century sophists and, more important still, of the "atomic" philosophers Democritus and Leucippus), but it does not necessarily follow that because a problem had not yet been given philosophical expression, it could not be conceived. The myth of Oedipus itself—like the stories of attempts to escape a predicted fate so frequent in the *Histories* of Sophocles' friend Herodotus—poses the problem in poetic form, and one of the functions of myth in preliterate societies, as Lévi-Strauss has so brilliantly demonstrated, is to raise deeply disturbing problems that will later demand more precise formulation.

Even though what remains of early Greek literature shows no verbal consciousness of the ideas we associate with freedom of the will, there is abundant evidence, from the earliest times, for a related concept that is in fact almost inseparable from it: individual responsibility. No one can be held fully responsible for actions committed under some kind of external constraint, and in early Greek belief such constraint might be exerted by a host of nonhuman powers. When Agamemnon, in Homer's *Iliad*, makes his apologies to Achilles for the harsh treatment which led to the death of so many heroes, he tries to evade responsibility; he is claiming, in other words, that he did not act freely.

> I am not responsible
> but Zeus is, and Destiny, and Erinys the mist-walking
> who in assembly caught my heart in the savage delusion
> on that day I myself stripped from him the prize of Achilleus.
> Yet what could I do? It is the god who accomplishes all things.
> (19.86–90, trans. Richmond Lattimore)

The context suggests that this is merely an excuse (Achilles, in his reply, does not even refer to Agamemnon's lengthy development of this theme—over fifty lines long). But the negative implication of this and many similar passages is clear: that a man *is* responsible for those actions which are not performed under constraint, which are the expression of his free will. The question of Oedipus' responsibility for what happens (and what has happened) is, as we shall see, posed in the play; it is also discussed much later, in *Oedipus at Colonus,* which deals with Oedipus' old age and death.

It is interesting to note that in those later centuries, when the Stoic philosophers do pose the problem in abstract form, they start from this same mythical base, the oracle given to Laius.

Chrysippus uses this oracle to illustrate his almost completely determinist position (the only freedom he allows man is that of a dog tied to a moving cart); Carneades reinterprets the oracle to allow man a little more freedom; Alexander of Aphrodisias takes up the challenge on the same ground, and Cicero debates the meaning of this same oracular prophecy. As long as Greek philosophy lasts, the discussion of Oedipus' freedom or his subjection to fate goes on—even in the commentaries on Plato by Albinus in the second and Calcidius in the sixth century A.D. It is from these endless (and inconclusive) discussions that Milton draws his famous description of the intellectual delights of the fallen angels:

> [they] reason'd high
> Of Providence, Foreknowledge, Will, and Fate,
> Fixt Fate, free will, foreknowledge absolute,
> And found no end, in wand'ring mazes lost. (*Paradise Lost* 2.658–61)

The end of Greek philosophy and the triumph of Christianity brought no end to the argument, only new terms in which to phrase it. St. Augustine writes his book *On Freedom of the Will* (*De Libero Arbitrio*) just as Cicero had written his *On Fate* (*De Fato*); Augustine is no longer concerned with the oracle given to Laius but he is just as tormented (as he claims all humanity is) by the contradiction between our free will and God's foreknowledge that we will sin. It was of course an argument that was to go further; Bergson, Croce, and Friedrich Engels, to name only a few, continue it into modern times. It has become much more complicated and sophisticated with the years; the terms of the opposition can be, and have been, continually redefined in philosophically elegant formulas that are designed, and may even seem, to abolish it; and of course modern analytical philosophers can dismiss the problem as a mere verbal misunderstanding. But to the ordinary man, now as in Sophocles' day, there is a problem in the coexistence of predictable pattern and free will, whether that pattern be thought of as divine providence, the will of history, or the influence of the stars.

There are two obvious ways of avoiding the contradiction,

both of them extreme positions and at opposite poles to each other; one might call them, to use a political metaphor, the right and the left. The right is all for order and pattern; it escapes the dilemma by dispensing with freedom altogether. It sees history, individual and general, as a rigidly determined succession of events in time. If you take such a view, whether Christian with St. Augustine—that all history is God's providential preparation of two cities, one of God, one of Satan, and that certain souls are predestined for salvation (or with Calvin, that other souls are destined for damnation)—or materialist and atheist with Marx and Engels, denying the freedom of history to all classes but the proletariat—"Freedom," wrote Engels, "is the recognition of necessity" (which is a German version of Chrysippus' dog tied to a cart)—if you take either of these determinist views, you have no antinomy, no contradiction. But you have no freedom, and, unless you happen to be one of the Christian or the Marxist elect, you have no future either.

What we have called the left, on the other hand, is all for freedom; to the devil with pattern and order, this party is for anarchy, the human will is absolutely free and nothing is predictable; there is no pattern of order in the universe, which is merely the operation of blind chance. If you deny the possibility of prediction and the existence of order, whether as an "atomic" theorist like Democritus, or out of sheer desperation, as Jocasta does in the play—"What should a man fear? It's all chance, / chance rules our lives" (1069–70)—you have abolished the logical contradiction. But you accept a blind, pointless, meaningless universe—the universe of the absurd.

Both of these extremes are of course repugnant to the human spirit and especially to that of the West, which is that of the Greeks. We want both the freedom of our will and the assurance of order and meaning; we want to eat our cake and have it too, and in this non-Christian and Christian are alike. But no matter what subtle distinctions we invent and refine, the basic contradiction remains. Insofar as any meaningful pattern or divine providence exists it must encroach to some extent on human freedom; if human freedom is unlimited, the possibility of pattern or order is denied. Whenever we are tempted to forget this uncomfortable fact we should look at what happens to the Christian version of the contradiction—God's foreknowledge that man would sin and man's freedom not to—under the scalpel of a satiric critic.

In that now much-neglected classic *Penguin Island,* Anatole France tells the story of an old half-blind Celtic saint, St. Mael, who goes off one day in his miraculous stone boat, is swept north by the current and lands on an ice floe. He is immediately surrounded by a flock of small, inquisitive, chattering creatures and being too short-sighted to see that they are penguins, he baptizes them. This raises grave theological difficulties for the celestial authorities, and in the council in heaven that meets to discuss the problem, doctors of the church and saints debate the fate of the baptized penguins. It is finally decided to turn them into human beings, and they are thus subject to the fate of man—the fall from grace, the expulsion from the garden, sin, work, disease and death, judgment and redemption. (As the Almighty remarks, they would have been much better off if they had gone on being penguins.) He closes the debate with a reminder to himself that though they will certainly fall from grace, they are nonetheless free not to do so. "However, my foreknowledge must not be allowed to interfere with their free will. So as not to limit human freedom, I hereby assume ignorance of what I know, I wind tightly over my eyes the veils which I have seen through, and in my blind clairvoyance, I allow myself to be surprised by what I have foreseen."

France is of course quite right; as a logical proposition, the two concepts are irreconcilable. The only way to believe in the pattern and the freedom at once is not as a logical proposition but as a mystery; the medium of exploration is not philosophy but religion—or art. We can say, as Tertullian defiantly said of the central Christian mystery, "I believe it precisely because it is absurd," or we can express the contradiction in poetic terms that transcend logic. It is significant that Plato's main discussion of the problem is not phrased in the cut and thrust of dialectic, but in the great myths, as in the myth of Er, where Socrates is no longer subject to questioning. Only a mood of religious humility or a work of art can hold in precarious coexistence the irreconcilable concepts. But for one form of art, the drama, this is a particularly dangerous subject. For the power of drama depends on our feeling that the actors are free, that their choice of action is significant. The dramatist who, like Sophocles, dares to base his drama on a story that seems to question if not rule out human freedom of action is walking a perilous tightrope.

The soul of drama, as Aristotle says, is plot—the action that demands and succeeds in engaging our attention so that we are no longer detached spectators but are involved in the progress of the stage events. Its outcome is important for us; in the greatest plots (and the plot of this play by Sophocles is perhaps the greatest) it is for the moment the most important thing in the world. But this engagement of the audience proceeds from an identification with the figures on stage, and this is not possible if we are made to feel that the action of the characters is not free, not effective. We expect to be made to feel that there is a meaningful relation between the hero's action and his suffering, and this is possible only if that action is free, so that he is responsible for the consequences.

There are of course external factors in our own lives that no force of our will can influence, and no one can object to their presence in the play. But the hero's will must be independent of those factors, not identified with them. As Macbeth, for example, is independent of the prophetic witches. Macbeth *chooses* to believe the witches and the vision of the dagger—and on this subject he says something very revealing:

> or art thou but
> A dagger of the mind, a false creation,
> Proceeding from the heat-oppressed brain?
> I see thee yet, in form as palpable
> As this which now I draw.
> Thou marshall'st me the way that I was going . . .   (2.1.37–42)

He *was going* anyway. If the witches had bewitched Macbeth, so that the murder of Duncan were not an act of his will, *Macbeth* would not be a tragedy—it would be a sort of science-fiction story in which a man is injected with a drug that makes him carry out the will of some external force. We might sympathize with him but could hardly be expected to engage ourselves emotionally with his actions, presented as a play. If Macbeth were injected with witches' brew or Oedipus with fate-serum, we could not regard them as tragic, or even dramatic.

In a play, then, the hero's will must be free, but something else is needed: it must have some causal connection with his suffering. If through no fault of his own the hero is crushed by a bulldozer in Act II, we are not impressed. Even though life is often like this—the absconding cashier on his way to Nicaragua is killed in a collision at the airport, the prominent statesman dies of a stroke in the midst of the negotiations he has spent years to bring about, the young lovers are drowned in a boating accident the day before their marriage—such events, the warp and woof of everyday life, seem irrelevant, meaningless. They are crude, undigested, unpurged bits of reality—to draw a metaphor from the late J. Edgar Hoover, they are "raw files." But it is the function of great art to purge and give meaning to human suffering, and so we expect that if the hero is indeed crushed by a bulldozer in Act II there will be some reason for it, and not just some reason but a good one, one which makes sense in terms of the hero's personality and action. In fact, we expect to be shown that he is in some way *responsible* for what happens to him.

If so, the hero obviously cannot be "fated," predestined or determined to act as he does. And, to get back finally to the *Oedipus* of Sophocles, Oedipus in the play *is* a free agent, and he is responsible for the catastrophe. For the plot of the play consists not of the actions which Oedipus was "fated" to perform, or rather, which were predicted; the plot of the play consists of his discovery that he has already fulfilled the prediction. And this discovery is entirely due to his action.

He dismisses Creon's politic advice to discuss the Delphic response in private; he undertakes a public and vigorous inquiry into the murder of Laius. He is the driving force which, against the reluctance of Tiresias, the dissuasion of Jocasta and the final supplication of the shepherd, pushes on triumphantly and disastrously to the discovery of the truth. If it had not been for Oedipus, the play persuades us, the truth would never have been discovered, or at least it would not have been discovered *now*. This presentation of the hero's freedom and responsibility in the context of the dreadful prophecy already unwittingly and unwillingly fulfilled is an artistic juxtaposition, a momentary illusion of full reconciliation between the two mighty opposites, freedom and destiny. It is an illusion because of course the question of responsibility for what happened *before* the play, of Oedipus' freedom in the context of divine prophecies fulfilled, is evaded. But it makes the play a triumphant tour de force, the like of which no other dramatist has ever attempted. Oedipus is the free agent who, by his own self-willed action, discovers that his own predicted destiny has already been fulfilled. This is why the play moves us as a spectacle of heroic action and why the figure of Oedipus, dominating the stage, arouses our admiration as well as our sympathy. It is noticeable that in Cocteau's masterpiece, where Oedipus is deliberately portrayed as a marionette in the hands of daemonic powers, the greatest dramatic excitement is generated by the action and speech not of Oedipus but of those divine powers Anubis and the Sphinx.

Oedipus' heroic achievement is the discovery of the truth, and that discovery is the most thoroughgoing and dreadful catastrophe the stage has ever presented. The hero who in his vigor, courage and intelligence stands as a representative of all that is creative in man discovers a truth so dreadful that the chorus which sums up the results of the great calculation sees in his fall the reduction of man to nothing.

> O the generations of men
> the dying generations—adding the total
> of all your lives I find they come to nothing . . .   (1311–13)

The existence of human freedom, dramatically represented in the *action* of Oedipus in the play, seems to be a mockery. The discovery to which it led is a catastrophe out of all proportion to the situation. Critics have tried, with contradictory results, to find some flaw in Oedipus' character that will justify his reversal. But there is nothing in his actions that can make it acceptable to us. The chorus' despairing summation, "come to nothing," echoes our own feelings as we watch Oedipus rush into the palace.

But this estimate of the situation is not the last word; in fact, it is contradicted by the final scene of the play. Oedipus' first thought, we are told by the messenger, was to kill himself—he asked for a sword—but he blinds himself instead. This action is one that the audience must have expected; it was mentioned in the earlier *Antigone,* for example (61–64), and Oedipus as the blind, exiled wanderer seems to have been one of the invariable elements in fifth-century versions of the myth. But, though the blindness was foreseen by Tiresias, Oedipus' action did not figure in the prophecies made to and about him by Apollo. When the messenger comes from inside the palace to describe the catastrophe he uses words which emphasize the independence of this action: "terrible things, and none done blindly now, / all done with a will" (1359–60). And as Oedipus, wearing a mask with blood running from the eye sockets, stumbles on stage, he makes the same distinction when the chorus asks him what power impelled him to attack his eyes:

>   Apollo, friends, Apollo—
>   he ordained my agonies—these, my pains on pains!
>   But the hand that struck my eyes was mine,
>   mine alone—no one else—
>   I did it all myself!   (1467–71)

These two passages suggest that in his decision to blind himself Oedipus is acting freely, that the intricate pattern of his destiny was complete when he knew the truth. To that terrible revelation some violent reaction was inevitable; the choice was left to him. He resisted the first suicidal impulse perhaps (though Sophocles is silent on the point) because of a latent conviction, fully and openly expounded in the last play (*Oedipus at Colonus,* 284–95, 612–16, 1101–31), that he was not to blame. He chose to blind himself, he tells the chorus, because he could not bear to see the faces of his children and his fellow-citizens. But his action has, in the context of this play, an impressive rightness; the man who, proud of his far-seeing intelligence, taunted Tiresias with his blindness now realizes that all his life long he has himself been blind to the dreadful realities of his identity and action.

The messenger's description of the horrors that took place inside the palace has prepared the audience for the spectacle of a broken man. So Oedipus seems to be at first, but very soon this bloodstained, sightless figure begins to reassert that magnificent imperious personality which was his from the beginning. He reproaches the chorus for wishing him dead rather than blind, defends his decision to blind himself, issues instructions to Creon, and finally has to be reminded that he is no longer master in Thebes. The despairing summation based on the fate of Oedipus—the great example (as the chorus calls him) that man is equal to nothing—is corrected by the reemergence of Oedipus as his old forceful self. Formidable as of old he may be, but with a difference. The confident tone in which the blind man speaks so regally is based on knowledge, knowledge of his own identity and of the truth of divine prophecy. This new knowledge, won at such a terrible price, makes clear what it was in the hero that brought about the disaster. It was ignorance.

In spite of his name, *Oidipous,* with its resemblance to the Greek word *oida* ("I know")—a theme that Sophocles hammers home with continual word-play—Oedipus, who thought he knew so much, did not even know who his mother and father were. But ignorance can be remedied, the ignorant can learn, and the force with which Oedipus now reasserts his presence springs from the truth he now understands: that the universe is not a field for the play of blind chance, and that man is not its measure. This knowledge gives him a new strength which sustains him in his misery and gives him the courage needed to go on living, though he is now an outcast, a man from whom his fellow-men recoil in horror.

The play then is a tremendous reassertion of the traditional religious view that man is ignorant, that knowledge belongs only to the gods—Freud's "theological purpose." And it seems to present at first sight a view of the universe as rigid on the side of order as Jocasta's was anarchic on the side of freedom. Jocasta thought that there was no order or design in the world, that dreams and prophecies had no validity; that man had complete freedom because it made no difference what he did—nothing made any sense. She was wrong; the design was there, and when she saw what it was she hanged herself. But the play now seems to give us a view of man's position that is just as comfortless as her acceptance of a meaningless universe. What place is there in it for human freedom and meaningful action?

Oedipus did have one freedom: he was free to find out or not find out the truth. This was the element of Sophoclean sleight-of-hand that enabled him to make a drama out of the situation which the philosophers used as the classic demonstration of man's subjection to fate. But it is more than a solution to an apparently insoluble dramatic problem; it is the key to the play's tragic theme and the protagonist's heroic stature. One freedom is allowed him: the freedom to search for the truth, the truth about the prophecies, about the gods, about himself. And of this freedom he makes full use. Against the advice and appeals of others, he pushes on, searching for the truth, the whole truth and nothing but the truth. And in this search he shows all those great qualities that we admire in him—courage, intelligence, perseverance, the qualities that make human beings great. This freedom to search, and the heroic way in which Oedipus uses it, make the play not a picture of man's utter feebleness caught in the toils of fate, but on the contrary, a heroic example of man's dedication to the search for truth, the truth about himself. This is perhaps the only human freedom, the play seems to say, but there could be none more noble.

OEDIPUS THE KING

CHARACTERS

OEDIPUS
king of Thebes

A PRIEST
of Zeus

CREON
brother of Jocasta

A CHORUS
of Theban citizens and their **LEADER**

TIRESIAS
a blind prophet

JOCASTA
the queen, wife of Oedipus

A MESSENGER
from Corinth

A SHEPHERD

A MESSENGER
from inside the palace

ANTIGONE, ISMENE
daughters of Oedipus and Jocasta

Guards and attendants

Priests of Thebes

TIME AND SCENE: *The royal house of Thebes. Double doors dominate the façade; a stone altar stands at the center of the stage.*

Many years have passed since OEDIPUS *solved the riddle of the Sphinx and ascended the throne of Thebes, and now a plague has struck the city. A procession of priests enters; suppliants, broken and despondent, they carry branches wound in wool and lay them on the altar.*

The doors open. Guards assemble. OEDIPUS *comes forward, majestic but for a telltale limp, and slowly views the condition of his people.*

OEDIPUS:
Oh my children, the new blood of ancient Thebes,
why are you here? Huddling at my altar,
praying before me, your branches wound in wool.
Our city reeks with the smoke of burning incense,
rings with cries for the Healer and wailing for the dead. 5
I thought it wrong, my children, to hear the truth
from others, messengers. Here I am myself—
you all know me, the world knows my fame:
I am Oedipus.

Helping a Priest to his feet.

Speak up, old man. Your years,
your dignity—you should speak for the others. 10
Why here and kneeling, what preys upon you so?
Some sudden fear? some strong desire?
You can trust me. I am ready to help,
I'll do anything. I would be blind to misery
not to pity my people kneeling at my feet. 15

PRIEST:
Oh Oedipus, king of the land, our greatest power!
You see us before you now, men of all ages
clinging to your altars. Here are boys,
still too weak to fly from the nest,
and here the old, bowed down with the years, 20
the holy ones—a priest of Zeus myself—and here
the picked, unmarried men, the young hope of Thebes.
And all the rest, your great family gathers now,
branches wreathed, massing in the squares,
kneeling before the two temples of queen Athena 25
or the river-shrine where the embers glow and die
and Apollo sees the future in the ashes.
                                  Our city—
look around you, see with your own eyes—
our ship pitches wildly, cannot lift her head
from the depths, the red waves of death . . . 30
Thebes is dying. A blight on the fresh crops
and the rich pastures, cattle sicken and die,
and the women die in labor, children stillborn,
and the plague, the fiery god of fever hurls down
on the city, his lightning slashing through us— 35
raging plague in all its vengeance, devastating
the house of Cadmus! And black Death luxuriates
in the raw, wailing miseries of Thebes.

Now we pray to you. You cannot equal the gods,
your children know that, bending at your altar.
But we do rate you first of men,
both in the common crises of our lives
and face-to-face encounters with the gods.
You freed us from the Sphinx, you came to Thebes
and cut us loose from the bloody tribute we had paid
that harsh, brutal singer. We taught you nothing,
no skill, no extra knowledge, still you triumphed.
A god was with you, so they say, and we believe it—
you lifted up our lives.
                So now again,
Oedipus, king, we bend to you, your power—
we implore you, all of us on our knees:
find us strength, rescue! Perhaps you've heard
the voice of a god or something from other men,
Oedipus . . . what do you know?
The man of experience—you see it every day—
his plans will work in a crisis, his first of all.

Act now—we beg you, best of men, raise up our city!
Act, defend yourself, your former glory!
Your country calls you savior now
for your zeal, your action years ago.
Never let us remember of your reign:
you helped us stand, only to fall once more.
Oh raise up our city, set us on our feet.
The omens were good that day you brought us joy—
be the same man today!
Rule our land, you know you have the power,
but rule a land of the living, not a wasteland.
Ship and towered city are nothing, stripped of men
alive within it, living all as one.

OEDIPUS:
                              My children,
I pity you. I see—how could I fail to see
what longings bring you here? Well I know
you are sick to death, all of you,
but sick as you are, not one is sick as I.
Your pain strikes each of you alone, each
in the confines of himself, no other. But my spirit
grieves for the city, for myself and all of you.
I wasn't asleep, dreaming. You haven't wakened me—
I have wept through the nights, you must know that,
groping, laboring over many paths of thought.
After a painful search I found one cure:
I acted at once. I sent Creon,
my wife's own brother, to Delphi—
Apollo the Prophet's oracle—to learn
what I might do or say to save our city.

Today's the day. When I count the days gone by
it torments me . . . what is he doing?
Strange, he's late, he's gone too long.
But once he returns, then, then I'll be a traitor
if I do not do all the god makes clear.

PRIEST:
Timely words. The men over there
are signaling—Creon's just arriving.

OEDIPUS:

                    Sighting CREON, *then turning
                    to the altar.*
                         Lord Apollo,
let him come with a lucky word of rescue,
shining like his eyes!

PRIEST:
Welcome news, I think—he's crowned, look,
and the laurel wreath is bright with berries.

OEDIPUS:
We'll soon see. He's close enough to hear—

> *Enter* CREON *from the side; his face is shaded with a wreath.*

Creon, prince, my kinsman, what do you bring us?
What message from the god?

CREON:
                    Good news.
I tell you even the hardest things to bear,
if they should turn out well, all would be well.

OEDIPUS:
Of course, but what were the god's *words*? There's no hope
and nothing to fear in what you've said so far.

CREON:
If you want my report in the presence of these people . . .

> *Pointing to the priests while drawing* OEDIPUS *toward the palace.*

I'm ready now, or we might go inside.

OEDIPUS:
                            Speak out,
speak to us all. I grieve for these, my people,
far more than I fear for my own life.

CREON:
                              Very well,
I will tell you what I heard from the god.
Apollo commands us—he was quite clear—
"Drive the corruption from the land,
don't harbor it any longer, past all cure,
don't nurse it in your soil—root it out!"

OEDIPUS:
How can we cleanse ourselves—what rites?
What's the source of the trouble?

CREON:
Banish the man, or pay back blood with blood.
Murder sets the plague-storm on the city.

OEDIPUS:
                         Whose murder?
Whose fate does Apollo bring to light?

CREON:
                              Our leader,
my lord, was once a man named Laius,
before you came and put us straight on course.

OEDIPUS:
                                   I know—
or so I've heard. I never saw the man myself.

CREON:
Well, he was killed, and Apollo commands us now—
he could not be more clear,
"Pay the killers back—whoever is responsible."

OEDIPUS:
Where on earth are they? Where to find it now,
the trail of the ancient guilt so hard to trace?

CREON:
"Here in Thebes," he said.
Whatever is sought for can be caught, you know,
whatever is neglected slips away.

OEDIPUS:
                                But where,
in the palace, the fields or foreign soil,
where did Laius meet his bloody death?

CREON:
He went to consult an oracle, Apollo said,
and he set out and never came home again.

OEDIPUS:
No messenger, no fellow-traveler saw what happened?
Someone to cross-examine?

CREON:
                          No,
they were all killed but one. He escaped,
terrified, he could tell us nothing clearly,
nothing of what he saw—just one thing.

OEDIPUS:
                                    What's that?
One thing could hold the key to it all,
a small beginning give us grounds for hope.

CREON:
He said thieves attacked them—a whole band,
not single-handed, cut King Laius down.

OEDIPUS:
                             A thief,   140
so daring, so wild, he'd kill a king? Impossible,
unless conspirators paid him off in Thebes.

CREON:
We suspected as much. But with Laius dead
no leader appeared to help us in our troubles.

OEDIPUS:
Trouble? Your *king* was murdered—royal blood!   145
What stopped you from tracking down the killer
then and there?

CREON:
                  The singing, riddling Sphinx.
She . . . persuaded us to let the mystery go
and concentrate on what lay at our feet.

OEDIPUS:

                                No,
I'll start again—I'll bring it all to light myself!
Apollo is right, and so are you, Creon,
to turn our attention back to the murdered man.
Now you have *me* to fight for you, you'll see:
I am the land's avenger by all rights,
and Apollo's champion too.
But not to assist some distant kinsman, no,
for my own sake I'll rid us of this corruption.
Whoever killed the king may decide to kill me too,
with the same violent hand—by avenging Laius
I defend myself.

To the priests.

        Quickly, my children.
Up from the steps, take up your branches now.

To the guards.

One of you summon the city here before us,
tell them I'll do everything. God help us,
we will see our triumph—or our fall.

OEDIPUS and CREON enter the palace, followed by the guards.

PRIEST:
Rise, my sons. The kindness we came for
Oedipus volunteers himself.
Apollo has sent his word, his oracle—
Come down, Apollo, save us, stop the plague.

The priests rise, remove their branches and exit to the side.

Enter a CHORUS, *the citizens of Thebes, who have not heard the news that* CREON *brings. They march around the altar, chanting.*

CHORUS:
                              Zeus!
Great welcome voice of Zeus, what do you bring?
What word from the gold vaults of Delphi   170
comes to brilliant Thebes? Racked with terror—
                    terror shakes my heart
and I cry your wild cries, Apollo, Healer of Delos
I worship you in dread . . . what now, what is your price?
some new sacrifice? some ancient rite from the past   175
come round again each spring?—
        what will you bring to birth?
Tell me, child of golden Hope
    warm voice that never dies!

You are the first I call, daughter of Zeus   180
deathless Athena—I call your sister Artemis,
heart of the market place enthroned in glory,
                    guardian of our earth—
I call Apollo, Archer astride the thunderheads of heaven—
O triple shield against death, shine before me now!   185
If ever, once in the past, you stopped some ruin
launched against our walls
        you hurled the flame of pain
far, far from Thebes—you gods
    come now, come down once more!

                              No, no
the miseries numberless, grief on grief, no end—
too much to bear, we are all dying
O my people . . .
   Thebes like a great army dying
and there is no sword of thought to save us, no
and the fruits of our famous earth, they will not ripen
no and the women cannot scream their pangs to birth—
screams for the Healer, children dead in the womb
             and life on life goes down
                         you can watch them go
   like seabirds winging west, outracing the day's fire
down the horizon, irresistibly
             streaking on to the shores of Evening
                                         Death
so many deaths, numberless deaths on deaths, no end—
Thebes is dying, look, her children
stripped of pity . . .
   generations strewn on the ground
unburied, unwept, the dead spreading death
and the young wives and gray-haired mothers with them
cling to the altars, trailing in from all over the city—
Thebes, city of death, one long cortege
             and the suffering rises
                   wails for mercy rise
   and the wild hymn for the Healer blazes out
clashing with our sobs our cries of mourning—
   O golden daughter of god, send rescue
   radiant as the kindness in your eyes!

Drive him back!—the fever, the god of death
                         that raging god of war
not armored in bronze, not shielded now, he burns me,
battle cries in the onslaught burning on—
O rout him from our borders!
Sail him, blast him out to the Sea-queen's chamber
                         the black Atlantic gulfs
   or the northern harbor, death to all
where the Thracian surf comes crashing.
Now what the night spares he comes by day and kills—
the god of death.

                   O lord of the stormcloud,
you who twirl the lightning, Zeus, Father,
thunder Death to nothing!

Apollo, lord of the light, I beg you—
      whip your longbow's golden cord
showering arrows on our enemies—shafts of power
champions strong before us rushing on!

Artemis, Huntress,
torches flaring over the eastern ridges—
                   ride Death down in pain!

God of the headdress gleaming gold, I cry to you—
your name and ours are one, Dionysus—
   come with your face aflame with wine
                         your raving women's cries
      your army on the march! Come with the lightning
come with torches blazing, eyes ablaze with glory!
Burn that god of death that all gods hate!

> OEDIPUS *enters from the palace to address the* CHORUS, *as if addressing the entire city of Thebes.*

OEDIPUS:
You pray to the gods? Let me grant your prayers.   245
Come, listen to me—do what the plague demands:
you'll find relief and lift your head from the depths.

I will speak out now as a stranger to the story,
a stranger to the crime. If I'd been present then,
there would have been no mystery, no long hunt   250
without a clue in hand. So now, counted
a native Theban years after the murder,
to all of Thebes I make this proclamation:
if any one of you knows who murdered Laius,
the son of Labdacus, I order him to reveal   255
the whole truth to me. Nothing to fear,
even if he must denounce himself,
let him speak up
and so escape the brunt of the charge—
he will suffer no unbearable punishment,   260
nothing worse than exile, totally unharmed.

> OEDIPUS *pauses, waiting for a reply.*

                             Next,
if anyone knows the murderer is a stranger,
a man from alien soil, come, speak up.
I will give him a handsome reward, and lay up
gratitude in my heart for him besides.   265

> *Silence again, no reply.*

But if you keep silent, if anyone panicking,
trying to shield himself or friend or kin,
rejects my offer, then hear what I will do.
I order you, every citizen of the state
where I hold throne and power: banish this man— 270
whoever he may be—never shelter him, never
speak a word to him, never make him partner
to your prayers, your victims burned to the gods.
Never let the holy water touch his hands.
Drive him out, each of you, from every home. 275
He is the plague, the heart of our corruption,
as Apollo's oracle has just revealed to me.
So I honor my obligations:
I fight for the god and for the murdered man.

Now my curse on the murderer. Whoever he is, 280
a lone man unknown in his crime
or one among many, let that man drag out
his life in agony, step by painful step—
I curse myself as well . . . if by any chance
he proves to be an intimate of our house, 285
here at my hearth, with my full knowledge,
may the curse I just called down on him strike me!

These are your orders: perform them to the last.
I command you, for my sake, for Apollo's, for this country
blasted root and branch by the angry heavens. 290
Even if god had never urged you on to act,
how could you leave the crime uncleansed so long?
A man so noble—your king, brought down in blood—
you should have searched. But I am the king now,
I hold the throne that he held then, possess his bed 295
and a wife who shares our seed . . . why, our seed
might be the same, children born of the same mother
might have created blood-bonds between us
if his hope of offspring had not met disaster—
but fate swooped at his head and cut him short. 300
So I will fight for him as if he were my father,
stop at nothing, search the world
to lay my hands on the man who shed his blood,
the son of Labdacus descended of Polydorus,
Cadmus of old and Agenor, founder of the line: 305
their power and mine are one.

                         Oh dear gods,
my curse on those who disobey these orders!
Let no crops grow out of the earth for them—
shrivel their women, kill their sons,
burn them to nothing in this plague 310
that hits us now, or something even worse.
But you, loyal men of Thebes who approve my actions,
may our champion, Justice, may all the gods
be with us, fight beside us to the end!

LEADER:
In the grip of your curse, my king, I swear
I'm not the murderer, I cannot point him out.
As for the search, Apollo pressed it on us—
he should name the killer.

OEDIPUS:
                    Quite right,
but to force the gods to act against their will—
no man has the power.

LEADER:
                    Then if I might mention
the next best thing . . .

OEDIPUS:
                    The third best too—
don't hold back, say it.

LEADER:
                    I still believe . . .
Lord Tiresias sees with the eyes of Lord Apollo.
Anyone searching for the truth, my king,
might learn it from the prophet, clear as day.

OEDIPUS:
I've not been slow with that. On Creon's cue
I sent the escorts, twice, within the hour.
I'm surprised he isn't here.

LEADER:
                    We need him—
without him we have nothing but old, useless rumors.

OEDIPUS:
Which rumors? I'll search out every word.   330

LEADER:
Laius was killed, they say, by certain travelers.

OEDIPUS:
I know—but no one can find the murderer.

LEADER:
If the man has a trace of fear in him
he won't stay silent long,
not with your curses ringing in his ears.   335

OEDIPUS:
He didn't flinch at murder,
he'll never flinch at words.

> *Enter* TIRESIAS, *the blind prophet, led
> by a boy with escorts in attendance.
> He remains at a distance.*

LEADER:
Here is the one who will convict him, look,
they bring him on at last, the seer, the man of god.
The truth lives inside him, him alone.

OEDIPUS:
                              O Tiresias,
master of all the mysteries of our life,
all you teach and all you dare not tell,
signs in the heavens, signs that walk the earth!
Blind as you are, you can feel all the more
what sickness haunts our city. You, my lord,
are the one shield, the one savior we can find.

We asked Apollo—perhaps the messengers
haven't told you—he sent his answer back:
"Relief from the plague can only come one way.
Uncover the murderers of Laius,
put them to death or drive them into exile."
So I beg you, grudge us nothing now, no voice,
no message plucked from the birds, the embers
or the other mantic ways within your grasp.
Rescue yourself, your city, rescue me—
rescue everything infected by the dead.
We are in your hands. For a man to help others
with all his gifts and native strength:
that is the noblest work.

TIRESIAS:
                        How terrible—to see the truth
when the truth is only pain to him who sees!
I knew it well, but I put it from my mind,
else I never would have come.

OEDIPUS:
What's this? Why so grim, so dire?

TIRESIAS:
Just send me home. You bear your burdens,
I'll bear mine. It's better that way, 365
please believe me.

OEDIPUS:
                    Strange response . . . unlawful,
unfriendly too to the state that bred and reared you—
you withhold the word of god.

TIRESIAS:
                    I fail to see
that your own words are so well-timed.
I'd rather not have the same thing said of me . . . 370

OEDIPUS:
For the love of god, don't turn away,
not if you know something. We beg you,
all of us on our knees.

TIRESIAS:
                    None of you knows—
and I will never reveal my dreadful secrets,
not to say your own. 375

OEDIPUS:
What? You know and you won't tell?
You're bent on betraying us, destroying Thebes?

TIRESIAS:
I'd rather not cause pain for you or me.
So why this . . . useless interrogation?
You'll get nothing from me.

OEDIPUS:
                              Nothing! You,
you scum of the earth, you'd enrage a heart of stone!
You won't talk? Nothing moves you?
Out with it, once and for all!

TIRESIAS:
You criticize my temper . . . unaware
of the one *you* live with, you revile me.

OEDIPUS:
Who could restrain his anger hearing you?
What outrage—you spurn the city!

TIRESIAS:
What will come will come.
Even if I shroud it all in silence.

OEDIPUS:
What will come? You're bound to *tell* me that.

TIRESIAS:
I will say no more. Do as you like, build your anger
to whatever pitch you please, rage your worst—

OEDIPUS:
Oh I'll let loose, I have such fury in me—
now I see it all. You helped hatch the plot,
you did the work, yes, short of killing him
with your own hands—and given eyes I'd say
you did the killing single-handed!

TIRESIAS:
                              Is that so!
I charge you, then, submit to that decree
you just laid down: from this day onward
speak to no one, not these citizens, not myself.
You are the curse, the corruption of the land!

OEDIPUS:
You, shameless—
aren't you appalled to start up such a story?
You think you can get away with this?

TIRESIAS:
                              I have already.
The truth with all its power lives inside me.

OEDIPUS:
Who primed you for this? Not your prophet's trade.

TIRESIAS:
You did, you forced me, twisted it out of me.

OEDIPUS:
What? Say it again—I'll understand it better.

TIRESIAS:
Didn't you understand, just now?
Or are you tempting me to talk?

OEDIPUS:
No, I can't say I grasped your meaning.
Out with it, again!

TIRESIAS:
I say you are the murderer you hunt.

OEDIPUS:
That obscenity, twice—by god, you'll pay.

TIRESIAS:
Shall I say more, so you can really rage? 415

OEDIPUS:
Much as you want. Your words are nothing—
futile.

TIRESIAS:
    You cannot imagine . . . I tell you,
you and your loved ones live together in infamy,
you cannot see how far you've gone in guilt.

OEDIPUS:
You think you can keep this up and never suffer? 420

TIRESIAS:
Indeed, if the truth has any power.

OEDIPUS:
                              It does
but not for you, old man. You've lost your power,
stone-blind, stone-deaf—senses, eyes blind as stone!

TIRESIAS:
I pity you, flinging at me the very insults
each man here will fling at you so soon.

OEDIPUS:
                              Blind,
lost in the night, endless night that nursed you!
You can't hurt me or anyone else who sees the light—
you can never touch me.

TIRESIAS:
                    True, it is not your fate
to fall at my hands. Apollo is quite enough,
and he will take some pains to work this out.

OEDIPUS:
Creon! Is this conspiracy his or yours?

TIRESIAS:
Creon is not your downfall, no, you are your own.

OEDIPUS:
                                      O power—
wealth and empire, skill outstripping skill
in the heady rivalries of life,
what envy lurks inside you! Just for this,   435
the crown the city gave me—I never sought it,
they laid it in my hands—for this alone, Creon,
the soul of trust, my loyal friend from the start
steals against me . . . so hungry to overthrow me
he sets this wizard on me, this scheming quack,   440
this fortune-teller peddling lies, eyes peeled
for his own profit—seer blind in his craft!

Come here, you pious fraud. Tell me,
when did you ever prove yourself a prophet?
When the Sphinx, that chanting Fury kept her deathwatch here,
why silent then, not a word to set our people free?
There was a riddle, not for some passer-by to solve—
it cried out for a prophet. Where were you?
Did you rise to the crisis? Not a word,
you and your birds, your gods—nothing.   450
No, but I came by, Oedipus the ignorant,
I stopped the Sphinx! With no help from the birds,
the flight of my own intelligence hit the mark.

And this is the man you'd try to overthrow?
You think you'll stand by Creon when he's king?   455
You and the great mastermind—
you'll pay in tears, I promise you, for this,
this witch-hunt. If you didn't look so senile
the lash would teach you what your scheming means!

LEADER:
I would suggest his words were spoken in anger,   460
Oedipus . . . yours too, and it isn't what we need.
The best solution to the oracle, the riddle
posed by god—we should look for that.

TIRESIAS:
You are the king no doubt, but in one respect,
at least, I am your equal: the right to reply.   465
I claim that privilege too.
I am not your slave. I serve Apollo.
I don't need Creon to speak for me in public.

                                                So,
you mock my blindness? Let me tell you this.
You with your precious eyes,   470
you're blind to the corruption of your life,
to the house you live in, those you live with—
who *are* your parents? Do you know? All unknowing
you are the scourge of your own flesh and blood,
the dead below the earth and the living here above,   475
and the double lash of your mother and your father's curse
will whip you from this land one day, their footfall
treading you down in terror, darkness shrouding
your eyes that now can see the light!

                                                 Soon, soon
you'll scream aloud—what haven won't reverberate?   480
What rock of Cithaeron won't scream back in echo?
That day you learn the truth about your marriage,
the wedding-march that sang you into your halls,
the lusty voyage home to the fatal harbor!
And a crowd of other horrors you'd never dream   485
will level you with yourself and all your children.

There. Now smear us with insults—Creon, myself
and every word I've said. No man will ever
be rooted from the earth as brutally as you.

OEDIPUS:
Enough! Such filth from him? Insufferable—   490
what, still alive? Get out—
faster, back where you came from—vanish!

TIRESIAS:
I would never have come if you hadn't called me here.

OEDIPUS:
If I thought you would blurt out such absurdities,
you'd have died waiting before I'd had you summoned. 495

TIRESIAS:
Absurd, am I! To you, not to your parents:
the ones who bore you found me sane enough.

OEDIPUS:
Parents—who? Wait . . . who is my father?

TIRESIAS:
This day will bring your birth and your destruction.

OEDIPUS:
Riddles—all you can say are riddles, murk and darkness. 500

TIRESIAS:
Ah, but aren't you the best man alive at solving riddles?

OEDIPUS:
Mock me for that, go on, and you'll reveal my greatness.

TIRESIAS:
Your great good fortune, true, it was your ruin.

OEDIPUS:
Not if I saved the city—what do I care?

TIRESIAS:
Well then, I'll be going.
To his attendant.
Take me home, boy. 505

OEDIPUS:
Yes, take him away. You're a nuisance here.
Out of the way, the irritation's gone.

> *Turning his back on* TIRESIAS,
> *moving toward the palace.*

TIRESIAS:
                    I will go,
once I have said what I came here to say.
I will never shrink from the anger in your eyes—
you can't destroy me. Listen to me closely: 510
the man you've sought so long, proclaiming,
cursing up and down, the murderer of Laius—
he is here. A stranger,
you may think, who lives among you,
he soon will be revealed a native Theban   515
but he will take no joy in the revelation.
Blind who now has eyes, beggar who now is rich,
he will grope his way toward a foreign soil,
a stick tapping before him step by step.

> OEDIPUS *enters the palace.*

Revealed at last, brother and father both   520
to the children he embraces, to his mother
son and husband both—he sowed the loins
his father sowed, he spilled his father's blood!

Go in and reflect on that, solve that.
And if you find I've lied   525
from this day onward call the prophet blind.

> TIRESIAS *and the boy exit to the side.*

CHORUS:
                                    Who—
who is the man the voice of god denounces
resounding out of the rocky gorge of Delphi?
    The horror too dark to tell,
whose ruthless bloody hands have done the work?   530
His time has come to fly
    to outrace the stallions of the storm
                    his feet a streak of speed—
Cased in armor, Apollo son of the Father
lunges on him, lightning-bolts afire!   535
And the grim unerring Furies
            closing for the kill.
                        Look,
the word of god has just come blazing
flashing off Parnassus' snowy heights!
    That man who left no trace—   540
after him, hunt him down with all our strength!
Now under bristling timber
    up through rocks and caves he stalks
                    like the wild mountain bull—
cut off from men, each step an agony, frenzied, racing blind 545
but he cannot outrace the dread voices of Delphi
ringing out of the heart of Earth,
    the dark wings beating around him shrieking doom
                    the doom that never dies, the terror—

The skilled prophet scans the birds and shatters me with terror!
I can't accept him, can't deny him, don't know what to say,
I'm lost, and the wings of dark foreboding beating—
I cannot see what's come, what's still to come . . .
and what could breed a blood feud between
    Laius' house and the son of Polybus?　　　　　　　　　555
I know of nothing, not in the past and not now,
no charge to bring against our king, no cause
to attack his fame that rings throughout Thebes—
    not without proof—not for the ghost of Laius,
    not to avenge a murder gone without a trace.　　　　　　560

Zeus and Apollo know, they know, the great masters
    of all the dark and depth of human life.
But whether a mere man can know the truth,
whether a seer can fathom more than I—
there is no test, no certain proof　　　　　　　　　　　　　565
    though matching skill for skill
a man can outstrip a rival. No, not till I see
these charges proved will I side with his accusers.
We saw him then, when the she-hawk swept against him,
saw with our own eyes his skill, his brilliant triumph—　　570
    there was the test—he was the joy of Thebes!
    Never will I convict my king, never in my heart.

Enter CREON *from the side.*

CREON:
My fellow-citizens, I hear King Oedipus
levels terrible charges at me. I had to come.
I resent it deeply. If, in the present crisis, 575
he thinks he suffers any abuse from me,
anything I've done or said that offers him
the slightest injury, why, I've no desire
to linger out this life, my reputation in ruins.
The damage I'd face from such an accusation 580
is nothing simple. No, there's nothing worse:
branded a traitor in the city, a traitor
to all of you and my good friends.

LEADER:
                              True,
but a slur might have been forced out of him,
by anger perhaps, not any firm conviction. 585

CREON:
The charge was made in public, wasn't it?
I put the prophet up to spreading lies?

LEADER:
Such things were said . . .
I don't know with what intent, if any.

CREON:
Was his glance steady, his mind right 590
when the charge was brought against me?

LEADER:
I really couldn't say. I never look
to judge the ones in power.

The doors open. OEDIPUS *enters.*

Wait,
here's Oedipus now.

OEDIPUS:
You—here? You have the gall
to show your face before the palace gates?   595
You, plotting to kill me, kill the king—
I see it all, the marauding thief himself
scheming to steal my crown and power!
Tell me,
in god's name, what did you take me for,
coward or fool, when you spun out your plot?   600
Your treachery—you think I'd never detect it
creeping against me in the dark? Or sensing it,
not defend myself? Aren't you the fool,
you and your high adventure. Lacking numbers,
powerful friends, out for the big game of empire—   605
you need riches, armies to bring that quarry down!

CREON:
Are you quite finished? It's your turn to listen
for just as long as you've . . . instructed me.
Hear me out, then judge me on the facts.

OEDIPUS:
You've a wicked way with words, Creon,   610
but I'll be slow to learn—from you.
I find you a menace, a great burden to me.

CREON:
Just one thing, hear me out in this.

OEDIPUS:
                              Just one thing,
don't tell *me* you're not the enemy, the traitor.

CREON:
Look, if you think crude, mindless stubbornness   615
such a gift, you've lost your sense of balance.

OEDIPUS:
If you think you can abuse a kinsman,
then escape the penalty, you're insane.

CREON:
Fair enough, I grant you. But this injury
you say I've done you, what is it?   620

OEDIPUS:
Did you induce me, yes or no,
to send for that sanctimonious prophet?

CREON:
I did. And I'd do the same again.

OEDIPUS:
All right then, tell me, how long is it now
since Laius . . .

CREON:
          Laius—what did *he* do?

OEDIPUS:
                              Vanished,   625
swept from sight, murdered in his tracks.

CREON:
The count of the years would run you far back . . .

OEDIPUS:
And that far back, was the prophet at his trade?

CREON:
Skilled as he is today, and just as honored.

OEDIPUS:
Did he ever refer to me then, at that time?

CREON:
                              No,   630
never, at least, when I was in his presence.

OEDIPUS:
But you did investigate the murder, didn't you?

CREON:
We did our best, of course, discovered nothing.

OEDIPUS:
But the great seer never accused me then—why not?

CREON:
I don't know. And when I don't, *I* keep quiet.   635

OEDIPUS:
You do know this, you'd tell it too—
if you had a shred of decency.

CREON:
                    What?
If I know, I won't hold back.

OEDIPUS:
                    Simply this:
if the two of you had never put heads together,
we would never have heard about *my* killing Laius.   640

CREON:
If that's what he says . . . well, you know best.
But now I have a right to learn from you
as you just learned from me.

OEDIPUS:
                    Learn your fill,
you never will convict me of the murder.

CREON:
Tell me, you're married to my sister, aren't you?   645

OEDIPUS:
A genuine discovery—there's no denying that.

CREON:
And you rule the land with her, with equal power?

OEDIPUS:
She receives from me whatever she desires.

CREON:
And I am the third, all of us are equals?

OEDIPUS:
Yes, and it's there you show your stripes—   650
you betray a kinsman.

CREON:
                    Not at all.
Not if you see things calmly, rationally,
as I do. Look at it this way first:
who in his right mind would rather rule
and live in anxiety than sleep in peace?   655
Particularly if he enjoys the same authority.
Not I, I'm not the man to yearn for kingship,
not with a king's power in my hands. Who would?
No one with any sense of self-control.
Now, as it is, you offer me all I need,   660
not a fear in the world. But if I wore the crown . . .
there'd be many painful duties to perform,
hardly to my taste.
                    How could kingship
please me more than influence, power
without a qualm? I'm not that deluded yet,   665
to reach for anything but privilege outright,
profit free and clear.
Now all men sing my praises, all salute me,
now all who request your favors curry mine.
I am their best hope: success rests in me.   670
Why give up that, I ask you, and borrow trouble?
A man of sense, someone who sees things clearly
would never resort to treason.
No, I have no lust for conspiracy in me,
nor could I ever suffer one who does.   675

Do you want proof? Go to Delphi yourself,
examine the oracle and see if I've reported
the message word-for-word. This too:
if you detect that I and the clairvoyant
have plotted anything in common, arrest me,   680
execute me. Not on the strength of one vote,
two in this case, mine as well as yours.
But don't convict me on sheer unverified surmise.

How wrong it is to take the good for bad,
purely at random, or take the bad for good. 685
But reject a friend, a kinsman? I would as soon
tear out the life within us, priceless life itself.
You'll learn this well, without fail, in time.
Time alone can bring the just man to light—
the criminal you can spot in one short day. 690

LEADER:
                                      Good advice,
my lord, for anyone who wants to avoid disaster.
Those who jump to conclusions may go wrong.

OEDIPUS:
When my enemy moves against me quickly,
plots in secret, I move quickly too, I must,
I plot and pay him back. Relax my guard a moment, 695
waiting his next move—he wins his objective,
I lose mine.

CREON:
          What do you want?
You want me banished?

OEDIPUS:
                     No, I want you dead.

CREON:
Just to show how ugly a grudge can . . .

OEDIPUS:
                           So,
still stubborn? you don't think I'm serious? 700

CREON:
I think you're insane.

OEDIPUS:
                Quite sane—in my behalf.

CREON:
Not just as much in mine?

OEDIPUS:
                    You—my mortal enemy?

CREON:
What if you're wholly wrong?

OEDIPUS:
                     No matter—I must rule.

CREON:
Not if you rule unjustly.

OEDIPUS:
                Hear him, Thebes, my city!

CREON:
My city too, not yours alone!   705

LEADER:
Please, my lords.
                    Enter JOCASTA *from the palace.*
        Look, Jocasta's coming,
and just in time too. With her help
you must put this fighting of yours to rest.

JOCASTA:
Have you no sense? Poor misguided men,
such shouting—why this public outburst?   710
Aren't you ashamed, with the land so sick,
to stir up private quarrels?

To OEDIPUS.

Into the palace now. And Creon, you go home.
Why make such a furor over nothing?

CREON:
My sister, it's dreadful . . . Oedipus, your husband,   715
he's bent on a choice of punishments for me,
banishment from the fatherland or death.

OEDIPUS:
Precisely. I caught him in the act, Jocasta,
plotting, about to stab me in the back.

CREON:
Never—curse me, let me die and be damned   720
if I've done you any wrong you charge me with.

JOCASTA:
Oh god, believe it, Oedipus,
honor the solemn oath he swears to heaven.
Do it for me, for the sake of all your people.

The CHORUS *begins to chant.*

CHORUS:
>   Believe it, be sensible
>   give way, my king, I beg you!

OEDIPUS:
>   What do you want from me, concessions?

CHORUS:
>   Respect him—he's been no fool in the past
>   and now he's strong with the oath he swears to god.

OEDIPUS:
>   You know what you're asking?

CHORUS:
>   I do.

OEDIPUS:
>   Then out with it!

CHORUS:
>   The man's your friend, your kin, he's under oath—
>   don't cast him out, disgraced
>   branded with guilt on the strength of hearsay only.

OEDIPUS:
Know full well, if that is what you want
you want me dead or banished from the land.

CHORUS:
                                Never—
    no, by the blazing Sun, first god of the heavens!
        Stripped of the gods, stripped of loved ones,
    let me die by inches if that ever crossed my mind.
    But the heart inside me sickens, dies as the land dies
    and now on top of the old griefs you pile this,   740
    your fury—both of you!

OEDIPUS:
                                Then let him go,
    even if it does lead to my ruin, my death
    or my disgrace, driven from Thebes for life.
    It's you, not him I pity—your words move me.
    He, wherever he goes, my hate goes with him.   745

CREON:
    Look at you, sullen in yielding, brutal in your rage—
    you will go too far. It's perfect justice:
    natures like yours are hardest on themselves.

OEDIPUS:
    Then leave me alone—get out!

CREON:
                                I'm going.
    You're wrong, so wrong. These men know I'm right.   750

                            Exit to the side. The CHORUS *turns
                            to* JOCASTA.

CHORUS:
>Why do you hesitate, my lady
>why not help him in?

JOCASTA:
>Tell me what's happened first.

CHORUS:
>Loose, ignorant talk started dark suspicions
>and a sense of injustice cut deeply too.

JOCASTA:
>On both sides?

CHORUS:
>Oh yes.

JOCASTA:
>What did they say?

CHORUS:
>Enough, please, enough! The land's so racked already
>or so it seems to me . . .
>End the trouble here, just where they left it.

OEDIPUS:
You see what comes of your good intentions now?
And all because you tried to blunt my anger.

CHORUS:
>My king,
>I've said it once, I'll say it time and again—
> I'd be insane, you know it,
>senseless, ever to turn my back on you.
>You who set our beloved land—storm-tossed, shattered—
>straight on course. Now again, good helmsman,
>steer us through the storm!

The CHORUS *draws away, leaving* OEDIPUS *and* JOCASTA *side by side.*

JOCASTA:
                    For the love of god,
Oedipus, tell me too, what is it?
Why this rage? You're so unbending.

OEDIPUS:
I will tell you. I respect you, Jocasta, 770
much more than these men here . . .
                    Glancing at the CHORUS.
Creon's to blame, Creon schemes against me.

JOCASTA:
Tell me clearly, how did the quarrel start?

OEDIPUS:
He says *I* murdered Laius—I am guilty.

JOCASTA:
How does he know? Some secret knowledge 775
or simple hearsay?

OEDIPUS:
          Oh, he sent his prophet in
to do his dirty work. You know Creon,
Creon keeps his own lips clean.

JOCASTA:
                              A prophet?
Well then, free yourself of every charge!
Listen to me and learn some peace of mind: 780
no skill in the world,
nothing human can penetrate the future.
Here is proof, quick and to the point.

An oracle came to Laius one fine day
(I won't say from Apollo himself   785
but his underlings his priests) and it declared
that doom would strike him down at the hands of a son,
our son, to be born of our own flesh and blood. But Laius,
so the report goes at least, was killed by strangers,
thieves, at a place where three roads meet . . . my son—   790
he wasn't three days old and the boy's father
fastened his ankles, had a henchman fling him away
on a barren, trackless mountain.
                              There, you see?
Apollo brought neither thing to pass. My baby
no more murdered his father than Laius suffered—   795
his wildest fear—death at his own son's hands.
That's how the seers and all their revelations
mapped out the future. Brush them from your mind.
Whatever the god needs and seeks
he'll bring to light himself, with ease.   800

OEDIPUS:
                              Strange,
hearing you just now . . . my mind wandered,
my thoughts racing back and forth.

JOCASTA:
What do you mean? Why so anxious, startled?

OEDIPUS:
I thought I heard you say that Laius
was cut down at a place where three roads meet. 805

JOCASTA:
That was the story. It hasn't died out yet.

OEDIPUS:
Where did this thing happen? Be precise.

JOCASTA:
A place called Phocis, where two branching roads,
one from Daulia, one from Delphi,
come together—a crossroads. 810

OEDIPUS:
When? How long ago?

JOCASTA:
The heralds no sooner reported Laius dead
than you appeared and they hailed you king of Thebes.

OEDIPUS:
My god, my god—what have you planned to do to me?

JOCASTA:
What, Oedipus? What haunts you so?

OEDIPUS:
                              Not yet. 815
Laius—how did he look? Describe him.
Had he reached his prime?

JOCASTA:
                        He was swarthy,
and the gray had just begun to streak his temples,
and his build . . . wasn't far from yours.

OEDIPUS:
                                    Oh no no,
I think I've just called down a dreadful curse   820
upon myself—I simply didn't know!

JOCASTA:
What are you saying? I shudder to look at you.

OEDIPUS:
I have a terrible fear the blind seer can see.
I'll know in a moment. One thing more—

JOCASTA:
                        Anything,
afraid as I am—ask, I'll answer, all I can.   825

OEDIPUS:
Did he go with a light or heavy escort,
several men-at-arms, like a lord, a king?

JOCASTA:
There were five in the party, a herald among them,
and a single wagon carrying Laius.

OEDIPUS:
                        Ai—
now I can see it all, clear as day.   830
Who told you all this at the time, Jocasta?

JOCASTA:
A servant who reached home, the lone survivor.

OEDIPUS:
So, could he still be in the palace—even now?

JOCASTA:
No indeed. Soon as he returned from the scene
and saw you on the throne with Laius dead and gone, 835
he knelt and clutched my hand, pleading with me
to send him into the hinterlands, to pasture,
far as possible, out of sight of Thebes.
I sent him away. Slave though he was,
he'd earned that favor—and much more. 840

OEDIPUS:
Can we bring him back, quickly?

JOCASTA:
Easily. Why do you want him so?

OEDIPUS:
                         I am afraid,
Jocasta, I have said too much already.
That man—I've got to see him.

JOCASTA:
                      Then he'll come.
But even I have a right, I'd like to think, 845
to know what's torturing you, my lord.

OEDIPUS:
And so you shall—I can hold nothing back from you,
now I've reached this pitch of dark foreboding.
Who means more to me than you? Tell me,
whom would I turn toward but you   850
as I go through all this?

My father was Polybus, king of Corinth.
My mother, a Dorian, Merope. And I was held
the prince of the realm among the people there,
till something struck me out of nowhere,   855
something strange . . . worth remarking perhaps,
hardly worth the anxiety I gave it.
Some man at a banquet who had drunk too much
shouted out—he was far gone, mind you—
that I am not my father's son. Fighting words!   860
I barely restrained myself that day
but early the next I went to mother and father,
questioned them closely, and they were enraged
at the accusation and the fool who let it fly.
So as for my parents I was satisfied,   865
but still this thing kept gnawing at me,
the slander spread—I had to make my move.
                                                  And so,
unknown to mother and father I set out for Delphi,
and the god Apollo spurned me, sent me away
denied the facts I came for,   870
but first he flashed before my eyes a future
great with pain, terror, disaster—I can hear him cry,
"You are fated to couple with your mother, you will bring
a breed of children into the light no man can bear to see—
you will kill your father, the one who gave you life!"   875
I heard all that and ran. I abandoned Corinth,
from that day on I gauged its landfall only
by the stars, running, always running
toward some place where I would never see
the shame of all those oracles come true.   880
And as I fled I reached that very spot
where the great king, you say, met his death.

Now, Jocasta, I will tell you all.
Making my way toward this triple crossroad
I began to see a herald, then a brace of colts   885
drawing a wagon, and mounted on the bench . . . a man,
just as you've described him, coming face-to-face,
and the one in the lead and the old man himself
were about to thrust me off the road—brute force—
and the one shouldering me aside, the driver,   890
I strike him in anger!—and the old man, watching me
coming up along his wheels—he brings down
his prod, two prongs straight at my head!
I paid him back with interest!
Short work, by god—with one blow of the staff   895
in this right hand I knock him out of his high seat,
roll him out of the wagon, sprawling headlong—
I killed them all—every mother's son!

Oh, but if there is any blood-tie
between Laius and this stranger . . .   900
what man alive more miserable than I?
More hated by the gods? *I* am the man
no alien, no citizen welcomes to his house,
law forbids it—not a word to me in public,
driven out of every hearth and home.   905
And all these curses I—no one but I
brought down these piling curses on myself!
And you, his wife, I've touched your body with these,
the hands that killed your husband cover you with blood.

Wasn't I born for torment? Look me in the eyes!   910
I am abomination—heart and soul!
I must be exiled, and even in exile
never see my parents, never set foot
on native ground again. Else I am doomed
to couple with my mother and cut my father down . . .   915
Polybus who reared me, gave me life.

                          But why, why?
Wouldn't a man of judgment say—and wouldn't he be right—
some savage power has brought this down upon my head?

Oh no, not that, you pure and awesome gods,
never let me see that day! Let me slip   920
from the world of men, vanish without a trace
before I see myself stained with such corruption,
stained to the heart.

LEADER:
My lord, you fill our hearts with fear.
But at least until you question the witness,   925
do take hope.

OEDIPUS:
                    Exactly. He is my last hope—
I am waiting for the shepherd. He is crucial.

JOCASTA:
And once he appears, what then? Why so urgent?

OEDIPUS:
I will tell you. If it turns out that his story
matches yours, I've escaped the worst.   930

JOCASTA:
What did I say? What struck you so?

OEDIPUS:
                              You said *thieves*—
he told you a whole band of them murdered Laius.
So, if he still holds to the same number,
I cannot be the killer. One can't equal many.
But if he refers to one man, one alone,   935
clearly the scales come down on me:
I am guilty.

JOCASTA:
              Impossible. Trust me,
I told you precisely what he said,
and he can't retract it now;
the whole city heard it, not just I.   940
And even if he should vary his first report
by one man more or less, still, my lord,
he could never make the murder of Laius
truly fit the prophecy. Apollo was explicit:
my son was doomed to kill my husband . . . my son,   945
poor defenseless thing, he never had a chance
to kill his father. They destroyed him first.

So much for prophecy. It's neither here nor there.
From this day on, I wouldn't look right or left.

OEDIPUS:
True, true. Still, that shepherd,   950
someone fetch him—now!

JOCASTA:
I'll send at once. But do let's go inside.
I'd never displease you, least of all in this.

                              OEDIPUS *and* JOCASTA *enter the*
                              palace.

CHORUS:
>   Destiny guide me always
>   Destiny find me filled with reverence   955
>   pure in word and deed.
>   Great laws tower above us, reared on high
>   born for the brilliant vault of heaven—
>   Olympian Sky their only father,
>   nothing mortal, no man gave them birth,   960
>   their memory deathless, never lost in sleep:
>   within them lives a mighty god, the god does not
>   grow old.
>
>   Pride breeds the tyrant
>   violent pride, gorging, crammed to bursting
>   with all that is overripe and rich with ruin—   965
>   clawing up to the heights, headlong pride
>   crashes down the abyss—sheer doom!
>   No footing helps, all foothold lost and gone.
>   But the healthy strife that makes the city strong—
>   I pray that god will never end that wrestling: 970
>   god, my champion, I will never let you go.

But if any man comes striding, high and mighty
  in all he says and does,
no fear of justice, no reverence
for the temples of the gods—   975
  let a rough doom tear him down,
repay his pride, breakneck, ruinous pride!
If he cannot reap his profits fairly
  cannot restrain himself from outrage—
mad, laying hands on the holy things untouchable!   980

  Can such a man, so desperate, still boast
    he can save his life from the flashing bolts of god?
    If all such violence goes with honor now
      why join the sacred dance?

Never again will I go reverent to Delphi,   985
  the inviolate heart of Earth
or Apollo's ancient oracle at Abae
or Olympia of the fires—
  unless these prophecies all come true
for all mankind to point toward in wonder.   990
King of kings, if you deserve your titles
  Zeus, remember, never forget!
You and your deathless, everlasting reign.

  They are dying, the old oracles sent to Laius,
    now our masters strike them off the rolls.   995
    Nowhere Apollo's golden glory now—
      the gods, the gods go down.

Enter JOCASTA *from the palace,*
carrying a suppliant's branch wound
in wool.

JOCASTA:
Lords of the realm, it occurred to me,
just now, to visit the temples of the gods,
so I have my branch in hand and incense too.

Oedipus is beside himself. Racked with anguish,
no longer a man of sense, he won't admit
the latest prophecies are hollow as the old—
he's at the mercy of every passing voice
if the voice tells of terror.
I urge him gently, nothing seems to help,
so I turn to you, Apollo, you are nearest.

Placing her branch on the altar,
while an old herdsman enters from
the side, not the one just summoned
by the King but an unexpected
MESSENGER *from Corinth.*

I come with prayers and offerings . . . I beg you,
cleanse us, set us free of defilement!
Look at us, passengers in the grip of fear,
watching the pilot of the vessel go to pieces.

MESSENGER:

Approaching JOCASTA *and*
the CHORUS.

Strangers, please, I wonder if you could lead us
to the palace of the king . . . I think it's Oedipus.
Better, the man himself—you know where he is?

LEADER:
This is his palace, stranger. He's inside.
But here is his queen, his wife and mother
of his children.

MESSENGER:
                    Blessings on you, noble queen,
queen of Oedipus crowned with all your family—
blessings on you always!

JOCASTA:
And the same to you, stranger, you deserve it . . .   1020
such a greeting. But what have you come for?
Have you brought us news?

MESSENGER:
                    Wonderful news—
for the house, my lady, for your husband too.

JOCASTA:
Really, what? Who sent you?

MESSENGER:
                    Corinth.
I'll give you the message in a moment.   1025
You'll be glad of it—how could you help it?—
though it costs a little sorrow in the bargain.

JOCASTA:
What can it be, with such a double edge?

MESSENGER:
The people there, they want to make your Oedipus
king of Corinth, so they're saying now.   1030

JOCASTA.
Why? Isn't old Polybus still in power?

MESSENGER:
No more. Death has got him in the tomb.

JOCASTA:
What are you saying? Polybus, dead?—dead?

MESSENGER:
                                    If not,
if I'm not telling the truth, strike me dead too.

JOCASTA:
                    To a servant.
Quickly, go to your master, tell him this!   1035

You prophecies of the gods, where are you now?
This is the man that Oedipus feared for years,
he fled him, not to kill him—and now he's dead,
quite by chance, a normal, natural death,
not murdered by his son.   1040

OEDIPUS:
                        Emerging from the palace.
                Dearest,
what now? Why call me from the palace?

JOCASTA:
                        Bringing the MESSENGER *closer.*
Listen to *him,* see for yourself what all
those awful prophecies of god have come to.

OEDIPUS:
And who is he? What can he have for me?

JOCASTA:
He's from Corinth, he's come to tell you   1045
your father is no more—Polybus—he's dead!

OEDIPUS:
Wheeling on the MESSENGER.
What? Let me have it from your lips.

MESSENGER:
Well,
if that's what you want first, then here it is:
make no mistake, Polybus is dead and gone.

OEDIPUS:
How—murder? sickness?—what? what killed him? 1050

MESSENGER:
A light tip of the scales can put old bones to rest.

OEDIPUS:
Sickness then—poor man, it wore him down.

MESSENGER:
That,
and the long count of years he'd measured out.

OEDIPUS:
So!
Jocasta, why, why look to the Prophet's hearth,
the fires of the future? Why scan the birds 1055
that scream above our heads? They winged me on
to the murder of my father, did they? That was my doom?
Well look, he's dead and buried, hidden under the earth,
and here I am in Thebes, I never put hand to sword—
unless some longing for me wasted him away, 1060
then in a sense you'd say I caused his death.
But now, all those prophecies I feared—Polybus
packs them off to sleep with him in hell!
They're nothing, worthless.

JOCASTA:
>   There.
Didn't I tell you from the start?   1065

OEDIPUS:
So you did. I was lost in fear.

JOCASTA:
No more, sweep it from your mind forever.

OEDIPUS:
But my mother's bed, surely I must fear—

JOCASTA:
>   Fear?
What should a man fear? It's all chance,
chance rules our lives. Not a man on earth   1070
can see a day ahead, groping through the dark.
Better to live at random, best we can.
And as for this marriage with your mother—
have no fear. Many a man before you,
in his dreams, has shared his mother's bed.   1075
Take such things for shadows, nothing at all—
Live, Oedipus,
as if there's no tomorrow!

OEDIPUS:
>   Brave words,
and you'd persuade me if mother weren't alive.
But mother lives, so for all your reassurances   1080
I live in fear, I must.

JOCASTA:
>   But your father's death,
that, at least, is a great blessing, joy to the eyes!

OEDIPUS:
Great, I know . . . but I fear *her*—she's still alive.

MESSENGER:
Wait, who is this woman, makes you so afraid?

OEDIPUS:
Merope, old man. The wife of Polybus. 1085

MESSENGER:
The queen? What's there to fear in her?

OEDIPUS:
A dreadful prophecy, stranger, sent by the gods.

MESSENGER:
Tell me, could you? Unless it's forbidden
other ears to hear.

OEDIPUS:
            Not at all.
Apollo told me once—it is my fate— 1090
I must make love with my own mother,
shed my father's blood with my own hands.
So for years I've given Corinth a wide berth,
and it's been my good fortune too. But still,
to see one's parents and look into their eyes 1095
is the greatest joy I know.

MESSENGER:
                         You're afraid of that?
That kept you out of Corinth?

OEDIPUS:

                      My *father*, old man—
so I wouldn't kill my father.

MESSENGER:

                 So that's it.
Well then, seeing I came with such good will, my king,
why don't I rid you of that old worry now?

OEDIPUS:
What a rich reward you'd have for that!

MESSENGER:
What do you think I came for, majesty?
So you'd come home and I'd be better off.

OEDIPUS:
Never, I will never go near my parents.

MESSENGER:
My boy, it's clear, you don't know what you're doing.

OEDIPUS:
What do you mean, old man? For god's sake, explain.

MESSENGER:
If you ran from *them,* always dodging home . . .

OEDIPUS:
Always, terrified Apollo's oracle might come true—

MESSENGER:
And you'd be covered with guilt, from both your parents.

OEDIPUS:
That's right, old man, that fear is always with me.   1110

MESSENGER:
Don't you know? You've really nothing to fear.

OEDIPUS:
But why? If I'm their son—Merope, Polybus?

MESSENGER:
Polybus was nothing to you, that's why, not in blood.

OEDIPUS:
What are you saying—Polybus was not my father?

MESSENGER:
No more than I am. He and I are equals.   1115

OEDIPUS:
                          My father—
how can my father equal nothing? You're nothing to me!

MESSENGER:
Neither was he, no more your father than I am.

OEDIPUS:
Then why did he call me his son?

MESSENGER:
                       You were a gift,
years ago—know for a fact he took you
from my hands.

OEDIPUS:
                    No, from another's hands?
Then how could he love me so? He loved me, deeply...

MESSENGER:
True, and his early years without a child
made him love you all the more.

OEDIPUS:
                              And you, did you...
buy me? find me by accident?

MESSENGER:
                         I stumbled on you,
down the woody flanks of Mount Cithaeron.

OEDIPUS:
                              So close,
what were you doing here, just passing through?

MESSENGER:
Watching over my flocks, grazing them on the slopes.

OEDIPUS:
A herdsman, were you? A vagabond, scraping for wages?

MESSENGER:
Your savior too, my son, in your worst hour.

OEDIPUS:
                                   Oh—
when you picked me up, was I in pain? What exactly?

MESSENGER:
Your ankles . . . they tell the story. Look at them.

OEDIPUS:
Why remind me of that, that old affliction?

MESSENGER:
Your ankles were pinned together. I set you free.

OEDIPUS:
That dreadful mark—I've had it from the cradle.

MESSENGER:
And you got your name from that misfortune too, the name's still with you.

OEDIPUS:
                    Dear god, who did it?—
mother? father? Tell me.

MESSENGER:
                    I don't know.
The one who gave you to me, he'd know more.

OEDIPUS:
What? You took me from someone else?
You didn't find me yourself?

MESSENGER:
                    No sir,
another shepherd passed you on to me.

OEDIPUS:
Who? Do you know? Describe him.

MESSENGER:
He called himself a servant of . . .
if I remember rightly—Laius.

> JOCASTA *turns sharply.*

OEDIPUS:
The king of the land who ruled here long ago?   1145

MESSENGER:
That's the one. That herdsman was *his* man.

OEDIPUS:
Is he still alive? Can I see him?

MESSENGER:
They'd know best, the people of these parts.

> OEDIPUS *and the* MESSENGER *turn to the* CHORUS.

OEDIPUS:
Does anyone know that herdsman,
the one he mentioned? Anyone seen him   1150
in the fields, here in the city? Out with it!
The time has come to reveal this once for all.

LEADER:
I think he's the very shepherd you wanted to see,
a moment ago. But the queen, Jocasta,
she's the one to say.

OEDIPUS:
                    Jocasta,   1155
you remember the man we just sent for?
Is *that* the one he means?

JOCASTA:
                    That man . . .
why ask? Old shepherd, talk, empty nonsense,
don't give it another thought, don't even think—

OEDIPUS:
What—give up now, with a clue like this?   1160
Fail to solve the mystery of my birth?
Not for all the world!

JOCASTA:
                    Stop—in the name of god,
if you love your own life, call off this search!
My suffering is enough.

OEDIPUS:
                    Courage!
Even if my mother turns out to be a slave,   1165
and I a slave, three generations back,
you would not seem common.

JOCASTA:
                    Oh no,
listen to me, I beg you, don't do this.

OEDIPUS:
Listen to you? No more. I must know it all,
must see the truth at last.

JOCASTA:
                    No, please—
for your sake—I want the best for you!

OEDIPUS:
Your best is more than I can bear.

JOCASTA:
                        You're doomed—
may you never fathom who you are!

OEDIPUS:
                    To a servant.
Hurry, fetch me the herdsman, now!
Leave her to glory in her royal birth.

JOCASTA:
Aieeeeee—
         man of agony—
that is the only name I have for you,
that, no other—ever, ever, ever!

Flinging through the palace doors. A long, tense silence follows.

LEADER:
Where's she gone, Oedipus?
Rushing off, such wild grief . . .
I'm afraid that from this silence
something monstrous may come bursting forth.

OEDIPUS:
Let it burst! Whatever will, whatever must!
I must know my birth, no matter how common
it may be—I must see my origins face-to-face. 1185
She perhaps, she with her woman's pride
may well be mortified by my birth,
but I, I count myself the son of Chance,
the great goddess, giver of all good things—
I'll never see myself disgraced. She is my mother! 1190
And the moons have marked me out, my blood-brothers,
one moon on the wane, the next moon great with power.
That is my blood, my nature—I will never betray it,
never fail to search and learn my birth!

CHORUS:
Yes—if I am a true prophet 1195
    if I can grasp the truth,
        by the boundless skies of Olympus,
at the full moon of tomorrow, Mount Cithaeron
you will know how Oedipus glories in you—
you, his birthplace, nurse, his mountain-mother! 1200
And we will sing you, dancing out your praise—
you lift our monarch's heart!
    Apollo, Apollo, god of the wild cry
            may our dancing please you!
                                Oedipus—
            son, dear child, who bore you? 1205
Who of the nymphs who seem to live forever
mated with Pan, the mountain-striding Father?
Who was your mother? who, some bride of Apollo
the god who loves the pastures spreading toward the sun?
    Or was it Hermes, king of the lightning ridges? 1210
Or Dionysus, lord of frenzy, lord of the barren peaks—
did he seize you in his hands, dearest of all his lucky finds?—
    found by the nymphs, their warm eyes dancing, gift
to the lord who loves them dancing out his joy!

> OEDIPUS *strains to see a figure coming from the distance. Attended by palace guards, an old* SHEPHERD *enters slowly, reluctant to approach the king.*

OEDIPUS:
I never met the man, my friends . . . still,   1215
if I had to guess, I'd say that's the shepherd,
the very one we've looked for all along.
Brothers in old age, two of a kind,
he and our guest here. At any rate
the ones who bring him in are my own men,   1220
I recognize them.

> *Turning to the* LEADER.

But you know more than I,
you should, you've seen the man before.

LEADER:
I know him, definitely. One of Laius' men,
a trusty shepherd, if there ever was one.

OEDIPUS:
You, I ask you first, stranger,   1225
you from Corinth—is this the one you mean?

MESSENGER:
You're looking at him. He's your man.

OEDIPUS:

> *To the* SHEPHERD.

You, old man, come over here—
look at me. Answer all my questions.
Did you ever serve King Laius?

SHEPHERD:
                              So I did . . .   1230
a slave, not bought on the block though,
born and reared in the palace.

OEDIPUS:
Your duties, your kind of work?

SHEPHERD:
Herding the flocks, the better part of my life.

OEDIPUS:
Where, mostly? Where did you do your grazing?   1235

SHEPHERD:
                                            Well,
Cithaeron sometimes, or the foothills round about.

OEDIPUS:
This man—you know him? ever see him there?

SHEPHERD:
                        Confused, glancing from the
                        MESSENGER *to the King.*
Doing what?—what man do you mean?

OEDIPUS:
                        Pointing to the MESSENGER.
This one here—ever have dealings with him?

SHEPHERD:
Not so I could say, but give me a chance, 1240
my memory's bad . . .

MESSENGER:
No wonder he doesn't know me, master.
But let me refresh his memory for him.
I'm sure he recalls old times we had
on the slopes of Mount Cithaeron; 1245
he and I, grazing our flocks, he with two
and I with one—we both struck up together,
three whole seasons, six months at a stretch
from spring to the rising of Arcturus in the fall,
then with winter coming on I'd drive my herds 1250
to my own pens, and back he'd go with his
to Laius' folds.

To the SHEPHERD.
Now that's how it was,
wasn't it—yes or no?

SHEPHERD:
Yes, I suppose . . .
it's all so long ago.

MESSENGER:
Come, tell me,
you gave me a child back then, a boy, remember? 1255
A little fellow to rear, my very own.

SHEPHERD:
What? Why rake up that again?

MESSENGER:
Look, here he is, my fine old friend—
the same man who was just a baby then.

SHEPHERD:
Damn you, shut your mouth—quiet! 1260

OEDIPUS:
Don't lash out at him, old man—
you need lashing more than he does.

SHEPHERD:
                      Why,
master, majesty—what have I done wrong?

OEDIPUS:
You won't answer his question about the boy.

SHEPHERD:
He's talking nonsense, wasting his breath. 1265

OEDIPUS:
So, you won't talk willingly—
then you'll talk with pain.

The guards seize the SHEPHERD.

SHEPHERD:
No, dear god, don't torture an old man!

OEDIPUS:
Twist his arms back, quickly!

SHEPHERD:
                    God help us, why?—
what more do you need to know?   1270

OEDIPUS:
Did you give him that child? He's asking.

SHEPHERD:
I did . . . I wish to god I'd died that day.

OEDIPUS:
You've got your wish if you don't tell the truth.

SHEPHERD:
The more I tell, the worse the death I'll die.

OEDIPUS:
Our friend here wants to stretch things out, does he?   1275

                    Motioning to his men for torture.

SHEPHERD:
No, no, I gave it to him—I just said so.

OEDIPUS:
Where did you get it? Your house? Someone else's?

SHEPHERD:
It wasn't mine, no, I got it from . . . someone.

OEDIPUS:
Which one of them?
Looking at the citizens.
Whose house?

SHEPHERD:
No—
god's sake, master, no more questions!   1280

OEDIPUS:
You're a dead man if I have to ask again.

SHEPHERD:
Then—the child came from the house . . .
of Laius.

OEDIPUS:
A slave? or born of his own blood?

SHEPHERD:
Oh no,
I'm right at the edge, the horrible truth—I've got to say it!

OEDIPUS:
And I'm at the edge of hearing horrors, yes, but I must hear!

SHEPHERD:
All right! His son, they said it was—his son!
But the one inside, your wife,
she'd tell it best.

OEDIPUS:
My wife—
she gave it to you?   1290

SHEPHERD:
Yes, yes, my king.

OEDIPUS:
Why, what for?

SHEPHERD:
To kill it.

OEDIPUS:
Her own child,
how could she?   1295

SHEPHERD:
She was afraid—
frightening prophecies.

OEDIPUS:
What?

SHEPHERD:
          They said—
he'd kill his parents.

OEDIPUS:
But you gave him to this old man—why?   1300

SHEPHERD:
I pitied the little baby, master,
hoped he'd take him off to his own country,
far away, but he saved him for this, this fate.
If you are the man he says you are, believe me,
you were born for pain.   1305

OEDIPUS:
                    O god—
all come true, all burst to light!
O light—now let me look my last on you!
I stand revealed at last—
cursed in my birth, cursed in marriage,
cursed in the lives I cut down with these hands!   1310

> *Rushing through the doors with a
> great cry. The Corinthian
> MESSENGER, the SHEPHERD and
> attendants exit slowly to the side.*

CHORUS:
O the generations of men
the dying generations—adding the total
of all your lives I find they come to nothing . . .
        does there exist, is there a man on earth
who seizes more joy than just a dream, a vision?   1315
And the vision no sooner dawns than dies
blazing into oblivion.

You are my great example, you, your life
your destiny, Oedipus, man of misery—
I count no man blest.

                You outranged all men!   1320
     Bending your bow to the breaking-point
you captured priceless glory, O dear god,
and the Sphinx came crashing down,
            the virgin, claws hooked
like a bird of omen singing, shrieking death—   1325
like a fortress reared in the face of death
you rose and saved our land.

From that day on we called you king
we crowned you with honors, Oedipus, towering over all—
mighty king of the seven gates of Thebes.   1330

But now to hear your story—is there a man more agonized?
More wed to pain and frenzy? Not a man on earth,
the joy of your life ground down to nothing
O Oedipus, name for the ages—
  one and the same wide harbor served you 1335
                son and father both
son and father came to rest in the same bridal chamber.
How, how could the furrows your father plowed
bear you, your agony, harrowing on
in silence O so long?

                But now for all your power 1340
Time, all-seeing Time has dragged you to the light,
judged your marriage monstrous from the start—
the son and the father tangling, both one—
O child of Laius, would to god
  I'd never seen you, never never! 1345
    Now I weep like a man who wails the dead
and the dirge comes pouring forth with all my heart!
I tell you the truth, you gave me life
my breath leapt up in you
and now you bring down night upon my eyes. 1350

Enter a MESSENGER *from the palace.*

MESSENGER:
Men of Thebes, always first in honor,
what horrors you will hear, what you will see,
what a heavy weight of sorrow you will shoulder . . .
if you are true to your birth, if you still have
some feeling for the royal house of Thebes.   1355
I tell you neither the waters of the Danube
nor the Nile can wash this palace clean.
Such things it hides, it soon will bring to light—
terrible things, and none done blindly now,
all done with a will. The pains   1360
we inflict upon ourselves hurt most of all.

LEADER:
God knows we have pains enough already.
What can you add to them?

MESSENGER:
The queen is dead.

LEADER:
                Poor lady—how?

MESSENGER:
By her own hand. But you are spared the worst,
you never had to watch . . . I saw it all,
and with all the memory that's in me
you will learn what that poor woman suffered.

Once she'd broken in through the gates,
dashing past us, frantic, whipped to fury,
ripping her hair out with both hands—
straight to her rooms she rushed, flinging herself
across the bridal-bed, doors slamming behind her—
once inside, she wailed for Laius, dead so long,
remembering how she bore his child long ago,
the life that rose up to destroy him, leaving
its mother to mother living creatures
with the very son she'd borne.
Oh how she wept, mourning the marriage-bed
where she let loose that double brood—monsters—
husband by her husband, children by her child.
                                         And then—
but how she died is more than I can say. Suddenly
Oedipus burst in, screaming, he stunned us so
we couldn't watch her agony to the end,
our eyes were fixed on him. Circling
like a maddened beast, stalking, here, there,
crying out to us—
            Give him a sword! His wife,
no wife, his mother, where can he find the mother earth
that cropped two crops at once, himself and all his children?
He was raging—one of the dark powers pointing the way,
none of us mortals crowding around him, no,
with a great shattering cry—someone, something leading him on—
he hurled at the twin doors and bending the bolts back
out of their sockets, crashed through the chamber.

And there we saw the woman hanging by the neck,   1395
cradled high in a woven noose, spinning,
swinging back and forth. And when he saw her,
giving a low, wrenching sob that broke our hearts,
slipping the halter from her throat, he eased her down,
in a slow embrace he laid her down, poor thing . . .   1400
then, what came next, what horror we beheld!

He rips off her brooches, the long gold pins
holding her robes—and lifting them high,
looking straight up into the points,
he digs them down the sockets of his eyes, crying, "You,   1405
you'll see no more the pain I suffered, all the pain I caused!
Too long you looked on the ones you never should have seen,
blind to the ones you longed to see, to know! Blind
from this hour on! Blind in the darkness—blind!"
His voice like a dirge, rising, over and over   1410
raising the pins, raking them down his eyes.
And at each stroke blood spurts from the roots,
splashing his beard, a swirl of it, nerves and clots—
black hail of blood pulsing, gushing down.

These are the griefs that burst upon them both,   1415
coupling man and woman. The joy they had so lately,
the fortune of their old ancestral house
was deep joy indeed. Now, in this one day,
wailing, madness and doom, death, disgrace,
all the griefs in the world that you can name,   1420
all are theirs forever.

LEADER:
                    Oh poor man, the misery—
has he any rest from pain now?

                         A voice within, in torment.

MESSENGER:
                         He's shouting,
"Loose the bolts, someone, show me to all of Thebes!
My father's murderer, my mother's—"
No, I can't repeat it, it's unholy.   1425
Now he'll tear himself from his native earth,
not linger, curse the house with his own curse.
But he needs strength, and a guide to lead him on.
This is sickness more than he can bear.
                    The palace doors open.
                    Look,
he'll show you himself. The great doors are opening—   1430
you are about to see a sight, a horror
even his mortal enemy would pity.

                         Enter OEDIPUS, *blinded, led by a*
                         boy. He stands at the palace steps, as
                         if surveying his people once again.

CHORUS:
                            O the terror—
    the suffering, for all the world to see,
    the worst terror that ever met my eyes.
    What madness swept over you? What god,   1435
    what dark power leapt beyond all bounds,
    beyond belief, to crush your wretched life?—
    godforsaken, cursed by the gods!
    I pity you but I can't bear to look.
    I've much to ask, so much to learn,   1440
    so much fascinates my eyes,
    but you . . . I shudder at the sight.

OEDIPUS:
                            Oh, Ohh—
    the agony! I am agony—
    where am I going? where on earth?
        where does all this agony hurl me?   1445
    where's my voice?—
        winging, swept away on a dark tide—
    My destiny, my dark power, what a leap you made!

CHORUS:
To the depths of terror, too dark to hear, to see.

OEDIPUS:
>   Dark, horror of darkness   1450
> *my* darkness, drowning, swirling around me
> crashing wave on wave—unspeakable, irresistible
>   headwind, fatal harbor! Oh again,
> the misery, all at once, over and over
>   the stabbing daggers, stab of memory   1455
> raking me insane.

CHORUS:
>   No wonder you suffer
> twice over, the pain of your wounds,
> the lasting grief of pain.

OEDIPUS:
>   Dear friend, still here?
> Standing by me, still with a care for me,
>   the blind man? Such compassion,   1460
>   loyal to the last. Oh it's you,
>   I know you're here, dark as it is
>   I'd know you anywhere, your voice—
> it's yours, clearly yours.

CHORUS:
>   Dreadful, what you've done . . .
> how could you bear it, gouging out your eyes?   1465
> What superhuman power drove you on?

OEDIPUS:
    Apollo, friends, Apollo—
he ordained my agonies—these, my pains on pains!
    But the hand that struck my eyes was mine,
    mine alone—no one else—
            I did it all myself!
    What good were eyes to me?
    Nothing I could see could bring me joy.

CHORUS:
No, no, exactly as you say.

OEDIPUS:
                What can I ever see?
    What love, what call of the heart
can touch my ears with joy? Nothing, friends.
    Take me away, far, far from Thebes,
    quickly, cast me away, my friends—
this great murderous ruin, this man cursed to heaven,
    the man the deathless gods hate most of all!

CHORUS:
Pitiful, you suffer so, you understand so much . . .
I wish you had never known.

OEDIPUS:
                    Die, die—
whoever he was that day in the wilds
who cut my ankles free of the ruthless pins,
    he pulled me clear of death, he saved my life   *1485*
    for this, this kindness—
                    Curse him, kill him!
If I'd died then, I'd never have dragged myself,
my loved ones through such hell.

CHORUS:
Oh if only . . . would to god.

OEDIPUS:
                        I'd never have come to this,
    my father's murderer—never been branded
    mother's husband, all men see me now! Now,
    loathed by the gods, son of the mother I defiled
    coupling in my father's bed, spawning lives in the loins
that spawned my wretched life. What grief can crown this grief?
        It's mine alone, my destiny—I am Oedipus!

CHORUS:
How can I say you've chosen for the best?
Better to die than be alive and blind.

OEDIPUS:
What I did was best—don't lecture me,
no more advice. I, with *my* eyes,
how could I look my father in the eyes
when I go down to death? Or mother, so abused . . .
I have done such things to the two of them,
crimes too huge for hanging.
                                Worse yet,
the sight of my children, born as they were born,
how could I long to look into their eyes?
No, not with these eyes of mine, never.
Not this city either, her high towers,
the sacred glittering images of her gods—
I am misery! I, her best son, reared
as no other son of Thebes was ever reared,
I've stripped myself, I gave the command myself.
All men must cast away the great blasphemer,
the curse now brought to light by the gods,
the son of Laius—I, my father's son!

Now I've exposed my guilt, horrendous guilt,
could I train a level glance on you, my countrymen?
Impossible! No, if I could just block off my ears,
the springs of hearing, I would stop at nothing—
I'd wall up my loathsome body like a prison,
blind to the sound of life, not just the sight.
Oblivion—what a blessing . . .
for the mind to dwell a world away from pain.

O Cithaeron, why did you give me shelter?
Why didn't you take me, crush my life out on the spot?
I'd never have revealed my birth to all mankind.

O Polybus, Corinth, the old house of my fathers,
so I believed—what a handsome prince you raised—
under the skin, what sickness to the core.
Look at me! Born of outrage, outrage to the core.

O triple roads—it all comes back, the secret,
dark ravine, and the oaks closing in
where the three roads join . . .
You drank my father's blood, my own blood
spilled by my own hands—you still remember me? 1535
What things you saw me do? Then I came here
and did them all once more!

                       Marriages! O marriage,
you gave me birth, and once you brought me into the world
you brought my sperm rising back, springing to light
fathers, brothers, sons—one murderous breed— 1540
brides, wives, mothers. The blackest things
a man can do, I have done them all!

                       No more—
it's wrong to name what's wrong to do. Quickly,
for the love of god, hide me somewhere,
kill me, hurl me into the sea 1545
where you can never look on me again.

                    Beckoning to the CHORUS *as they*
                  shrink away.

                       Closer,
it's all right. Touch the man of grief.
Do. Don't be afraid. My troubles are mine
and I am the only man alive who can sustain them.

                  Enter CREON *from the palace,*
                  attended by palace guards.

LEADER:
Put your requests to Creon. Here he is, 1550
just when we need him. He'll have a plan, he'll act.
Now that he's the sole defense of the country
in your place.

OEDIPUS:
            Oh no, what can I say to him?
How can I ever hope to win his trust?
I wronged him so, just now, in every way. 1555
You must see that—I was so wrong, so wrong.

CREON:
I haven't come to mock you, Oedipus,
or to criticize your former failings.
                              Turning to the guards.
                     You there,
have you lost all respect for human feelings?
At least revere the Sun, the holy fire   1560
that keeps us all alive. Never expose a thing
of guilt and holy dread so great it appalls
the earth, the rain from heaven, the light of day!
Get him into the halls—quickly as you can.
Piety demands no less. Kindred alone   1565
should see a kinsman's shame. This is obscene.

OEDIPUS:
Please, in god's name . . . you wipe my fears away,
coming so generously to me, the worst of men.
Do one thing more, for your sake, not mine.

CREON:
What do you want? Why so insistent?   1570

OEDIPUS:
Drive me out of the land at once, far from sight,
where I can never hear a human voice.

CREON:
I'd have done that already, I promise you.
First I wanted the god to clarify my duties.

OEDIPUS:
The god? His command was clear, every word: 1575
death for the father-killer, the curse—
he said destroy me!

CREON:
So he did. Still, in such a crisis
it's better to ask precisely what to do.

OEDIPUS:
So miserable—
you would consult the god about a man like me? 1580

CREON:
By all means. And this time, I assume,
even you will obey the god's decrees.

OEDIPUS:
I will,
I will. And you, I command you—I beg you . . .
the woman inside, bury her as you see fit.
It's the only decent thing, 1585
to give your own the last rites. As for me,
never condemn the city of my fathers
to house my body, not while I'm alive, no,
let me live on the mountains, on Cithaeron,
my favorite haunt, I have made it famous. 1590
Mother and father marked out that rock
to be my everlasting tomb—buried alive.
Let me die there, where they tried to kill me.

Oh but this I know: no sickness can destroy me,
nothing can. I would never have been saved 1595
from death—I have been saved
for something great and terrible, something strange.
Well let my destiny come and take me on its way!

About my children, Creon, the boys at least,
don't burden yourself. They're men,
wherever they go, they'll find the means to live.
But my two daughters, my poor helpless girls,
clustering at our table, never without me
hovering near them . . . whatever I touched,
they always had their share. Take care of them,
I beg you. Wait, better—permit me, would you?
Just to touch them with my hands and take
our fill of tears. Please . . . my king.
Grant it, with all your noble heart.
If I could hold them, just once, I'd think
I had them with me, like the early days
when I could see their eyes.

> ANTIGONE *and* ISMENE, *two small children, are led in from the palace by a nurse.*

What's that?
O god! Do I really hear you sobbing?—
my two children. Creon, you've pitied me?
Sent me my darling girls, my own flesh and blood!
Am I right?

CREON:
Yes, it's my doing.
I know the joy they gave you all these years,
the joy you must feel now.

OEDIPUS:
Bless you, Creon!
May god watch over you for this kindness,
better than he ever guarded me.
Children, where are you?
Here, come quickly—

Groping for ANTIGONE *and* ISMENE,
*who approach their father cautiously,
then embrace him.*

Come to these hands of mine,
your brother's hands, your own father's hands
that served his once bright eyes so well—
that made them blind. Seeing nothing, children,
knowing nothing, I became your father, 1625
I fathered you in the soil that gave me life.

How I weep for you—I cannot see you now . . .
just thinking of all your days to come, the bitterness,
the life that rough mankind will thrust upon you.
Where are the public gatherings you can join, 1630
the banquets of the clans? Home you'll come,
in tears, cut off from the sight of it all,
the brilliant rites unfinished.
And when you reach perfection, ripe for marriage,
who will he be, my dear ones? Risking all 1635
to shoulder the curse that weighs down my parents,
yes and you too—that wounds us all together.
What more misery could you want?
Your father killed his father, sowed his mother,
one, one and the selfsame womb sprang you— 1640
he cropped the very roots of his existence.

Such disgrace, and you must bear it all!
Who will marry you then? Not a man on earth.
Your doom is clear: you'll wither away to nothing,
single, without a child.

Turning to CREON.

                    Oh Creon,   1645
you are the only father they have now . . .
we who brought them into the world
are gone, both gone at a stroke—
Don't let them go begging, abandoned,
women without men. Your own flesh and blood!   1650
Never bring them down to the level of my pains.
Pity them. Look at them, so young, so vulnerable,
shorn of everything—you're their only hope.
Promise me, noble Creon, touch my hand!

> *Reaching toward* CREON, *who draws back.*

You, little ones, if you were old enough   1655
to understand, there is much I'd tell you.
Now, as it is, I'd have you say a prayer.
Pray for life, my children,
live where you are free to grow and season.
Pray god you find a better life than mine,   1660
the father who begot you.

CREON:
                    Enough.
You've wept enough. Into the palace now.

OEDIPUS:
I must, but I find it very hard.

CREON:
Time is the great healer, you will see.

OEDIPUS:
I am going—you know on what condition?   1665

CREON:
Tell me. I'm listening.

OEDIPUS:
Drive me out of Thebes, in exile.

CREON:
Not I. Only the gods can give you that.

OEDIPUS:
Surely the gods hate me so much—

CREON:
You'll get your wish at once.

OEDIPUS:
                        You consent?   1670

CREON:
I try to say what I mean; it's my habit.

OEDIPUS:
Then take me away. It's time.

CREON:
Come along, let go of the children.

OEDIPUS:
                No—
don't take them away from me, not now! No no no!

Clutching his daughters as the guards wrench them loose and take them through the palace doors.

CREON:
Still the king, the master of all things?   1675
No more: here your power ends.
None of your power follows you through life.

Exit OEDIPUS *and* CREON *to the palace. The* CHORUS *comes forward to address the audience directly.*

CHORUS:
People of Thebes, my countrymen, look on Oedipus.
He solved the famous riddle with his brilliance,
he rose to power, a man beyond all power.
Who could behold his greatness without envy?
Now what a black sea of terror has overwhelmed him.
Now as we keep our watch and wait the final day,
count no man happy till he dies, free of pain at last.

Exit in procession.

OEDIPUS AT COLONUS

INTRODUCTION

SOPHOCLES died some time in the year 406–5 B.C., but the Athenians did not see this last play performed until the festival of Dionysus in the spring of 401 B.C. In the intervening five years they had tasted the bitterness of total defeat and unconditional surrender. The peace terms of 404 were harsh: the Athenians were reduced to military impotence by the surrender of their few remaining ships and the destruction of their fortifications; the democratic institutions under which they had lived for almost exactly a century were replaced by a Spartan-backed reactionary dictatorship—the Thirty Tyrants, who ruled by terror. It could, however, have been worse; the Thebans and Corinthians argued for the annihilation of Athens—enslavement of the population, destruction of the city—but the Spartans were unwilling to go so far. And when their puppet regime provoked an uprising by its excesses they did not intervene vigorously enough to save it; by 401 Athens was once again a democracy, and the worst effects of the years of civil war were mitigated by an enlightened act of amnesty. But it was not the same Athens; gone forever were the confidence and daring, the sense of unlimited horizons characteristic of the Periclean city.

The audience that saw Sophocles' *Oedipus at Colonus* in 401 B.C. must have been profoundly moved, for it is, among other things, a valedictory celebration of Athens as it was in its time of greatness. Sophocles must have known when he wrote it that the city was headed for defeat, perhaps destruction; in this play he brings Oedipus to Athens, or rather to the nearby village of Colonus, his own birthplace, where the blind exile from Thebes is to receive Athenian protection and, in return, guarantee victory for Athens over Thebes in some future war. This victory will be won on the site of his grave; but, for that to happen, its location must remain a secret, known only to the rulers of his adopted city.

How much of this strange story is Sophoclean invention we do not know, but it seems likely that there was at least a local tradition that linked the death of Oedipus with Colonus. Sophocles may be glancing at the obscurity of such local lore when he has the citizen speak to Oedipus of

> the spirit of the place . . .
> not much honored in legends, more in the hearts
> of us who live here, love it well. (74–76)

In any case, though Oedipus speaks of going to Colonus to die in Euripides' *Phoenician Women* (produced long before our play), the motif of the secret grave at Colonus and its power over the future meets us nowhere else in the Oedipus legends. Such a protective grave however is not an unknown phenomenon in Greek tragedy. Eurystheus, in Euripides' *Sons of Heracles*, promises the Athenians that if they will bury him in front of Athena's temple he will be "a resident alien, conferring favor and safety on the city" and "a bitter enemy" to the Peloponnesians "when they come here in force." And Orestes, in the final play of the *Oresteia*, makes a similar promise to the Athenians as he thanks them for the verdict of their court which frees him from the Furies: if his descendants ever make war on Athens, he says,

> We ourselves, even if we must rise up from the grave,
> will deal with those who break the oath I take—
> baffle them with disasters, curse their marches . . .
> (*The Eumenides*, 781–83, trans. Robert Fagles)

These passages are not mere tragic convention; they reflect deep-seated popular belief. Typical is the story Herodotus tells about the Spartan search for the bones of Orestes. They had been told by the oracle at Delphi that they would never defeat their hostile neighbors, the Tegeans, until they removed the bones of Orestes to Sparta. After a long search they found them, on Tegean soil; once they succeeded in removing them, without the Tegeans realizing what had happened, they were steadily victorious over their enemy. And in the early days of the naval offensive against Persia, so Plutarch tells us, the Athenians, after wiping out the pirates based on the rocky island of Scyros, discovered the bones of their own hero Theseus, who had died there, and brought them back reverently to Athens for burial in Attic earth. "This is not our doing," said Themistocles in Herodotus, after the Persian defeat at Salamis, "it is the work of gods and heroes . . ." By "heroes" he does not mean the men who fought the battle but the dead heroes, protectors of Greek earth, worshiped and placated by sacrifice on their graves. When this cult of heroes began we do not know—there is no trace of it in Homer, where the word *hêrôs* seems to mean no more than "nobleman"—but by the fifth century it was a widespread religious phenomenon.

These sacrificial ceremonies took place at the grave (real or supposed) of the hero; usually he was one of the great figures of Homeric saga—Achilles, Ajax, Hector all had their places, some of them more than one—and sometimes he was believed to possess healing or prophetic powers, like Asclepius, or to send prophetic dreams, like Amphiaraus. More often he was thought of simply as an angry spirit whose wrath had to be appeased by sacrifice. The heroes followed in death the fierce code they had lived by: to help their friends and harm their enemies.

But heroic cult was not exclusively reserved for ancestral figures of the remote past; we know of at least two fifth-century men who were paid such honors after their death. One was Brasidas, the Spartan general, who, in a campaign like that waged by Lawrence of Arabia, liberated the cities of the North Aegean from Athenian domination in the early years of the Peloponnesian War. After his death in a battle that saved the principal city of Amphipolis from an Athenian counterattack in 422 B.C., he was buried inside the city walls and given heroic sacrifice. The other, strangely enough, was Sophocles himself. This extraordinary honor was paid him not because of his eminence as a dramatist or his services to the city but because he had been the official host of the healing hero Asclepius when his cult was introduced into Athens. Sophocles was accorded heroic worship under the name *Dexion*—The Receiver. We know from an inscription found on the west slope of the Acropolis that the cult of *Dexion* was still active in the second half of the fourth century.

Though his grave will not be the scene of sacrifice (for its location is to be kept secret from all except Theseus and his descendants) Oedipus is to become such a figure: his grave will be the site of a battle in which an invading army will be defeated. This is the destiny Oedipus dimly foresaw at the end of the earlier play. In its final scene, the blind outcast begs Creon to expel him from Thebes, to let him die on the barren mountains. But then he corrects himself; somehow he knows that this will not be the manner of his death. "I have been saved / for something great and terrible, something strange" (1596–97). The last play shows us the fulfillment of that prophetic insight.

The setting of the play distinguishes it sharply from its predecessors; the stage door is not the entrance to the palace of a ruler, Creon or Oedipus, but the shadowed edge of a thick wood. Such places filled the Greeks with awe and not a little fear. Yeats understood this, as he did so much about the Greeks: "When Oedipus at Colonus went into the Wood of the Furies," he wrote, "he felt the same creeping in his flesh that an Irish countryman feels in certain haunted woods in Galway and in Sligo." The wood is indeed sacred to the Furies, those grim goddesses whose special province is the punishment of wrongdoers, especially those who wrong their parents. In Aeschylus' *Oresteia* they pursued the matricide Orestes, only to lose their prey when an Athenian court acquitted him; they then turned their wrath against Athens, but the goddess Athena offered them honors and a home in her city, and they became protecting deities of the Athenian land. So they are not only "The Terrible Goddesses . . . / Daughters of Earth, Daughters of the Darkness" but also "the Kindly Ones, / the Eumenides" (46–50).

Toward their sacred grove come two actors to open the play. Their entrance is a long-drawn-out movement through the *parodos*—the passage between the end of the spectators' benches and the stage building—to center stage. One of them represents a young girl; the other, a blind man feeling his way with a stick and leaning on his daughter's arm, is a pitiful sight, as we know from the reaction of his son Polynices later in the play:

> wrapped in such rags—appalling—
> the filth of years clings to his old withered body,
> wasting away the skin, the flesh on his ribs . . .
> and his face, the blind sockets of his eyes,
> and the white hair wild, flying in the wind!
> And all of a piece with this, I'm afraid, the scraps
> he packs to fill his shriveled belly. (1421–27)

We learn, from his very first words, that this wreck of a human being is Oedipus, once King of Thebes. For him the place he has come to is just one more way station in his vagrant life as a beggar. "Where are we now? What land, what city of men? / Who will receive the wandering Oedipus today?" (2–3). But when he hears, from the local citizen who orders him to move away from the sacred grove, the name of the Kindly Ones, he is a changed man. He had been all compliance, as befits a beggar—

> We have come
> to learn from the citizens . . .
> and carry out their wishes to the end. (12–14)

But now he is defiant; he will not leave. "I shall never leave my place in this new land, / this is my refuge!" (53–54).

This peremptory refusal to move is followed by something even more unexpected: Oedipus gives the citizen a message for Theseus, King of Athens, and the message is as incomprehensible as the beggar's change of attitude. "Simply tell him this: / with a small service he may gain a great deal" (86–87). The citizen goes off, not to Theseus, but to consult the inhabitants of the nearby village of Colonus; they will soon, in the persons of the chorus, come to see for themselves. Meanwhile Oedipus, assured by Antigone that they are alone, addresses the goddesses of the grove. We learn now the reason for his sudden assumption of authority, the explanation of his enigmatic phrase: "this is the sign, the pact that seals my fate" (55). At Delphi, when as a young man he was given the terrible prophecies that came eventually to fulfillment, he was also promised an end to his sufferings: "my promised rest / after hard years weathered" (107-8). And the place of his rest was to be "the grounds of the Awesome Goddesses" (110). This prophecy also explains his message to Theseus: he was to be "a blessing to the hosts I live among" (113). From this place he now intends never to move, and though he makes some concessions in the next scene, leaving the actual precinct of the Eumenides for profane ground, he will not go offstage from this moment until he leaves the earth forever. The play's movement will be that of the other characters, friendly or hostile, around this fixed center. He will not be induced to move by force, threats or persuasion; he will leave only when the lightning and thunder summon him to "some great consummation at the end" (126).

In spite of the self-imposed immobility of the protagonist the play is not static; in fact it is, by the standards of Greek tragedy, remarkable for the variety and intensity of its stage action. The impressive entrance of Oedipus and Antigone is the first in a series of highly dramatic appearances: the citizen with his terrified, peremptory order to move off; the chorus hunting the sacrilegious trespasser; Ismene in a broad traveling hat, riding a colt and bringing surprising news; Theseus with his warm welcome for the blind outcast; Creon with his soldiers, his lying speech and his violent hands laid on the old man; Theseus' sudden entry in the nick of time; the triumphant return of Antigone and Ismene, rescued by Theseus; and the final surprise, the arrival of Polynices. The exits are no less effective: Ismene goes to perform the purificatory rites for the Furies and, as we learn later, is seized by Creon and his armed men; Antigone is dragged off by Creon's soldiers as Oedipus gropes in the dark to help her; Creon leaves, under arrest, to go with Theseus to the rescue of the two girls; Polynices, in spite of the pleas of Antigone, departs for Thebes to fulfill the curse of his father—to kill and be killed by his own brother—and, in what is perhaps the most spectacular exit in all Greek tragedy, the blind man walks with sure swift steps as he leads Theseus and the daughters toward the place where his mortal existence will end. But quite apart from all the vigorous stage action created by the basic plot—the succession of assaults on Oedipus' resolve to confer on Athens the gift within his power—the play also generates dramatic excitement through its exploration of a unique theme: the transformation of Oedipus the mortal man into the *hêrôs* he is to be in his grave. In the last hours of his life on the earth, he begins to exercise the powers of the daemonic figure he is destined to become.

When Oedipus first appears, he is the visible fulfillment of the prophecy Tiresias made in the earlier play:

> Blind who now has eyes, beggar who now is rich,
> he will grope his way toward a foreign soil,
> a stick tapping before him step by step. (517–19)

And his mood now corresponds to his condition:

> it's little I ask
> and get still less, but quite enough for me.
> Acceptance—that is the great lesson suffering teaches,
> suffering and the long years . . . (4–7)

It is hard to recognize in this broken man the vigorous, confident figure of the earlier play, the man who answered the riddle of the Sphinx, who was "crowned . . . with honors . . . towering over all— / mighty king of the seven gates of Thebes" (1329–30). But the news that he is in the grove of the Eumenides brings the old Oedipus to life in this tired old man: the same confident assertiveness—"I shall never leave my place in this new land" (53)—the same sense of his own worth—"whatever I say, there will be great vision / in every word I say" (89–90). And from this point he never retreats; his sense of mission and power, far from faltering as he stands helpless before the assaults of his enemies, fills him with sure prophetic insight and daemonic rage. His last earthly action before he goes to the mysterious grave to which the gods summon him is the tremendous curse he pronounces on his ingrate son.

The play has often been compared to Shakespeare's *King Lear*, and indeed there are many parallels in action, theme and character. But in its movement the ancient play is the reverse of the modern. Lear's rage comes early on, as he first feels the sting of the "serpent's tooth" and curses his daughters. He curses Goneril first, in specific and terrifying terms.

> Hear, Nature, hear! . . .
> Suspend thy purpose if thou didst intend
> To make this creature fruitful!
> Into her womb convey sterility!
> Dry up in her the organs of increase . . . (1.4.284–88)

Spurned by Regan in turn, he threatens both of them, but in sputtering incoherence which foreshadows the madness that will descend on him in the storm on the heath.

> No, you unnatural hags!
> I will have such revenges on you both
> That all the world shall—I will do such things—
> What they are, yet I know not; but they shall be
> The terrors of the earth. (2.4.280–84)

But much later when, defeated and captured together with Cordelia, he is sent off to prison, it is the old man who comforts the young woman with counsel of acceptance:

> Come, let's away to prison;
> We two alone will sing like birds i' th' cage:
> When thou dost ask me blessing, I'll kneel down,
> And ask of thee forgiveness: so we'll live,
> And pray, and sing, and tell old tales, and laugh
> At gilded butterflies, and hear poor rogues
> Talk of court news . . . (5.3.8–14)

This is the mood in which Oedipus begins: "Acceptance . . . the great lesson suffering teaches . . ." (6–7). He ends in the inhuman fury of his repudiation of his son and the unearthly sureness with which, still blind, he leads Theseus and his daughters toward the secret place where his buried corpse will give protection to Athens and bring destruction on his enemies.

The stages of this transformation, from abject beggar to daemonic power, are defined for us in familiar terms: Oedipus' relation to and comprehension of the Apolline prophecies which, in this play as in the other, hedge his destiny. It is the memory of the old prophecy—that he would find rest in the grove of the Eumenides—that spurs the first expression of his new-found assurance. But Apollo promised more than rest. Oedipus was to be, in death, a dispenser of good and evil—"a blessing to the hosts I live among, / disaster to those who sent me, drove me out!" (113-14). Not until his other daughter, Ismene, comes to bring him news from Thebes will he begin to understand the full meaning of this prophecy. At the moment he is no power in the land but a "harried ghost of a man . . . no more / the flesh and blood of old" (133-35) and must hide in the sacred grove from the chorus, which now comes on stage to question the trespasser. He agrees to leave the forbidden ground in exchange for a promise of protection, but the promise is broken when the chorus learns his identity. He has to plead with them for refuge and later answer their prurient questions about his past. But as he defends that past and states his essential innocence, the confident mood returns, and he tells them in authoritative tones that he comes

>   as someone sacred, someone filled
> with piety and power, bearing a great gift
> for all your people. (312-14)

The chorus will wait for Theseus, their king, to decide. But before he arrives, Oedipus learns from Ismene that his sons, Eteocles in command of Thebes and Polynices backed by a foreign army from Argos, are at war.

For these sons Oedipus has nothing but angry feelings, as we learn from his bitter outburst that points the contrast between their indifference to his suffering and the devoted service of the two girls. But there is more than this behind his anger. As we learn later, he had cursed them for their ingratitude even before he was expelled from Thebes. In the old epic poem that dealt with these events the curse was provoked by actions on the part of the sons which seem trivial by comparison with their terrible consequences—they gave him the haunch of the roast instead of the choice cut from the shoulder, for example. But Sophocles makes no reference to these traditional details: he leaves us to attribute Oedipus' fatal curse to his anger at the sons' indifference to his fate; later, face-to-face with Polynices, he will even charge him with responsibility for his father's lamentable condition. What he now learns from Ismene is what the outcome of the war between the sons may depend on, and once again prophecies are involved. The Thebans have been told by Apollo that victory over Argos depends on Oedipus: "They are in your hands, the oracle says, / their power rests in you" (429-30). Now he learns, as we do, the nature of the gift he can make to Athens: his grave, if it is on foreign soil, will be the site of a Theban defeat. Creon, acting for Eteocles, will come to try to lure him back to Thebes, but, Ismene warns him, they will not bury him in Theban soil, not with his father's blood on his hands. They will bury him just at the frontier, where he can be of no use to any other city. On these terms Oedipus will never go: "they will never get me in their clutches—never!" (453). And when he hears that both his sons knew of the prophecy but made no move to bring him home, his anger blazes out and he renews the terms of the curse he had pronounced on them:

> may the great gods
> never quench their blazing, fated strife!
> May it rest in my hands alone—
> now their spears are lifting tip to tip—
> to bring their fighting to its bitter end.
> I'd see that the one who holds the scepter now
> would not last long, nor would the exile ever
> return again! (469-76)

This is the same curse he had pronounced on them at the time when, as he says, Thebes expelled him and "my own sons who could have swept to the rescue, / . . . they did nothing, they refused!" (493-94). The Greek word for curse, *ara*, is also the word for "prayer"; a curse is just a prayer for someone to come to harm. And so Oedipus expresses his will here, as a wish, a prayer, something not in his power but a gift of the gods. Yet he has some inner sense that his wish will be granted:

> precious little good will ever come to them
> from lording over Thebes. That much I know,
> now that I hear the oracles my dear one brings
> and brood on the old prophecies, stored
> in the depths of all my being,
> that Apollo has fulfilled for me at last. (506–11)

Now his mind is fully made up. The dream that he might be welcomed back to Thebes has gone forever; Athens is to be his eternal home; to Athens will go the victory his grave confers. Oedipus the blind outcast found it hard to believe Ismene's news that his decrepit body was an object to be sought after—"What good could anyone get from the like of me?" (428). Now he understands fully the prophecy given to him so long ago. "The gods are about to raise you to your feet—" Ismene told him (432); by his choice of a place to die he can make history, become a presence in the soil feared by some and thanked by others.

Even the frightened and suspicious chorus is impressed. They now accept the stranger but warn him he must make a ritual appeasement of the spirits on whose forbidden ground he has trespassed. The careful instructions for carrying out the ritual reinforce the religious solemnity that surrounds the action of this mystery play from start to finish. Ismene goes to perform the rites and (as we learn later) to be captured by Creon; the chorus now has their chance to probe fully into the horrors of Oedipus' past. They do not spare his feelings. In spite of his appeals, they demand, as a return for their concession, answers to their questions, confirmation of all the rumors they have heard. Oedipus is forced to rehearse it all, to the shocked outcries of the old men: the marriage with his mother, the daughters who are actually his sisters, the blood of his father on his hands. But he ends this recital of horrors with a claim that he is not a guilty man. As before (284–95) he pleads both self-defense and ignorance of identity in the matter of Laius' death, but this time the plea of ignorance is more explicit, and the affirmation of innocence in the eyes of the law is more emphatic:

the man I murdered—he'd have murdered me!
I am innocent! Pure in the eyes of the law,
blind, unknowing, I, I came to this! (614–16)

The arrival of Theseus puts a stop to the importunate probing of the chorus; his treatment of Oedipus is a stunning contrast. No personal questions: "I know all about you, son of Laius" (621). He asks only what the suppliant desires, and promises, as one who has known exile himself, to do all he can to help. He does not know, as yet, that Oedipus comes bringing a gift. No wonder Oedipus sounds his praises: "so magnanimous, so noble! Your few words / spare me the need to draw things out at length" (642–43).

Theseus is of course the representative Athenian hero, mythic founder of the unity of Attica under the city of Athens, the prototype of Athenian heroic endeavor and civilized living. Sophocles here presents him as a picture of the humane greatness of Athens in its best days, of the compassion that had long since vanished under the harsh pressures of protracted war and revolution. Pericles' ideal Athens of the Funeral Speech is re-created here in all its generosity: "We alone do good to our neighbors," Pericles said, "not upon a calculation of interest, but in the confidence of freedom and in a frank and fearless spirit." This Athens deserves the gift of Oedipus, the future victory over a Thebes that we shall see represented by the violence and lies of Creon, the hypocrisy and fratricidal hate of Polynices. But Theseus still has to learn what advantage will come to Athens because of his generosity, and when he is told what the gift will be, he learns also that it may bring trouble—"My sons will force you to send me back to Thebes" (663). He cannot understand why Oedipus does not want to go home and reproves the old man for his stubborn anger. But Oedipus will accept no rebuke and reproves Theseus in his turn. "Wait till you hear me out, then criticize me—" (667). Told that the grave of Oedipus will be the scene of a Theban defeat on Attic soil, Theseus is incredulous; these cities are at peace. "And how on earth could conflict ever come / between your city and mine?" (684–85). The answer is one of the most famous passages in Sophocles:

> Oh Theseus,
> dear friend, only the gods can never age,
> the gods can never die. All else in the world
> almighty Time obliterates, crushes all
> to nothing. (685–89)

Nothing mortal can resist the changes Time brings: not bodily strength, not friendship between man and man, still less between city and city. No man can be confident of the future; human confidence is based on total ignorance. It is the lesson Oedipus himself learned long ago in Thebes, and he reads it to Theseus now with all the authority of his empty eye sockets and dreadful name.

But he does not abide by the doctrine he preaches; he goes on to prophesy. Athens and Thebes are at peace now, but "a day will come when the treaties of an hour, / the pacts firmed with a handclasp will snap—" (701–2). And as he foresees the day of his vengeance on the Thebans who have wronged him, his words reverberate with an unearthly tone, the daemonic wrath which, in Greek belief, was the characteristic quality of so many of the beings they honored with heroic sacrifice. He looks forward to "some far-off day when my dead body, slumbering, buried / cold in death, will drain their hot blood down" (704–5). Apollo's prophecy had no such detailed vision; this stems from a growth of some new prophetic power in Oedipus himself. But he still claims Apollo as his authority: "if Zeus is still Zeus and Apollo the son of god / speaks clear and true" (706–7). He does not yet prophesy the future on his own authority. That will be the final stage of his transformation.

Theseus is convinced; he accepts the gift Oedipus offers. He promises protection to the old man not just as a suppliant but as a full citizen of Athens, for so he makes him now: "I will settle him / in our land, a fellow-citizen with full rights" (723–24). So Athena, in the Aeschylean trilogy, offered a home and a place in the city's worship to those Eumenides whose grove is the background of this play and who, like Oedipus, brought powers and blessings to the land. Oedipus is no longer a helpless vagrant, a stateless refugee, but a citizen of Athens, and the chorus now sings the praises of that city in a choral hymn that re-creates for us the beauty and glory of Athens as Sophocles knew and loved it in the great days of peace and prosperity. It celebrates the countryside of Attica—the trees, the nightingales, the ivy, narcissus and crocus, the rivers, the olive groves, the horses, the sea. But every detail recalls some aspect of the city that presided over all this fruitful landscape. "The Reveler Dionysus" and the "wine-dark ivy" recall not only the wine of the Attic countryside but the theater, perhaps the supreme glory of the city where it first came to birth. The narcissus, "crown of the Great Goddesses," invokes the memory of Persephone, lured by that flower to her capture by Hades; she and her mother Demeter were worshiped in the famous mysteries at Eleusis in Attica, and it was on Athenian soil that Triptolemos, protégé of the two great goddesses, taught man to cultivate the grain. The olive, gift of Athena to Athens, produced that oil which was exported in decorated vases made of Attic clay to every quarter of the Greek world. The horses, Poseidon's gift to Athens, are still to be seen on the remains of the great frieze which ran round the inside of the Parthenon portico; they are the spirited mounts of those Athenian aristocratic youngsters who, in the play, will soon ride to rescue Oedipus' daughters from Creon and his men. And the ship, Poseidon's other gift, was the instrument of Athenian empire; for most of Sophocles' long life span, no ship had sailed the Aegean Sea against Athens' will.

Yet in this lyrical praise of Attic landscape and Athenian greatness there sounds a note of sadness; the hymn of praise is also a requiem. The nightingale, mourning for her butchered son Itys, is a bird of lamentation; the narcissus and the crocus, both associated with the mysteries of Eleusis and the life beyond death, were planted on graves. As Sophocles wrote these marvelous lines the power of Athens was at its lowest ebb; defeat stared her in the face; invading armies had wrecked the fertility and shattered the peace of the Attic countryside. A Theban cavalry raid, just a few years before the production of the play, had been routed close to Athens, perhaps at Colonus; it is certain that the annual procession along the sacred way from Athens to

Eleusis had been prevented for some years past by the Spartan force, which held a permanent strongpoint in Attica at Decelea. The olive trees of the farms had long since been chopped down and burned by the invaders; the young horsemen of the frieze were long since dead, fallen in the inconclusive land battles of the middle years of the war or worked to death as prisoners in the quarries at Syracuse; and Athenian sea power was outfought and soon to be annihilated by a Spartan fleet financed by Persian subsidies.

Yet the sadness in these lines is not that of despair. For the same details that hint at death speak also of immortality. The mysteries of the Great Goddesses promised the initiates a blessed existence in a future life, and the olive is "a creation self-creating, never conquered" (794); Herodotus tells the story of the sacred olive tree on the Acropolis which, burned by the Persians, grew fresh shoots the very next day. The Athens Sophocles knew in his youth and manhood is to die, but become immortal; he sings of his city in the last grim days of the war as he remembered it in the time of greatness and glory and, partly thanks to him, this is how we remember it still. At Colonus now there is a bus garage surrounded by an industrial slum. But to those whose ears have been charmed by Sophocles' siren song the name will always suggest horses, the nightingale, the laurel and the olive, and, though the words in their context refer to Colonus, Athens itself, "the noblest home on earth / . . . glistening, brilliant in the sun" (763–64).

Oedipus had warned Theseus (745–48) of trouble to come, and the great ode in praise of Athens is hardly finished when it appears—in the person of Creon, accompanied by an armed bodyguard. His reassuring speech to the chorus—"I haven't come here with any thought of force" (830)—is as big a lie as his offer to Oedipus—"return to Thebes, the house of your fathers!" (861). Ismene has already told her father what the Thebans really intend, and Oedipus rejects his invitation with anger and contempt. The fierce accusation that follows reminds us of his equally fierce attack on Creon in the earlier play. Their final interview is like their first. In both Creon is condemned out of hand, with the same vindictive wrath, but this time the sentence is just. In Oedipus' scornful rejection of Creon in this scene we see some of the reasons for his bitterness against Thebes, but his indictment ends with a new manifestation of some more than human strength that is growing in him, a new prophecy, more explicit.

> Well that is not your destiny, no, *this* is—
> my curse, my fury of vengeance
> rooted deep in your soil for all time to come!
> And for my sons, this legacy: a kingdom in my realm,
> room enough to die in—six feet of earth.   (896–900)

The source of this, as of all he knows, is "Apollo and Zeus himself, Apollo's father" (904). This knowledge is imparted, not to the proud, vigorous and successful royal figure of the first play, but to the blind, decrepit old man who cannot even see, much less prevent, the violence offered to himself and his daughters. At the end of the scene Creon has Antigone dragged off to join Ismene, whom he has already seized, and is about to lay hands on Oedipus himself when Theseus comes to the rescue.

His harsh indictment of Creon as a violater of the laws of hospitality is the other side of the generous welcome he extended to Oedipus. The Athenians are mobilized for the pursuit, to recapture the daughters, but Creon is not finished yet. He now tries to drive a wedge between Theseus and Oedipus by dwelling on the polluted nature, the criminal past, of the suppliant Athens has taken in; he supports his glib self-justification—that he never dreamed Athens would protect "a creature so corrupt" (1077)—with a reference to "the Mount of Ares," where mankind's first court of law, the Areopagus, was inaugurated by Athena herself. Oedipus' wounds are not allowed to close; after the recital of his past misfortunes dragged from him by the insistent chorus, he now has to listen while his enemy presents him as an object of loathing and disgust in an attempt to turn his only friend against him.

He reacts with vigor. And his long speech takes up the question that the earlier play had raised implicitly by the background of its action, but did not explicitly discuss: the question of his responsibility for the things he did and which the god predicted. His crimes were committed, he says, against his will. Perhaps the gods were exacting from him punishment for the crimes of his fathers (a familiar doctrine in archaic Greek literature), but he rejects vehemently the idea that there was "something criminal deep inside" him which demanded such punishment (1104). He puts to Creon the question raised by the earlier play:

> tell me: if, by an oracle of the gods,
> some doom were hanging over my father's head
> that he should die at the hands of his own son,
> how, with any justice, could you blame *me*?
> I wasn't born yet . . . (1106-10)

And the actions that were predicted were committed in ignorance; he killed his father "blind to whom I killed" (1115) and married his mother, both of them unwitting—"I knew nothing, she knew nothing" (1123). He places the responsibility squarely on the shoulders of the gods: "And the gods led me on" (1140). This defense is not contested, by Creon or anyone else; Oedipus stands cleared, in his own eyes and those of Athens, of any moral guilt.

He is still, however, a polluted being, stained with his father's blood; and in ancient Greek belief the act of killing, even if no blame could be attached to it, cut a man off from communion with his fellow-men until ritual purification could confer a sort of absolution. But for Oedipus the facts of patricide and incest are beyond purification, and Sophocles emphasizes this with a dramatic scene. When Theseus returns with the daughters and restores them to their father, Oedipus, in an outpouring of gratitude moves, groping in the dark, toward the king to clasp his hand. And then suddenly checks his movement—

> What am I saying?
> You touch me? How could I ask? So wretched,
> a man stained to the core of his existence! (1284-86)

Theseus does not contradict him; he simply ignores the matter. But he does not touch him either; Oedipus is indeed a polluted being and will go to the grave still an untouchable (except for his daughters, who are the fruits of his unholy union).

Yet this condition, almost intolerable for a human being, is not at all inappropriate for the wrathful hero he is to become. Many of the heroes whose tombs were sacred places had been, like Oedipus, men set apart from normal humanity because of the enormity of their violent actions or the strangeness of their end—the great Ajax, for example, who died by his own hand after an unsuccessful attempt to kill the commanders of the Greek host at Troy, or the lesser Ajax, who raped Athena's priestess Cassandra in her temple and was drowned on his way home. And, in Sophocles' own century, Cleomedes of Astypalaea, denied the prize in an athletic contest, went in a mad rage to the school on his native island and, like Samson among the Philistines, brought the roof down on the children, killing them all. He disappeared in the temple of Athena and the Delphic oracle told his bereaved fellow-citizens to pay him heroic honors. Oedipus, too, will disappear, to await the day when the descendants of Creon and his men will take their stand on his secret grave, and their blood will drain down into the earth to satisfy his wrath.

With Theseus' return the action seems complete; it is time for the signs that Oedipus was told to expect—"earthquake, thunder perhaps, or the flashing bolt of Zeus" (116)—his final summons. But there is still one more trial he must face, one more test of his heroic resolution, a second challenge to his choice of Athens as beneficiary of his power over the future. Creon came with deceitful persuasion and resorted to force, but there is a new arrival who is alone, helpless, a suppliant at the nearby altar of Poseidon. Theseus has only to mention the name of Argos and Oedipus knows who it is: Creon came to enlist him on the side of Eteocles, but this is the other brother, Polynices, begging for the gift of victory his father can bestow. Oedipus does not want to hear him; the voice of his son is loathsome to him. He rejects Theseus' urgent pleas on the suppliant's behalf. It is Antigone who wins a hearing for the brother whose body she will one day bury at the cost of her own life. And she pleads with her father for more than a hearing; she is clearly asking for forgiveness, reconciliation.

> Many other men have rebellious children,
> quick tempers too . . . but they listen to reason,
> they relent, the worst rage in their natures
> charmed away by the soothing spells of loved ones.   (1356–59)

These are words that might well soothe the anger of an ordinary father, but Oedipus is now in the last hours of his mortal life, and the attributes of his future state are growing to full maturity, eclipsing his mortal faculties.

But to the chorus Oedipus is still just what he seems to be—a broken blind old man; the first two stanzas of the song with which they close this scene are a melancholy descant on the miseries of extreme old age. "Not to be born is best / when all is reckoned in . . ." (1388–89); this is a familiar Greek saying (it is found in almost this exact form in the sixth-century poet Theognis), but Sophocles adapts it to his dramatic theme: the chorus' vision of the blind old man as the supreme example of man's helpless misery "once his youth slips by." Death comes as a release as "envy and enemies, rage and battles, bloodshed" assail him and last of all the naked feebleness of old age—"stripped of power, companions, stripped of love" (1392–97). The closing stanza compares Oedipus to "some great headland fronting the north" (1401) which must endure the buffeting of weather from every quarter. It is an image of suffering, but it is also an image of endurance—the headland will outlive the storms. And as the choral song dies away, the last assault on Oedipus' resolve is unleashed: his son Polynices comes to enlist his aid for the attack on Thebes.

His shocked self-reproach when he sees the miserable condition of the father he has neglected, his call for forgiveness and his talk of "cures for all the past wrongs done" (1435)—all this is met by a stubborn silence; Oedipus will not speak to him. Polynices turns to Antigone for help, but all she can do is advise him to make his appeal; something he says may touch his father's heart. And so he launches out on his long speech of self-justification, full of hatred for his brother, of vengeful pride in the might of the army he has marshaled against his own city, of condescending pity for his father: he can even compare their conditions—"we both fawn on the world for shelter, / you and I, we share the same fate" (1509–10). Nothing could be further from the truth. Oedipus comes to Athens not to beg but to give. And he maintains his contemptuous silence. The chorus leader implores him to say something, anything, before sending Polynices away.

It will not be what his son wants to hear, says Oedipus, but he will speak. And he turns on Polynices with a torrential hard rage that is the product of anger long pent up. His denunciation of both his sons for their dereliction of duty would seem even more justified to Greek ears than it does to ours today; sons were expected to repay their parents for their upbringing by supporting them in their old age. In Athens, one of the questions asked of all aspirants to public office was: "Do you treat your parents well?" The law prescribed penalties for those who mistreated their parents, and we know of suits brought by parents against children for failure to provide support. Beyond the laws made by men, the all-seeing Furies, in front of whose grove Oedipus arraigns his son, stood ready to punish transgressors, if the law should fail.

Oedipus does more than refuse to help Polynices capture Thebes; he prophesies disaster for the expedition.

> Impossible—you'll never tear that city down. No,
> you'll fall first, red with your brother's blood
> and he stained with yours—equals, twins in blood.   (1554–56)

These are, as he says, the curses he had leveled at his sons before, and he calls on those curses now to stand beside him. But what was before a prayer, a wish, is now delivered as an unqualified prophecy; he knows the future and he predicts it, not in the name of Apollo and Zeus, but in his own. The man who in the earlier play cast scorn on oracular prophecy—"why look to the Prophet's hearth, / the fires of the future?" (1054–55)—and raged in anger at the blind seer Tiresias has become a prophetic voice himself.

Moreover, as he delivers the curse that he has summoned to back his repudiation of his son, the tremendous lines Sophocles puts in his mouth express a fury that is more than human; this is the outraged voice of some unearthly power, intent on exacting the full price for injustice, of that grim spirit which, hidden in the ground, will one day drink Theban blood. Creon could argue and return threat for threat, but to this inhuman wrath no reply is imaginable and Polynices makes none. He recognizes at once that this is true prophecy; his cause is doomed and so is he. But he will not turn back, nor will he breathe a word of the dreadful knowledge he now possesses to his comrades in arms. He rejects his sister's plea to give up the attack on Thebes, and as he recovers from the initial shock inflicted by his father's overwhelming curse, he begins to regain courage; as in all Greek stories of destiny and prediction, he resolves to ignore the prophetic voice and avoid the doom it has foretold. To Antigone's agonized appeal—"Don't you see? / You carry out father's prophecies to the finish!" (1614–15)—he replies by dismissing the prophecy as a mere wish (1618). But it is not just a wish, as it was in Oedipus' earlier speech; it is the true shape of the future, as Polynices must realize when he asks his sisters to see to his burial. He cannot, however, go to lead his army in this mood; since the prophecy is against him he will dismiss it and with it prophecy in general. As for his future—"that's in the hands of a dark power, destiny— / whether we live or die, who knows?" (1641–42). The Greek word translated "a dark power, destiny" is *daimôn*, which can mean both "destiny" and "a supernatural being." Polynices does not realize the sense in which his words are true, that the *daimôn* in whose hands his future lies is the blind old man who has now assumed the powers that should rightly be his only when he is buried in a hero's grave.

And almost at once the thunder sounds; Oedipus is summoned by the gods. Theseus must be with him in his last moments, to receive the gift: "the power that age cannot destroy, / the heritage stored up for you and Athens" (1718–19). And Oedipus, as if the gods had given him back his eyes, leads Theseus and his daughters off the stage. The girls move to guide his steps as they have for so long and over so many roads, but he does not need them now.

> I stand revealed at last, look,
> a strange new role for me—I am your guide
> as you were once your father's. (1750–52)

He will guide them, as we learn from the messenger later, to a place in the Colonus countryside, midway between a bowl scooped out in the stone and the Rock of Thoricus (Sophocles' audience knew these places, though they mean nothing to us). There he prepares his living body for its last journey, with the bathing and libations administered to the dead. The thunder comes again, this time from below, and Oedipus takes leave of his daughters and sends them away. The chorus, after his exit, had prayed that Oedipus' passing would be an easy one: "Not in pain, not by a doom / that breaks the heart with mourning" (1771–72). And so it is. He simply vanishes, and leaves Theseus, the one man who knows the secret site where he lies,

> shielding his eyes,
> both hands spread out against his face as if—
> some terrible wonder flashed before his eyes . . . (1872–74)

Before Oedipus goes to his eternal home, however, the gods speak to him; these are the only words, apart from the riddling prophecies of Apollo, that the gods speak in either play. " 'You, you there, Oedipus—what are we waiting for? / You hold us back too long! We must move on, move on!' " (1844–45). Though he does not become a god, that "we" defines him as one who is now no longer human, one who belongs to the realm of those unseen powers that preside in mysterious ways over the destinies of men and nations.

And in the last scene of all we see those destinies in the making; the play looks forward now to the future. As the daughters mourn their loss, their thoughts turn to home, to Thebes, where brother faces brother and Oedipus' prophecies are to be fulfilled.

The play ends with Theseus' promise to send Antigone back to Thebes, as she requests, in a vain attempt to prevent the fratricidal duel on which Polynices is intent. She must know in her heart that she cannot prevent it; what she does after brother has killed brother we know from the earlier play, *Antigone*.

This is no happy ending, nor was it meant to be. That Oedipus has become a protective hero of the Athenian land, with power over his enemies, is perhaps some kind of recognition on the part of the gods that they had used him, to his cost, for a tremendous demonstration of the fact that human knowledge at its greatest is ignorance compared with theirs. But for the children of his doomed house there is to be no escape. The brothers will die by each other's hand and Antigone will prove herself the most stubbornly heroic of them all. Like her father, both as king in Thebes and beggar at Colonus, she will pursue her purpose in the face of opposition, threats and death itself with that heroic courage which is the one shaft of light in the dark universe of Sophoclean tragedy. It is a universe governed by powers in whose justice man must assert, in ignorance and with little hope of confirmation, a desperate belief.

Yet in the last play of all, that belief seems more solidly based than in the first. Antigone dies without a sign from those gods whose laws she defended; she prays that her persecutor will be punished but she does not live to see that prayer fulfilled. In the first of the two Oedipus plays the god who predicted his strange destiny speaks only through prophecies but never explains them; Oedipus must work his way unaided to an understanding of his fate and ground whatever hopes he has for the future on an untutored intuition that he is reserved for some extraordinary end. But the last play is full of divine signs and wonders, of prophecies that promise rather than threaten, and in the end the gods speak directly to Oedipus in words which clearly imply that in some mysterious sense he now belongs to them. The last play is still tragic in its outcome—Oedipus dies, Polynices and Antigone are doomed—but in it, for one man and for one moment, the silent gods speak, and the gulf between human and divine is bridged.

OEDIPUS AT COLONUS

CHARACTERS

OEDIPUS
formerly king of Thebes

ANTIGONE
his daughter

A CITIZEN
of Colonus

A CHORUS
of old citizens of Colonus and their **LEADER**

ISMENE
daughter of Oedipus, sister of Antigone

THESEUS
king of Athens

CREON
king of Thebes, brother-in-law of Oedipus

POLYNICES
son of Oedipus, brother of Antigone and Ismene

A MESSENGER

Guards and attendants of Theseus and bodyguard of Creon

TIME AND SCENE: *The grove of the Furies at Colonus looms in the background, while Athens lies in the distance to the right. Immediately to the right rises an heroic statue of a horseman; to the left, a rocky ledge overshadowed by the woods. A larger outcropping of rock stands in the foreground, with a stone altar at the center of the stage.*

Several years have passed since OEDIPUS *was expelled from Thebes. He enters from the left—the direction of that city—a broken, blind old man in filthy rags, led by a young woman, his daughter* ANTIGONE.

OEDIPUS:
My child, child of the blind old man—Antigone,
where are we now? What land, what city of men?
Who will receive the wandering Oedipus today?
Not with gifts but a pittance . . . it's little I ask
and get still less, but quite enough for me.
Acceptance—that is the great lesson suffering teaches,
suffering and the long years, my close companions,
yes, and nobility too, my royal birthright.

Child, look, do you see some place to rest?
Public grounds or groves reserved for the gods?
Give me your arm and sit me down—
we must find out where we are. We have come
to learn from the citizens, strangers from citizens,
and carry out their wishes to the end.

ANTIGONE:
Father, old and broken Oedipus, the towers
crowning the city, so far as I can see,
are still a good way off, but this is holy ground,
you can sense it clearly. Why, it's bursting
with laurel, olives, grapes, and deep in its heart,
listen . . . nightingales, the rustle of wings—
they're breaking into song.

                          Here, bend a knee and sit.
It's a rough rock, father, but then for an old man
you have come a long hard way from home.

OEDIPUS:
Then sit me down, watch over the blind man.

ANTIGONE:
No need to teach me that, not after all these years.

Helping him to sit on the rocky ledge just beside the grove.

OEDIPUS:
Now, dear, can you tell me where we are?

ANTIGONE:
The city is Athens, that I know, but not this place.

OEDIPUS:
Of course it's Athens—
the roads are crowded with people telling us of Athens.

ANTIGONE:
Very well, you want me to leave you here alone
and go and find its name?

OEDIPUS:
                Please, child,
if anyone really lives here.

ANTIGONE:
                    Oh there's life, all right.
No need to leave you—there's a man, near us—
I can see him.

*A CITIZEN of Colonus approaches
from the right.*

OEDIPUS:
            Where?
Coming toward us, already on his way?   35

ANTIGONE:
No, he's here. Whatever you think is best,
say it now, the man's right here.

OEDIPUS:
Friend, my daughter sees for the both of us . . .
she says you've come to find out who we are,
and lucky for us too: you can explain some things,   40
give us some light—

CITIZEN:
            Stop!
No more questions, not till you leave that seat!
Get up—it's holy ground, you mustn't walk on it.

OEDIPUS:
What is this ground? What god is worshiped here?

CITIZEN:
It's untouchable, forbidden—no one lives here.   45
The Terrible Goddesses hold it for themselves,
the Daughters of Earth, Daughters of the Darkness.

OEDIPUS:
                                Who?
Tell me their awesome names so I can pray to them.

CITIZEN:
The Ones who watch the world, the Kindly Ones,
the Eumenides—that's what people call them here. 50
In other places other names are proper.

OEDIPUS:
                              Oh—
then let them receive their suppliant with kindness!
I shall never leave my place in this new land,
this is my refuge!

CITIZEN:
            What do you mean?

OEDIPUS:
This is the sign, the pact that seals my fate. 55

CITIZEN:
Well I, for one, I'd never roust you from your seat.
I wouldn't dare, not without orders from the city,
not till I report what I am doing.

                    Turns to leave.

OEDIPUS:
                    For the love of god,
stranger, don't refuse me, vagabond that I am—
I beg you, tell me what I need to know. 60

CITIZEN:
Speak up. I won't refuse you, you'll see.

OEDIPUS:
                         Tell me,
what is this place where we have set our feet?

CITIZEN:
Whatever *I* know, you'll learn it all from me.
All that lies before you is hallowed ground.
The dread lord Poseidon holds it in his hands,
and another power lifts his torch nearby, the Titan,
Prometheus, and the spot you're standing on
is called the Brazen Threshold of this earth,
the holy bulwark of Athens.
And the rich, bordering plowlands claim Colonus,
that horseman there,

Pointing to the heroic statue.
        their founding father.
His name lives on in us—it is our heritage:
all his people carry on his name.
                So that,
you see, is the spirit of the place, old stranger,
not much honored in legends, more in the hearts
of us who live here, love it well.

OEDIPUS:
                So,
there are people really living on these lands?

CITIZEN:
Yes indeed, all of us named for that hero there.

OEDIPUS:
Do you have a king or a common public voice?

CITIZEN:
A king in the city governs all these parts.

OEDIPUS:
And who is he? Who holds the reins of power and speech?

CITIZEN:
Theseus—we call him Theseus, the son of Aegeus,
the king who came before him.

OEDIPUS:
                            Please,
could a messenger, one of your people go to him?

CITIZEN:
Why? To give him news or bring him here?

OEDIPUS:
Simply tell him this:
with a small service he may gain a great deal.

CITIZEN:
And what's there to gain from a man who cannot see?

OEDIPUS:
Whatever I say, there will be great vision
in every word I say.

CITIZEN:
                     Listen, friend,
you keep out of danger now, you hear me?
You've noble blood, I can see that,
your hard luck aside.
You stay here, just where you appeared,
till I go and tell our people what you say—
our neighbors, not in the town but here.
They'll do the deciding for you, whether
you're going to stay or you'll be moving on.

                     Exit, right.

OEDIPUS:
Dear, is the stranger gone?

ANTIGONE:

                    Gone.
Say what you want to say, father,   100
all's quiet—only I am here.

OEDIPUS:

                  Reaching out his hands in prayer.
You queens of terror, faces filled with dread!
Since yours is the first holy ground
where I've sat down to rest in this new land,
I beg you, don't be harsh to Apollo, harsh to me.   105
When the god cried out those lifelong prophecies of doom
he spoke of *this* as well, my promised rest
after hard years weathered—
I will reach my goal, he said, my haven
where I find the grounds of the Awesome Goddesses   110
and make their home my home. There I will round
the last turn in the torment of my life:
a blessing to the hosts I live among,
disaster to those who sent me, drove me out!
And he warned me signs of all these things will come   115
in earthquake, thunder perhaps, or the flashing bolt of Zeus.

And now I know it, now some omen from you, my queens,
some bird on the wing that fills my heart with faith
has led my slow steps home to your green grove.
Yes, how else could you be the first I've met   120
in all the roads I've traveled?—you and I,
ascetic and sober, we who drink no wine—
or found this solemn seat, this raw unhewn rock?

Now, goddesses, just as Apollo's voice foretold,
grant my life at last some final passage, 125
some great consummation at the end.
Unless—who knows?—I am beneath your dignity,
slave as I am to the worst relentless pains
that ever plagued a man. Come, hear my prayer,
you sweet daughters born of primeval Darkness! 130
Hear me, city named for mighty Athena—Athens,
honored above all cities on the earth!
Pity this harried ghost of a man,
this Oedipus . . . Oedipus is no more
the flesh and blood of old.

ANTIGONE:
                    Quiet. 135
Here come some men, bent with age,
coming to search out your resting place.

OEDIPUS:
I'll be quiet, but hurry, move me away,
hide me in the woods till I can hear
what they have to say and know their mood— 140
knowledge will safeguard everything we do.

> ANTIGONE *helps* OEDIPUS *withdraw
> into the grove. Enter a* CHORUS *of
> old men from the right, the citizens
> of Colonus. Some chant singly,
> others chant in groups.*

CHORUS:
Look for the man! Who is he? where's he hiding?—
where's he gone, rushed away, where now?
   That man, of all men on earth
the most shameless, desperate man alive!
Look for him, press the search now
scour every inch of the ground!
   A wanderer, wandering fugitive
that old man—no native, a stranger
else he'd never set foot where none may walk,
this grove of the Furies, irresistible, overwhelming—
Oh we tremble to say their names, filing by,
not a look, not a sound, not a word
moving our lips in silence
silent reverence, oh pass by, pass by . . .
   but now one's come, the rumors say
who fears the Furies not at all—
the man we look for, scanning
round and round this holy precinct,
cannot find him
               cannot find his hiding

OEDIPUS:

> *Emerging from the grove with*
> ANTIGONE, *as the* CHORUS *draws*
> *back from him in horror.*

                    Here—
I am the man you want! I see by sound alone,
as people say of the blind.

CHORUS:
               Oh dreadful—
dreadful to see him, dreadful to hear—

OEDIPUS:
                                Don't,
I beg you, don't look on me as an outlaw.

LEADER:
God save us! You, old man, who are you?   165

OEDIPUS:
One not quite in the first ranks of fortune,
you guardians of the land.
Obviously, or I'd never grope along
with another's eyes to point the way,
leaning my old hulk on weaker shoulders.   170

CHORUS:
Oh blind, blind, poor man . . . no eyes, no sight—
tell me, were you blind from birth?
    Your life a life of pain
and the years long, it's all too clear
but at least if I can help it, if I have any power   175
you won't bring down new curses on your head!
    You've gone too far, too far—
but before you stumble one step more
invading the sacred glade, rapt in silence
the deep green lawns where the bowl brims libations   180
running with holy water swirling honey—
                                Stop—
sufferer, stranger, you must not trespass!
Move, come down among us now—
closer, a good safe way from the grove,
        you hear, old traveler, man of grief?   185
Do you have an appeal to make before our session?
Move!—move off forbidden ground, come down
where the law permits us all to speak,
till then hold back
            be silent—not a word!

OEDIPUS:
Antigone, what now?—what do you think?

ANTIGONE:
                              Father,
it's best to obey the customs of the people:
give in if we must, and listen closely too.

OEDIPUS:
Reach out your hand to me . . .

ANTIGONE:
                       There, you feel it?

OEDIPUS:
Oh strangers, let me suffer no injustice—
now I've trusted you, now I've left my shelter.

CHORUS:
                                Never!
No one will ever drag you from this place of rest—
   never, old man, not against your will.

Leaning on ANTIGONE, OEDIPUS
*begins to move forward, groping,
slowly.*

OEDIPUS:
Still farther?

CHORUS:
         Come forward, a little more.

OEDIPUS:
Still more?

CHORUS:
                Help him along, young one,
you can see the way.

ANTIGONE:
                        Come, father, follow me   200
with your frail, blind steps, follow me, father,
I will lead you on.

CHORUS:
                    Patience, stranger—
here in a strange land, poor man,
hate with a will
whatever the city holds in rooted hatred,   205
honor what the city holds in love.

OEDIPUS:
    Then come, my child, lead me on
to the sacred, lawful ground
where we may speak and we may listen—
and no more fighting with necessity.   210

                        *Reaching the large outcropping of
                        rock at the center of the stage.*

CHORUS:
Here—no farther. This base of native rock,
    never lift a foot from this firm threshold.

OEDIPUS:
So, far enough?

CHORUS:
            Just enough, you hear me?

OEDIPUS:
Now may I sit down?

CHORUS:
                    Move to the side a little,
you're right at the rock's edge—now crouch down.

ANTIGONE:
Father, I'll help you; calm now, easy . . .

OEDIPUS:
Oh dear gods—

ANTIGONE:
              . . . step by step, our steps together,
lean your aged body on my loving arm.

> *Helping him down, gently.*

OEDIPUS:
Oh so ruined, doomed.

CHORUS:
                    So helpless . . .
    there now, rest at ease, and tell us,
    who were your parents?—who are you, old man,
    led by the hand in hardship? Tell us,
    what's your fatherland?

OEDIPUS:
                    Fatherland, friends?
I am an exile! Oh but don't—

LEADER:
                    Don't what, old man?
What are you holding back?

OEDIPUS:
                    No no! Don't ask who I am—
no more probing, testing—stop—no more!

LEADER:
What—why?

OEDIPUS:
My birth, so dreadful . . .

LEADER:
More, speak up!

OEDIPUS:
My child, oh, oh, what can I say?

LEADER:
What is your lineage, stranger?
Tell us—who was your father?

OEDIPUS:
God help me! 230
Dear girl, what must I suffer now?

ANTIGONE:
Say it. You're driven right to the edge.

OEDIPUS:
Then speak I will—no way to hide it now.

LEADER:
You're wasting time, the two of you.
Out with it, quickly. 235

OEDIPUS:
Do you know a son of Laius? Oh . . .

LEADER:
Oh no!

OEDIPUS:
Born of the royal blood of Thebes?

LEADER:
                              Dear god—

OEDIPUS:
... and the wretched, suffering Oedipus?

LEADER:
                              You, you're *that* man—?

OEDIPUS:
Please, don't be afraid, whatever I say—

LEADER:
O—ohhh!

OEDIPUS:
          My destiny, very hard ...   240
                    Drawing back, the CHORUS *all
                    but drowns his words with cries
                    of horror.*
Antigone, what will they do to us now?

LEADER:
Out with you! Out of our country—far away!

OEDIPUS:
But your promise—
won't you make good on your promise?

CHORUS:
Fate will never punish a man   245
for returning harm first done to him.
Deceit matched by deceit, the tables turned:
treachery pays you back in pain, not kindness.
You—out of this place of rest, away, faster!
Off and gone from the land—before you fix   250
some greater penalty on our city.

ANTIGONE:
                          Oh strangers,
you, with all the compassion in your hearts—
since you cannot endure my father, old as he is,
hearing the dreadful things he did against his will,
pity me at least, good strangers, my despair,   255
I beg you!—beg you for my father, beg you
with eyes that still can look into your eyes.
I implore you, look—
like a daughter sprung of your own blood,
I beg that my shattered father find compassion.   260
We throw ourselves on your mercy as on a god,
in all our misery. Hear us! Oh say Yes—
grant us the help we never dreamed to see!
I beg you now by all that you hold dear, by child,
by wife, by earthly possessions, by your gods!   265
Look through all humanity: you'll never find
a man on earth, if a god leads him on,
who can escape his fate.

LEADER:
                          You must know,
child of Oedipus, we pity you both,
we're moved by your misfortunes.   270
But we dread what the gods may do . . .
we've no authority, we cannot go beyond
our first commands—you must leave.

OEDIPUS:
Then what's the good of glory, magnificent renown,
if in its flow it streams away to nothing?
If Athens, Athens
is that rock of reverence all men say it is,
the only city on earth to save the ruined stranger,
the only one to protect him, give him shelter—
where are such kindnesses for me? First
you raise me up from my seat in the grove,
then you drive me off the land, terrified
by my name alone, surely not my physique
nor what I've done.

          Since *my* acts, at least,
were acts of suffering more than actions outright—
but I cannot bear to tell you the whole story
of mother and father . . .
that's what makes you fear me, well I know.

                                 But no, no—
how could you call me guilty, how by nature?
I was attacked—I struck in self-defense.
Why even if I had known what I was doing,
how could that make me guilty? But in fact,
knowing nothing, no, I went . . . the way I went—
but the ones who made me suffer, they knew full well,
they wanted to destroy me.

                         So, strangers,
I beg you by the gods, with the same kindness
that raised me up before, save me now!
Never honor the gods in one breath
and take the gods for fools the next.
Remember, they are watching over us always,
eyes trained on the mortals who respect them,
eyes trained on the worst transgressors.
There is no escape, ever,
not for a single godless man in all the world.

Now with the gods' help, don't cloud the fame, 305
the radiance of Athens,
don't descend to naked acts of outrage.
But just as you have taken up the suppliant,
pledged yourselves—rescue, guard me to the end!
Don't reject me as you look into the horror 310
of my face, these sockets raked and blind.
I come as someone sacred, someone filled
with piety and power, bearing a great gift
for all your people. And when your ruler comes,
whoever is your leader, you will hear it all 315
and know it all, and meanwhile
as we wait together, do not be unjust.

LEADER:
You fill me with awe, you must, old man—
you express your arguments with such force.
But I'll be more at ease 320
if the lords of the realm decide these matters for me.

OEDIPUS:
Where is he now, strangers, the ruler of your land?

LEADER:
In the city where his father ruled the country,
and the man who brought us here has gone to get him.

OEDIPUS:
What? You think he'll have such regard, such care 325
for a blind man, he'll come to us in person?

LEADER:
Without a doubt, soon as he hears your name.

OEDIPUS:
My name . . . and who's to tell him that?

LEADER:
It's a long way to Athens. Crowded too,
and travelers' rumors spread like wildfire—
soon as he learns, don't worry, he'll be here.
Your name, old stranger, echoes through the world.
Even at rest or indisposed to move,
when Theseus hears it's you, he'll come at once.

OEDIPUS:
Then let him come with a blessing for his city,
for Oedipus too. The good man helps himself.

ANTIGONE:
Scanning the distance eagerly.
Dear god, what to say? to think?—father!

OEDIPUS:
Now what, child? Antigone!

ANTIGONE:
                I can see
a woman coming toward us, riding a sleek colt,
and the broad brim of her hat's low on her face,
shading her from the sun. What can I say?
Is it or isn't it?—am I losing my mind?
Yes—no—I can't say . . . poor girl, it's she,
it must be—
      Look, her eyes glistening—
smiling at me, she's coming closer, waving,
oh it's clear, it's no one else—
dear sister, dear Ismene!

OEDIPUS:
            What are you saying, child?

ANTIGONE:
I see your daughter, my own sister—
you'll know her at once, by her voice.

Enter ISMENE *from the left.*

ISMENE:
Father—
sister—the two words I love the most,
I love to say the most! So hard to find you,
now I can hardly see you through my tears.

OEDIPUS:
Child, you've come?

ISMENE:
Oh father! Your fate so cruel,
I can barely look—

OEDIPUS:
Ismene, you're really here?

ISMENE:
Yes, and what a journey I had.

OEDIPUS:
Touch me, dear one.

ISMENE:
Let me hold you both!

OEDIPUS:
Oh my children—sisters!

ISMENE:
                    Such wretched straits.

OEDIPUS:
Hers and mine?

ISMENE:
                    And mine too, my pain the third.

OEDIPUS:
Little one, why have you come?

ISMENE:
                              For you, father,
concern for you.

OEDIPUS:
                    Longing for me, you mean?

ISMENE:
                                        That,
and to bring you the news myself, in my own words,
with the only servant left that I can trust.

OEDIPUS:
And the boys, your brothers, where are they?
Can't they do their part?

ISMENE:
                    They are—
where they are . . . now's their darkest hour.

OEDIPUS:
                                So,   365
just like Egyptians, aren't they? Heart and soul!
The same habits, same way they live their lives.
There it's the men who loll about indoors,
doing the work of women at the loom,
but the wives are out and working,   370
winning the daily bread, day in, day out.
Look at yourselves, children. Your brothers,
who should perform this labor, tend the hearth
like girls, but you, you take their place,
shouldering all your father's grinding sorrows. 375

Antigone, from the time she left her childhood behind
and came into full strength, has volunteered for grief,
wandering with me, leading the old misery, hungry,
feet cut through the bristling woods . . .
an eternity—worn down by the drenching rains, 380
the scorching suns at noon. Hard labor,
but you endured it all, never a second thought
for home, a decent life, so long as your father
had some care and comfort.

                    Turning to ISMENE.

                        And you, child,
in the early days, all unknown to Thebes   385
you left the city, brought your father the oracles,
any prophecy said to touch his life.
You were my faithful guard, you took that part
when I was an exile from the land. Now again,
Ismene, what news do you bring your father?   390
What mission brings you far from home?
You haven't come empty-handed, well I know,
not without some word to rouse my fears.

ISMENE:
Whatever I suffered on the way, father,
trying to find your resting place and shelter, 395
let's pass over that . . . I haven't the heart
to rake up all that pain again, twice over.
But the dark clouds just closing in around
your two doomed sons—I've come to tell you that.

At first they were eager to leave the throne to Creon, 400
not to pollute the city any longer:
they saw how the blight on the race,
ages old, clung to your long-suffering house.
But now some god, some sinister twist of mind
has gripped them both, some fatal, murderous rivalry— 405
they grab for power, the scepter and the crown.
Now the younger, like some hot-blooded boy,
strips his elder brother Polynices,
seizes the throne and drives him from his homeland.
But the exile—a flood of rumors fills our ears— 410
the exile's fled to Argos ringed in hills,
he embraces new kinsmen, bound by marriage,
and a whole massed army of new friends.
Soon, he tells them, Argos in arms
will drag the plain of Thebes from glory 415
or lift its name in praises to the stars.

This is no mere flurry of words, father,
it's action, terrible action!
And when the gods will shower pity on you
and your ordeals, I simply cannot tell. 420

OEDIPUS:
What? You'd begun to hope the gods
would look on me, deliver me at last?

ISMENE:
Yes, father, just now, with the latest oracles . . .

OEDIPUS:
What are they? What are the prophecies, my child?

ISMENE:
Soon, soon the men of Thebes will want you greatly, 425
once you are dead, and even while you're alive—
they need you for their welfare, their survival.

OEDIPUS:
What good could anyone get from the like of me?

ISMENE:
They are in your hands, the oracle says,
their power rests in you.

OEDIPUS:
                So, 430
when I am nothing—then am I a man?

ISMENE:
                        Yes!
The gods are about to raise you to your feet—
till now they were bent on your destruction.

OEDIPUS:
It costs them little to raise an old man!
Someone crushed in younger days.

ISMENE:
                      That may be, 435
but Creon, at any rate—make no mistake,
he's coming for you, for just this reason.
Soon, not late, I warn you.

OEDIPUS:
To do what, my child? Be clearer—tell me.

ISMENE:
To settle you near the fatherland of Thebes,
to have you in their power,
but you may not set foot within the borders.

OEDIPUS:
What earthly use am I to them, deposited
beyond the gates?

ISMENE:
              Your tomb will curse them
if it lacks the proper rites.

OEDIPUS:
                    Of course,
it takes no god from the blue to teach us that.

ISMENE:
That's why they want to keep you close at hand,
a good strong ally,
not in a land where you can be your own master.

OEDIPUS:
But surely they will shroud my corpse with Theban dust?

ISMENE:
No, not with your father's blood on your hands,
that's forbidden, father!

OEDIPUS:
Then they will never get me in their clutches—never!

ISMENE:
Then some day this will be a heavy curse on Thebes . . .

OEDIPUS:
How, child?—when, what fatal rendezvous?

ISMENE:
That day, by the force of your great rage,
that day they take their stand upon your tomb.

OEDIPUS:
All you say, child, who told you this?

ISMENE:
                        The men,
the envoys sent to Apollo's hearth at Delphi.

OEDIPUS:
Those were the very words the god spoke—
about *my* future?

ISMENE:
            So they reported,
coming back to Thebes.

OEDIPUS:
                Tell me—my sons,
has either of them heard any word of this?

ISMENE:
Oh they both have, they know it all too well.

OEDIPUS:
And still—those ingrates! they heard it all and still
they love the crown more than their own father—
the chance to bring me back.

ISMENE:
It hurts me to hear it . . .
I must bear it just the same.

OEDIPUS:
                          No, no, may the great gods
never quench their blazing, fated strife!   470
May it rest in my hands alone—
now their spears are lifting tip to tip—
to bring their fighting to its bitter end.
I'd see that the one who holds the scepter now
would not last long, nor would the outcast   475
ever return again! When I, their own father
was drummed off native ground, disgraced,
they didn't lift a finger, didn't defend me, no,
they just looked on, they watched me driven from home,
they heard the heralds cry my sentence—exile!   480

Say it . . . that was exactly what I wanted then,
the city granted me my heart's desire. Not at all!
That first day, true, when all my rage was seething,
my dearest wish was death,
stoning to death in public—I couldn't find a soul   485
to satisfy my passion. But then, as time wore on
and the smoldering fever broke and died at last,
and I began to feel my rage had far outrun my wrongs,
I'd lashed myself too much for what I'd done,
once, long ago—then, when it suited them,   490
the city wheeled and marched me off the land,
brutally, after all that time—
and my own sons who could have swept to the rescue,
sons to their father, they did nothing, they refused!
For want of one small word from those two princes 495
I was rooted out, a beggar, an outcast,
fugitive forever.

                    Oh thank god for you!
My two girls, dear sisters, young as you are,
as far as the life within you lends you power
I have my daily bread, safe-conduct through the land   500
and all the lovely kindnesses of kinship.
But your two brothers turn their backs
on their own father, for throne, for scepter,
the tyrant's iron grip upon the realm. Never,
they will never win this Oedipus for their champion!   505
And precious little good will ever come to them
from lording over Thebes. That much I know,
now that I hear the oracles my dear one brings
and brood on the old prophecies, stored
in the depths of all my being,   510
that Apollo has fulfilled for me at last.
                                     So,
let them send Creon himself to hunt me down,
and whoever else is high and mighty in the city.
If you, my friends, you and your champions,
the Awesome Goddesses who guard your people—   515
if you are willing to rise to my defense,
you will win a great deliverer for your state
and mortal punishment for my mortal enemies.

LEADER:
Oedipus, you deserve all the pity in our hearts,
you and your children here. First your appeal,   520
and now you add your power to save our land.
Let me advise you, for your own good.

OEDIPUS:
                             Oh friend,
I will do anything. Guide me now, my friend.

LEADER:
Come, you must appease those Spirits now.
When you arrived, you trespassed on their ground. 525

OEDIPUS:
How, with what rites? Teach me, friend.

LEADER:
First, there is a spring that runs forever:
gather libations from it, holy water.
See that your hands are clean before you touch it.

OEDIPUS:
And when I collect the water, pure and clear? 530

LEADER:
There are bowls waiting, work of a master-craftsman.
Cover the rim and handles at the mouth.

OEDIPUS:
With what—sprays of leaves, strips of weaving?

LEADER:
Take tufts of wool, just cut from a young lamb.

OEDIPUS:
                                            Good,
and then, what is the last rite I must perform? 535

LEADER:
Pour out the holy water, stand and face the east.

OEDIPUS:
Do I pour the offerings from the bowls you mentioned?

LEADER:
Yes. Pour from all three, but empty out the last.

OEDIPUS:
And what do I fill the third with? Tell me that.

LEADER:
Water. Honey. But no wine, add no wine.   540

OEDIPUS:
And there in the shadows underneath the leaves,
once the earth has drunk its fill, what then?

LEADER:
Take up sprays of olive, three times nine,
and with both hands, hand following hand,
lay them there and crown them with this prayer.

OEDIPUS:
                                                    The prayer—
I must learn the prayer, the greatest thing by far.

LEADER:
Simply this: "As we call you Powers of Kindness,
so from the springs of kindness in your heart
receive your suppliant now and save his life."
That is the prayer,   550
your own, or someone praying for you.
But pray in silence, do not raise your voice,
then withdraw and never look behind.
If you will do all this, I'd stand beside you,
fearing nothing—otherwise, my friend,   555
I would be terrified for you.

OEDIPUS:
                    Children,
you hear what the strangers say,
the people of these parts?

ANTIGONE:
I've heard it all. Tell us what to do.

OEDIPUS:
I cannot go myself, not in this condition,
strength gone, sight gone, a double share of pain.
One of you go and carry out these rites.
One soul is enough,
I know, to pay the debt for thousands,
if one will go to the gods in all good faith.
Quickly—do it now. Just don't leave me alone.
I'm too weak to move these old bones . . . abandoned,
cut off from any guide to lead the way.

ISMENE:
Then I'll go, I'll perform the rites.
Where do I find the place? I have to know.

LEADER:
The other side of the grove, child.
If there's anything you need, there's a guardian
at the spot and he'll instruct you.

ISMENE:
                    I'm on my way.
Antigone, you stay here, watch over father.
If there's any work for a parent's sake,
we must take the work in stride.

ISMENE exits left. The CHORUS *gathers around* OEDIPUS *and begins to chant.*

CHORUS:
                        A terrible thing, my friend,
to wake an old grief, laid to rest so long . . .
nevertheless I long to learn—

OEDIPUS:
                What now?

CHORUS:
That dreadful agony you faced—no recovery,
no way out—that agony you lived through.

OEDIPUS:
                         No!   580
For the sake of kindness toward a guest,
don't lay bare the cruelty I suffered!

CHORUS:
But the rumor spreads throughout the world,
it will not die—I want to hear it, friend,
hear the truth from you.

OEDIPUS:
              Oh no . . .   585

CHORUS:
Bear up, I beg you.

OEDIPUS:
          Dear gods—

CHORUS:
                      Grant me my wish,
just as I grant you yours.

OEDIPUS:
                    I have suffered, friends,
the worst horrors on earth, suffered against my will,
I swear to god, not a single thing self-willed—

CHORUS:
                                        What?—how?

OEDIPUS:
Thebes married me to disaster! Thebes bound me fast,   590
so blind, to a bride who was my curse, my ruin, my—

CHORUS:
                                                Mother?
I've heard it, I can't believe—you filled that bed
with infamy . . . with your own mother?

OEDIPUS:
Misery—it's death to hear those words!
Oh strangers, and these two girls,   595
born of my blood—

CHORUS:
                    What? Say it!

OEDIPUS:
Daughters, both so cursed—

CHORUS:
                    O Zeus!

OEDIPUS:
                                —sprang from the same womb,
the same mother brought us all to birth!

CHORUS:
                                        So they,
why they're your children, then in the same breath—

OEDIPUS:
My sisters, yes, their father's sisters!   600

CHORUS
Horrible . . .

OEDIPUS:
               Horrible, countless horrors
sweeping over me, over and over!

CHORUS:
                              What you've suffered—

OEDIPUS:
Suffered unforgivable, unforgettable . . .

CHORUS:
What you've done!

OEDIPUS:
           No, not done—

CHORUS:
                         What then?

OEDIPUS:
                                    Received,
received as a gift, a prize to break the heart—   605
Oh would to god I'd never served my city,
never won the prize they handed up to me!

CHORUS:
                              So wretched,
doomed—but then too, you spilled the blood?—

OEDIPUS:
Why that? what more do you need to know?

CHORUS:
You killed your father?

OEDIPUS:
                    Oh no no,
the second stab—wound on wound!

CHORUS:
                        You, you murdered—

OEDIPUS:
Murdered, but not without some justice—

CHORUS:
What in the world?

OEDIPUS:
            By all rights, I—

CHORUS:
                    What?

OEDIPUS:
                        I'll tell you:
the man I murdered—he'd have murdered me!
I am innocent! Pure in the eyes of the law,
blind, unknowing, I, I came to this!

Enter THESEUS, *with his royal guard, from the right.*

LEADER:
Look, our king, Theseus, son of Aegeus—
your message brought him here.

THESEUS:
In the old days I often heard your legend,
the bloody mutilation of your eyes . . .   620
I know all about you, son of Laius.
And now, seeing you at this crossroads,
beyond all doubt I know you in the flesh.
Your rags, your ravaged face—
it's all too clear, they show me who you are,   625
and in all compassion I would ask you, Oedipus,
doomstruck Oedipus, why are you here?
What appeal do you bring to Athens and to me?
You and the young girl, helpless at your side.

Tell me all. Your story, your fortunes   630
would have to be grim indeed to make me turn
my back on you. I too, I remember well,
was reared in exile just like you,
and in strange lands, like no man else on earth,
I grappled dangers pressing for my life.   635
Never, I tell you, I will never shrink
from a stranger, lost as you are now,
or fail to lend a hand and save a life.
I am only a man, well I know,
and I have no more power over tomorrow,   640
Oedipus, than you.

OEDIPUS:
                    Oh Theseus,
so magnanimous, so noble! Your few words
spare me the need to draw things out at length.
Who I am, and the father who gave me life,
and my native land—you name them all exactly.
So now there is nothing left for me to tell
but my desire, and then the story's finished.

THESEUS:
Yes, tell me that. I want to know.

OEDIPUS:
I come with a gift for you,
my own shattered body . . . no feast for the eyes,
but the gains it holds are greater than great beauty.

THESEUS:
Gains? What do you claim to carry with you?

OEDIPUS:
Soon you will learn it all, not quite yet, I think.

THESEUS:
And when will the gifts you offer come to light?

OEDIPUS:
When I am dead, and you have put my body in the grave.

THESEUS:
You ask for the final things of life, but all between
you wipe from memory, or count as nothing.

OEDIPUS:
                                            True.
There, in that last kindness, I harvest all the rest.

THESEUS:
Then the gift you ask of me is very little.

OEDIPUS:
Oh beware—there is nothing slight about it, 660
not the struggle it will breed.

THESEUS:
                    You mean . . .
something between your offspring and myself?

OEDIPUS:
My sons will force you to send me back to Thebes.

THESEUS:
Why? If you want to go, it's wrong to remain an exile.

OEDIPUS:
Oh no—when *I* was willing, *they* refused!

THESEUS:
                        You fool! 665
Anger is not what your misfortunes call for.

OEDIPUS:
Wait till you hear me out, then criticize me—
spare me now.

THESEUS:
            Tell me more . . .
I must not judge you, not without more to go on.

OEDIPUS:
I have suffered terribly, Theseus, 670
wrongs on wrongs, no end.

THESEUS:
You mean the ancient troubles of your house?

OEDIPUS:
No, no—all Greece rings with talk of that.

THESEUS:
What then? How do your griefs exceed
the griefs of all mankind?

OEDIPUS:
                      Here, look at me,   675
rooted out of my country by my sons,
my own flesh and blood. My doom is never
to return again—I killed my father!

THESEUS:
Then how could they call you home—
to settle you outside?   680

OEDIPUS:
A god, the voice of a god is forcing them on.

THESEUS:
What do they fear, what dreadful prophecies?

OEDIPUS:
Thebes is doomed to be struck down in this land.

THESEUS:
And how on earth could conflict ever come
between your city and mine?

OEDIPUS:
                              Oh Theseus,
dear friend, only the gods can never age,
the gods can never die. All else in the world
almighty Time obliterates, crushes all
to nothing. The earth's strength wastes away,
the strength of a man's body wastes and dies—
faith dies, and bad faith comes to life,
and the same wind of friendship cannot blow forever,
holding steady and strong between two friends,
much less between two cities.
For some of us soon, for others later,
joy turns to hate and back again to love.
And even if all is summer sunshine now
between yourself and Thebes,
infinite Time, sweeping through its rounds
gives birth to infinite nights and days . . .
and a day will come when the treaties of an hour,
the pacts firmed with a handclasp will snap—
at the slightest word a spear will hurl them to the winds—
some far-off day when my dead body, slumbering, buried
cold in death, will drain their hot blood down,
if Zeus is still Zeus and Apollo the son of god
speaks clear and true.
                              Enough. It's no pleasure
to break the silence of these mysteries.
Let me end where I began.
Just defend your word to the last, and you
will never say you welcomed Oedipus for nothing,
a useless citizen in this land of yours,
unless the gods defeat my dearest hopes.

LEADER:
                              My king,
for some time this man has seemed determined
to carry out such promises for our country.

THESEUS:
Such kindness—who could reject such a man?
First, in any case, Oedipus is our ally:
by mutual rights we owe him hospitality
What's more, he has come to beg our gods for help
and render no small benefit to our country   720
in return, to me as well.
So I respect his claims, I'll never reject
the gifts he offers, no, I will settle him
in our land, a fellow-citizen with full rights.

And if it pleases our friend to remain here,   725
I command you, old men, guard him well.
But if he'd rather come along with me—
what is your pleasure, Oedipus?
The choice is yours. Whatever you decide,
I will stand behind you all the way.   730

OEDIPUS:
Oh god bless such men!

THESEUS:
                                What would you like?
Will you come home with me?

OEDIPUS:
                                Gladly,
if the gods were willing. But *this* is the place where . . .

THESEUS:
What will you do here? Not that I'd oppose you.

OEDIPUS:
—Where I will triumph over those who drove me out.   735

THESEUS:
Your very presence here, from all you say,
will be a mighty blessing.

OEDIPUS:
So it will,
if only you keep your guarantees to me
and act them out to the end.

THESEUS:
Have no fear.
Trust me, Oedipus, I will never betray you.

OEDIPUS:
And I will never bind you with an oath,
never impugn your honor.

THESEUS:
My word is my bond.
You have nothing more to gain than that.

OEDIPUS:
And what will you do when . . .

THESEUS:
What do you fear?

OEDIPUS:
Men will come—

THESEUS:
These men will attend to them.

OEDIPUS:
                                              Take care! 745
Since you are leaving me—

THESEUS:
                        Don't teach me what to do.

OEDIPUS:
I'm forced, I'm so afraid.

THESEUS:
                        Not I, I have no fear.

OEDIPUS:
But you don't know the threats—

THESEUS:
                                I do know this:
no one can take you away from here against my will.
Men have threatened for ages, blustered their threats   750
to nothing in their rage. But once a man
regains his self-control, all threats are gone.
As for these men of Thebes, something tells me . . .
though they thunder with talk of taking you off,
they'll find some heavy seas to block their way,   755
rough sailing in the end.
                          Take heart,
I urge you, even without my firm resolve—
didn't Apollo send you here himself?
Rest assured, no matter if I'm away,
I know my name will shield you well,   760
you'll never come to grief.

Exit THESEUS *with his guard to the left. The* CHORUS *gathers around* OEDIPUS.

CHORUS:
                    Here, stranger,
here in the land where horses are a glory
you have reached the noblest home on earth
Colonus glistening, brilliant in the sun—
    where the nightingale sings on,   765
her dying music rising clear,
hovering always, never leaving,
down the shadows deepening green
    she haunts the glades, the wine-dark ivy,
dense and dark the untrodden, sacred wood of god   770
rich with laurel and olives never touched by the sun
untouched by storms that blast from every quarter—
    where the Reveler Dionysus strides the earth forever
    where the wild nymphs are dancing round him
        nymphs who nursed his life.   775

And here it blooms, fed by the dews of heaven
lovely, clustering, morning-fresh forever,
narcissus, crown of the Great Goddesses
    Mother and Daughter dying
into life from the dawn of time,   780
and the gold crocus bursts like break of day
and the springs will never sleep, will never fail,
    the fountainhead of Cephisus flowing nomad
quickening life forever, fresh each day—
life rising up with the river's pure tide   785
flowing over the plains, the swelling breast of earth—
    nor can the dancing Muses bear to leave this land
    or the Goddess Aphrodite, the charioteer
        with the golden reins of love.

And there is a marvel here, I have not heard its equal   790
nothing famed in the vast expanse of Asia, nothing
like it in Pelops' broad Dorian island
    ever sprang to light—
a creation self-creating, never conquered,
a terror to our enemies and their spears,   795
it flourishes to greatness in our soil,
    the gray-leafed olive, mother, nurse of children,
perennial generations growing in her arms—
neither young nor old can tear her from her roots,
the eternal eyes of Guardian Zeus   800
    look down upon her always,
            great Athena too
    her eyes gray-green and gleaming as the sea.

And I have another praise to sound in song
a mighty gift bestowed our mother-city   805
the splendor of a majestic, ancient god
    the pride and power of our earth—
the glory of horses, glory of young horses
the glorious rippling sinews of the sea!
O Poseidon, you have throned her in this power,   810
    lord god of the sea-lanes, you were first
to forge the bit and bridle, first to curb
the fiery rage of stallions in these roads—
and your ship flies like a marvel past the land
    your long flashing oars whipping the sea   815
        mounting the white manes of the sea
        racing the sea-nymphs dancing past the prow!

ANTIGONE:
Looking left, alarmed.
Oh Athens, praised above any land on earth,
now turn your glowing praises into action!

OEDIPUS:
What now, child?

ANTIGONE:
Creon—he's closing on us, 820
not without an escort, father.

OEDIPUS:
Dear old men, some action—please—
defend me to the end!

LEADER:
Nothing to fear,
you have our promise. I may be old
but the power of my country never ages. 825

Enter CREON, *left, with his bodyguard.*

CREON:
Noble old men, the pride of your land,
I seem to catch a glint of fear in your eyes,
a sudden shudder at my arrival. Don't be afraid,
and don't greet me with anything uncivil.
I haven't come here with any thought of force, 830
I am too old for that,
and I know the city I have reached is strong,
if any in Greece is strong—a great power.
No, I have been sent, despite my age,
to persuade this old man here 835
to return with me to the land of his fathers.

I haven't come on my own initiative either:
I bear the mandate of my entire people
since it fell to me, by ties of blood,
to mourn his pains as no one else in Thebes.
                                    So,   840
poor pitiful Oedipus, hear me now, come home!
Your whole people summon you, rightly so,
and I first among them, just as I—
unless I am the most callous man alive—
grieve for your sorrows most of all, old man,   845
now that I see you ground down in misery,
a derelict, beggar, stumbling on forever,
stripped of the bare essentials,
only a frail girl to lean your weight on . . .
Dear god, I never dreamed she'd sink so low—   850
degraded, helpless thing. Always tending you,
crushed by the gloom and poverty of your life.
And at her ripe age unmarried, look, a prize
for the first rough hand.
                        There, heaven help me,
is that painful enough—the shame I heap on you?   855
Well, it mortifies me too, and all our people.
But who can hide the appalling facts with you
out here on the roads? *You* can, Oedipus.
Now, by our fathers' gods, listen to me,
hide your own disgrace, consent—   860
return to Thebes, the house of your fathers!
Take friendly leave of Athens, she deserves it,
but Thebes has first claim. Respect her well,
justly so—years ago your city gave you birth.

OEDIPUS:
What brazen gall! You'd stop at nothing! 865
From any appeal at all you'd wring
some twisted, ingenious justice of your own!
Why must you attack me so, twice over,
catching me in the traps where I would suffer most?

First, in the old days, when I was sick to death 870
with the horror of my life,
when I lusted to be driven into exile,
you refused that favor—for all my prayers.
But then, when I'd had my fill of rage at last
and living on in the old ancestral house seemed sweet . . . 875
then you were all for cutting, casting me away—
these ties of blood you maunder on about
meant nothing to you then. And now,
again, when you see me welcomed well,
embraced by this great city and all her sons, 880
again you'd attack me, drag me off and away,
your oily language smoothing your brutality.

What's the joy of it? Who wants your kindness now?
Just imagine, Creon, someone giving you nothing,
refusing every help, and you craving it so— 885
but then, when your heart's desire was sated,
then he gave you all, when the favor
was no favor any more. Look at me, Creon:
wouldn't you find that pleasure empty—ashes?
That's precisely how your offers strike me now: 890
your words like honey—your actions, drawn swords.

I'll say it to these men too, I'll show how false you are.
You, you've come to take me, not to take me home
but plant me just outside your borders, just
to keep your city free of harm from Athens.
Well that is not your destiny, no, *this* is—
my curse, my fury of vengeance
rooted deep in your soil for all time to come!
And for my sons, this legacy: a kingdom in my realm,
room enough to die in—six feet of earth.

Now then, don't I see the fate of Thebes
more vividly than you? Oh so much more,
the sources of all I know are so much stronger:
Apollo and Zeus himself, Apollo's father.
But here you are, you fraud, lies on your lips,
your tongue whetted, double-edged. Well plead away—
you'll reap your own destruction, nothing can save you.
Enough. I can't convince you, I know that—get out!
Suffer us to live here . . . even in these straits
our life is not as pitiful as you'd think,
so long as we find joy in every hour.

CREON:
                              Tell me,
which of us suffers more from this tirade?
Whom are you hurting more, me or you?

OEDIPUS:
Nothing could please me more, Creon,
than if you fail to convince my friends here—
as fully as you fail with me.

CREON:
Burnt-out husk of a man—look, you see?
Not even the years can bring you to your senses.
Must you disgrace old age?

OEDIPUS:
You and your wicked way with words, Creon—   920
I've never known an honest man
who can plead so well for any plea whatever.

CREON:
Ah, but it's one thing to run off at the mouth,
quite another to hit the mark head-on.

OEDIPUS:
As if you were brief but to the point.   925

CREON:
Not to you, a mind as crude as yours.

OEDIPUS:
                              Away—
I shout it out in the name of these men too!
Stop harassing me here, blockading
the haven where I am destined to live on.

CREON:
I call these men—not you—to witness this,   930
the abuse you fling in the teeth of loved ones!—
and if I ever get my hands on you—

OEDIPUS:
                              And who
could tear me away from these allies by force?

CREON:
                              I warn you,
even without that, we have ways to make you suffer.

OEDIPUS:
By doing what?— 935
what have you got behind your threats, your bluster?

CREON:
Your two children. One I've seized just now
and sent her off—now I'll take the other.

OEDIPUS:
                                    Oh no . . .

CREON:
You'll have more to groan about in a moment.

OEDIPUS:
. . . you've taken my child? 940

CREON:
This one too—it won't be long, I promise you!

OEDIPUS:
Oh friends, friends! What will you do?—forsake me now?
Won't you drive this infidel off your land?

LEADER:
Move, stranger—out with you, faster!
You're bent on a new crime now, 945
what you've done is criminal.

CREON:
To his guards.
You there—time to escort her off.
By force, if she won't go freely.

ANTIGONE:
> Lost, lost!
Where to run? where do I go for help?—
what gods, what men?

> > CREON *moves toward* ANTIGONE.

LEADER:
> What are you doing, stranger? 950

CREON:
I won't touch the old man, but the girl's mine.

OEDIPUS:
Lords of the land!

LEADER:
> It's criminal, stranger, wrong!

CREON:
It's right!

LEADER:
> Right?—how?

CREON:
> I only take what's mine.

> > *Laying his hands on* ANTIGONE,
> > *as the* CHORUS *comes forward.*

OEDIPUS:
O Athens!

CHORUS:
          What are you doing, stranger? Let her go!
We'll come to blows in a moment, test our strength.

Moving toward CREON.

CREON:
Keep away!

CHORUS:
          Not from you—hellbent on this!

CREON:
I warn you, it's war with Thebes if you lay a hand on me.

OEDIPUS:
See? Didn't I tell you?

CHORUS:
          Take your hands off her,
give her up at once.

CREON:
          No commands—you have no power.

CHORUS:
Release her now, I tell you!

CREON:

To the guards with ANTIGONE
in hand.
          And I tell you—move out.

CHORUS:
> Come to the rescue! come, my countrymen—
> Athens, our Athens is laid low by force—
> come, come to the rescue!

ANTIGONE:
They tear me away—help me, strangers, friends!

OEDIPUS:
Where are you, child? I need you!   965

Groping for her.

ANTIGONE:
—Overwhelming me, dragging me off!

OEDIPUS:
Your hands, dear—touch me.

ANTIGONE:
> I can't, I'm helpless . . .

CREON:

Wheeling on the guards, as they drag away ANTIGONE *to the left.*

Go—now!

OEDIPUS:
> Oh god, dear god—

CREON:
                              These two sticks—
at least they'll never prop your steps again.
But since you're bent on defeating your own country,   970
your own kin—who commissioned me to do their will,
royal blood that I am—defeat us if you must.
Given time, you'll see this well, I know:
you do yourself no good, not now, not years ago,
indulging your rage despite the pleas of loved ones—   975
blind rage has always been your ruin.

                    Turning to go, but the CHORUS
                    blocks his way.

LEADER:
Stop where you are, stranger.

CREON:
                         Hands off me.

LEADER:
I'll never let you go—
Surrender those young girls.

CREON:
                         By heaven,
you'll give my city a greater hostage in a moment—   980
I'll seize more than his two daughters!

LEADER:
What are you going—?

CREON:
                    That old man—I'll seize him too!

LEADER:
Brave words.

CREON:
                    Actions too, now—unless, perhaps,
the king of the country blocks my way!

OEDIPUS:
Shameless words! Would you lay hands on me?   985

CREON:
No more from you—quiet.

OEDIPUS:
                    No!—
let the Powers of this place permit me,
let me break their sacred silence, one more curse.
You, you swine—with my eyes gone, you ripped away
the helpless darling of my eyes, my light in darkness!   990
So may the great god of the sun, the eye of the day
that sees all things, grant you and all your race
a life like mine—blind old age at last!

CREON:
Men of Athens, look, do you see this?

OEDIPUS:
They see you and me: they know my pain's a fact,   995
my revenge is empty breath.

CREON:
                    No holding back,
not now—alone as I am, old and slow,
I'll take that man by force.

                        Turning for OEDIPUS:

OEDIPUS:
No no!

CHORUS:
You're filled with arrogance, stranger,
brazen if you think you'll bring this off! 1000

CREON:
I do!

CHORUS:
Then it's the end of Athens, Athens is no more!

CREON:
The weak can defeat the strong in a case as just as mine.

OEDIPUS:
You hear what he is saying?

CHORUS:
Words for the wind—
god knows, he'll never act them out.

CREON:
God knows, not you!

Laying hold of OEDIPUS.

CHORUS:
What outrage—

CREON:
Outrage you will grin and bear. 1005

CHORUS:
O my people, all of you, lords of the land,
come quickly, come with a vengeance, quick,
before they cross our borders!

Enter THESEUS, *left, with full armed guard.*

THESEUS:
                         Why this shouting?
What's the trouble, what could alarm you so?—
interrupting me at the altar, my sacrifice   1010
to Poseidon, guardian of Colonus. Tell me,
I have to know it all. It's brought me
here on the run, a hard forced march.

OEDIPUS:
Dear friend! I know your voice—
I have suffered terrible things, just now,   1015
at the hands of that man there.

THESEUS:
                   What's wrong?
Who's tormenting you? Tell me.

OEDIPUS:
                       Creon there,
you're looking at him—he's making off
with my children, tearing them away,
the pair of them, my last, best support!   1020

THESEUS:
What are you saying?

OEDIPUS:
            All I suffered,
now you've heard it all.

THESEUS:
> *To his men.*

Quickly, one of you, to the altars!
Force our people to break off the rites,
make a dash for it, all of them,   1025
foot soldiers, cavalry, full gallop—
go where the two highways meet, hurry!—
before the girls are past that point
and I'm a mockery to my enemy here,
easy game for the first brutal hand.   1030
Go, I tell you, quickly.

> *A soldier rushes out, left.* THESEUS
> *turns to* CREON.

As for this . . .
if my anger went as far as he deserves,
he'd never slip through my fingers unscathed.
But now the barbaric law he imports himself,
that, no other, will bring its man to heel.   1035

You, you'll never leave this land until you return
those young girls, produce them before my eyes.
What you've done humiliates me
and your own country, the race that gave you life.
You have come to a city that practices justice,   1040
that sanctions nothing without law, but you,
you flout our authorities, make your inroads,
seize your prizes, commandeer at will!
Tell me, did you imagine Athens stripped of men,
peopled by slaves? Myself worth nothing?

                              No, 1045
it wasn't Thebes that trained you in your treachery:
Thebes makes no habit of rearing lawless sons.
Nor would she ever praise you if she learned
you're plundering me, plundering our gods,
dragging away their helpless suppliants by force. 1050
Never, I tell you, if I'd set foot on your soil,
even if I'd the most just claims on earth—
never without the sanction of your king,
whoever he might be, I'd never drag and plunder.
I would know how a stranger should conduct himself 1055
in the midst of citizens. But you disgrace a city
that deserves the opposite—your native city, too.
And the fullness of your years that brings you
ripe old age has emptied out your senses.

I've said it once, I'll say it one last time: 1060
someone had better bring those children back at once,
unless you'd like to remain here in our country,
a resident alien here for all time to come,
and not by your own free will—by force.
And I tell you this, believe me, 1065
from my lips and from the bottom of my heart.

LEADER:
You see what trouble you're in now, stranger?
You seem to come from a righteous people,
but your actions show you up for what you are.

CREON:
                                                Not at all,
I never thought your city unmanly, son of Aegeus,   1070
not injudicious either, as you suggest,
not when I did what I have done.
I simply judged that none of your people
could ever be so infatuated with kin of mine
as to shelter them against my will. And I knew   1075
they'd never harbor a father-killer . . . worse,
a creature so corrupt, exposed as the mate,
the unholy husband of his own mother.

Far better judgment—I knew as well as you—
resides on the Mount of Ares,   1080
in the great court that regulates your land.
Surely you could never suffer a fugitive
like him to live with you, within your walls.
Clinging to that belief I tried to take my prize.
Nor would I have bothered, but there he was,   1085
calling down his withering curses on myself
and all my sons. In the face of such attacks
I thought it only right to strike in self-defense.

So oppose me any way you like. My isolation
leaves me weak, however just my cause.   1090
But opposing you, old as I am,
I'll stop at nothing, match you blow for blow.
A man's anger can never age and fade away,
not until he dies. The dead alone feel no pain.

OEDIPUS:
Unctuous, shameless—where do you think your insults   1095
do more damage, my old age or yours? Bloodshed,
incest, misery, all your mouth lets fly at me,
I have suffered it all, and all against my will!
Such was the pleasure of the gods, raging,
perhaps, against our race from ages past.   1100
But as for me alone—
say my unwilling crimes against myself
and against my own were payment from the gods
for something criminal deep inside me . . . no, look hard,
you'll find no guilt to accuse me of—I am innocent!   1105

Come, tell me: if, by an oracle of the gods,
some doom were hanging over my father's head
that he should die at the hands of his own son,
how, with any justice, could you blame *me*?
I wasn't born yet, no father implanted me,   1110
no mother carried me in her womb—
I didn't even exist, not then! And if,
once I'd come to the world of pain, as come I did,
I fell to blows with my father, cut him down in blood—
blind to what I was doing, blind to whom I killed—   1115
how could you condemn that involuntary act
with any sense of justice?

                        And my mother . . .
wretched man, have you no shame? Your own sister!
Her marriage—forcing me to talk of that marriage!
Oh I'll tell it all, I won't be silent, not now, 1120
you and your blasphemous mouth have gone so far.
She was my mother, yes, she bore me—
oh the horror—I knew nothing, she knew nothing!—
and once she'd borne me then she bore me children,
her disgrace. But at least I know one thing: 1125
you slander her and me of your own free will,
but I made her my bride against my will,
I repeat this to the world against my will. No,
I'll not be branded guilty, not in that marriage,
not in the murder of my father, all those crimes 1130
you heap on me relentlessly, harrowing my heart.

One thing, answer me just one thing. If,
here and now, a man strode up to kill you,
you, you self-righteous—what would you do?
Investigate whether the murderer were your father 1135
or deal with him straight off? Well I know,
as you love your life, you'd pay the killer back,
not hunt around for justification. Well that,
that was the murderous pass *I* came to,
and the gods led me on, 1140
and my father would only bear me out, I know,
if he came back to life and met me face-to-face!

But you, you lack all justice, counting it well and good
to spew out anything at all—no line drawn between
what a man may say and things too dark to tell— 1145
you lash me with these charges, here, before these men.
And you flatter the fine, noble name of Theseus,
you exclaim how firmly Athens has been governed,
but piling on your praises you forget *this*:
if any land knows how to respect the gods 1150
with solemn rites, Athens excels them all.
And you were scheming to steal me out of Athens,
seize an old man, a suppliant—
you'd already carried off my daughters!

So now I cry to those Great Goddesses, 1155
I beg them, I storm them with my prayers—
Come to the rescue, fight for me, my champions!
So you can learn your lesson, Creon, learn
what breed of men stands guard around this city.

LEADER:
Our friend is a good man, my king. 1160
His fate has practically destroyed him;
he deserves our help.

THESEUS:
                    Enough words!
The criminals are escaping,
we the victims, we stand still.

CREON:
What would you have me do? I'm helpless. 1165

THESEUS:
Lead the way there, I'll escort you.
If you are holding the children close by
point them out to us. If the men who took them
are on the loose now, we can save our breath—
others will ride them down. They'll never escape
and cross our borders, never thank their gods for victory.
Come, move out! The spoiler's spoiled, I tell you,
Fate has got the hunter in her traps—
whatever's won by treachery won't last long.

And you'll have no one to back you in your scheme.
I know you weren't alone, without accomplices
when you hit this pitch of daring, this outrage
that inspires you now. You trusted to someone
when you set about your work.
I must look to that, and never render the city
weaker than one man. You catch my meaning?
Or does all this strike you now as nonsense,
just as when you were plotting out your scheme?

CREON:
Talk your fill, on your own native soil—
I can't quarrel here.
Once at home, I'll know what to do.

THESEUS:
Threaten away, but march, now! Oedipus,
you stay here in peace, you trust to this:
unless I die first, I'll never stop
until I've placed your children in your hands.

OEDIPUS:
Bless you, Theseus, for your noble spirit,
bless you for all the loyal pains you take for us.

Exit THESEUS, CREON, *and the guard, left; the* CHORUS *groups and scans the distance, chanting.*

CHORUS:
    O god, to be there!—
where the warring armies wheel and charge—
soon, soon fighting hand-to-hand 1195
in the brazen cries of battle!
There where Apollo guards the pass
    or down that torchlit shore
where the Great Goddesses tend the awesome rites
offering life to mortals after death, their lips 1200
   sealed by the golden key of silence
pressed upon them by the priests—
there, I think, Theseus spurs the fighting!
He and the two young captives, virgin sisters
soon will join in the battle cries inside our borders 1205
   victory ringing in their hearts!

   Yes or soon they'll clash
swinging round the snowy crag
driving west on the pastures,
borne on racing horses 1210
chariots racing down the wind—
   the enemy will be crushed!
Terrible, the armored might of Colonus
terrible the sons of Theseus in their power!
   Look, their bridle irons flashing, 1215
the cavalry of Athens thundering headlong on!
They honor Athena, reigning queen of horsemen—
honor the Sea-lord, guardian of our earth
   the Mother's loving son.

Speaking out in separate voices.

—Now for the fight, or is it still to come? 1220

—I'm filled with hope, with longing—
soon I'll see them face-to-face!

—Terrible what they have suffered—
    terrible pain inflicted by their kinsman.

—Today is the day that Zeus brings some great work to birth!

—Like a seer I sense the glory in these struggles—
   Rush me, wing me into the whirlwind, O dear god,
like a dove at the thunderheads of heaven I'd look down
I'd scan these struggles, I would see their glory!

Regrouping as a chorus.

Hear me, marshal of all the gods, 1230
Zeus, all-seeing Zeus!
Grant our defenders triumph
power to carry out the attack
   power to carry home their prizes!
Hear me, daughter of Zeus, mighty Athena! 1235
Apollo, lord of the hunt—your sister Artemis
    racing the flights of dappled streaking deer!
Come down, you gods, I beg you, come like armies joined—
unite to save our land and all our people!

The LEADER *suddenly turns to*
OEDIPUS.

LEADER:
My wandering friend, you won't call me 1240
a false prophet now, your lookout hasn't lied—
I can see your daughters, there, coming closer,
and an escort brings them on!

OEDIPUS:
                    Where?
How—what are you saying?

> *Enter* ANTIGONE *and* ISMENE *from
> the left, escorted by attendants with*
> THESEUS *in the lead.*

ANTIGONE:
                    Father, father!
If only a god would give you back your eyes, 1245
then you could see this prince of men
who's brought us back to you!

OEDIPUS:
                    Child!
You're here, both of you in the flesh?

ANTIGONE:
Yes! His strong arms have saved us—
Theseus, and his loyal comrades. 1250

OEDIPUS:
Closer, children, come to your father!
Let me embrace you—I never thought I'd feel you,
hold you again.

ANTIGONE:
            All you want, all will be done—
I long for it, father, just as much as you.

OEDIPUS:
Where, where are you? 1255

ANTIGONE:
Here, both together.

OEDIPUS:
                    Dearest, sweet young girls!

ANTIGONE:
Dear to their father, all his children.

OEDIPUS:
                              My supports,
props of an old man . . .

ANTIGONE:
                    And we share your pain,
your fate is ours.

OEDIPUS:
              I've got my dear ones now. Now,
even if I should die, I'm not destroyed, not utterly, 1260
not with the two of you beside me. Come, little ones,
here, press hard! I'll wrap my arms around you,
closer, tighter—father together with his children!
And give me rest from the journey I've been through,
so lonely, cruel . . . and tell me what's happened, 1265
briefly as you can. For girls so young
speeches should be short.

ANTIGONE:
                    Here he is—

                    Turning to THESEUS.

he saved us. Hear it from him, father,
he did it all. That's how brief I'll be.

OEDIPUS:
Dear friend, don't wonder at this, if I go on and on . . .   1270
my heart is bursting—finding my children back,
beyond my dreams! The joy they bring me,
well I know, I owe it all to you,
you saved them, yes, no other man alive.
May the gods reward you just as I desire,   1275
you and your great country. Here among you,
you alone of all mankind—
I have discovered reverence, humanity
and lips that never lie. I know from experience,
know these things I repay with words of thanks.   1280
Whatever I have, I have through you alone,
no other man on earth.

                    Groping toward THESEUS.
                    Give me your right hand,
my king, let me touch it, if it's permitted,
kiss your face . . . wait—

                    He stops.
                    What am I saying?
You touch *me*? How could I ask? So wretched,   1285
a man stained to the core of his existence!
I ask you? Never! I wouldn't let you,
even if you were willing. No, the only ones
who can share my pain are those who've borne it with me.
Theseus, stay where you are and take my thanks!   1290
And give me your loyal care in time to come,
just as you have until this very hour.

THESEUS:
No wonder you draw things out a little
with your children, delighting in them so,
or that you'd prefer to have words with them   1295
before you turn to me. That doesn't offend me,
I assure you. It's not through words but actions
that I want to set the luster on my life.
And you have proof: I haven't failed in a thing
I swore to do for you, old man. Here I am,   1300
and I've brought your daughters back alive,
untouched, for all the threats against them.
And how the fight was won—
why fill the air with empty boasting?
You'll learn it from them, embracing your two children.   1305

But there was some talk that struck me, just now,
as I was coming here. Give me your advice.
It's little to tell, but strange, worth our wonder,
and a mere man should never neglect a thing
that comes his way.

OEDIPUS:
                What is it, Theseus?   1310
Tell me. I know nothing of what you're asking.

THESEUS:
A man, they say, not of your own city
but still a kinsman—out of the blue he's come
and flung himself on Poseidon's altar, a suppliant,
where I was sacrificing just before I came.   1315

OEDIPUS:
What's his country? What does he want,
sitting, waiting there?

THESEUS:
                    I just know this:
they say he asks for a brief word with you,
it shouldn't be much trouble.

OEDIPUS:
                         What does he want?
Clinging to the altar—it's no small matter.   1320

THESEUS:
He simply wants to confer with you, they say,
then go back the way he came, unharmed.

OEDIPUS:
Who on earth can he be?
This suppliant of the god . . .

THESEUS:
See if you have a relative in Argos,   1325
someone who might beg this favor of you.

OEDIPUS:
Friend—stop right there!

THESEUS:
                    What's the matter?

OEDIPUS:
Ask no more.

THESEUS:
            About what? Tell me.

OEDIPUS:
Well I know, I can hear it in your words—
I know who that suppliant is.

THESEUS:
                     Who in the world?   *1330*
And why should I have any objection to him?

OEDIPUS:
My son, king—that son I hate! His words alone
would cause me the greatest pain of any words,
any man alive.

THESEUS:
           But why? Can't you listen?
He cannot make you act against your will.   *1335*
Why should it hurt you just to hear him out?

OEDIPUS:
Just that voice, my king,
the sound is loathsome to his father.
Don't drive me, don't force me to yield in this!

THESEUS:
But don't his prayers exert some force too? 1340
Look to it, what if the god has powers
you should respect?

ANTIGONE:
               Father, listen to me,
young as I am to offer you advice.
Permit the king to satisfy himself,
his sense of conscience, and serve the god 1345
as he thinks best—and for us, for our sake,
yield, let our brother come! Have no fear,
he'll never wrench you away from your resolve,
not with an argument against your interests.
What's the harm then, just to hear him out? 1350
The worst crimes, you know, are exposed
in the very telling. Yes, and you're his father—
so even if he'd inflict on you the worst wrong,
the worst outrage, father, it isn't right
for you to strike back in kind.

Oh let him come! 1355
Many other men have rebellious children,
quick tempers too . . . but they listen to reason,
they relent, the worst rage in their natures
charmed away by the soothing spells of loved ones.
Look to the past, not the present, consider all 1360
you suffered through *your* father and mother—
look hard at that. You will see, I think,
what a dreadful outcome waits on dreadful anger.
You've good reason to remember, deprived of your eyes—
eyes that can never see the light again.
                                    Yield to us! 1365
It isn't good for men with a decent cause
to beg too long, or a man to receive help,
then fail to treat a fellow-victim kindly.

OEDIPUS:
                                    Child,
it's hard for me, this pleasure you win from me
with all your pleading. But if your heart is set, 1370
so be it.
                    Turning to THESEUS.
        Just one thing, my friend,
if that man is coming here, never
let him get me in his clutches—never!

THESEUS:
Once is enough for that, old man,
I don't need to hear that twice. 1375
I'm not about to boast, but trust to this:
your life is safe, so long as a god saves mine.

*Exit right, with the royal guard,
while the* CHORUS *gathers around*
OEDIPUS.

CHORUS:
Show me a man who longs to live a day beyond his time
   who turns his back on a decent length of life,
I'll show the world a man who clings to folly.   1380
For the long, looming days lay up a thousand things
closer to pain than pleasure, and the pleasures disappear,
      you look and know not where
when a man's outlived his limit, plunged in age
and the good comrade comes who comes at last to all,   1385
not with a wedding-song, no lyre, no singers dancing—
the doom of the Deathgod comes like lightning
      always death at the last.

            Not to be born is best
when all is reckoned in, but once a man has seen the light
   the next best thing, by far, is to go back   1390
back where he came from, quickly as he can.
For once his youth slips by, light on the wing
lightheaded . . . what mortal blows can he escape
      what griefs won't stalk his days?
Envy and enemies, rage and battles, bloodshed   1395
and last of all despised old age overtakes him,
stripped of power, companions, stripped of love—
the worst this life of pain can offer,
      old age our mate at last.

This is the grief he faces—I am not alone— 1400
like some great headland fronting the north
hit by the winter breakers beating down
from every quarter—so he suffers,
terrible blows crashing over him
head to foot, over and over 1405
down from every quarter—
now from the west, the dying sun
now from the first light rising
now from the blazing beams of noon
now from the north engulfed in endless night. 1410

ANTIGONE:
Look there—I think it's the stranger coming toward us,
but at least the man's without an escort, father,
and his eyes are streaming tears,
he's struggling on his way.

OEDIPUS:
               Who is he?

                Enter POLYNICES, *left.*

ANTIGONE:
The one we've had in mind from the start— 1415
it's Polynices, here.

POLYNICES:
                    Oh, what will I do?
Cry for my own miseries first, my sisters?
Or the miseries of my old father,
look, before my eyes. I find him here,
an outcast, here in a strange land with you,   1420
two weak girls. And wrapped in such rags—appalling—
the filth of years clings to his old withered body,
wasting away the skin, the flesh on his ribs . . .
and his face, the blind sockets of his eyes,
and the white hair wild, flying in the wind!   1425
And all of a piece with this, I'm afraid, the scraps
he packs to fill his shriveled belly. So late,
to my everlasting shame I learn all this so late.

                    Turning to OEDIPUS.

I am the worst man alive, I swear it,
in all that touches you, the care you need.   1430
Hear it from me, no one else. But think . . .
even Zeus himself, in all his works,
keeps Mercy beside him, poised beside his throne—
so let her stand beside you now, my father!
There are cures for all the past wrongs done,   1435
no way to make them worse, not now.
                                    What, silence?
Father, say something, anything—don't turn away from me!
Nothing in answer to me? You'd reject me,
send me away, cursed with silence?
Nothing to tell me why you're raging so?   1440

                    To ANTIGONE *and* ISMENE.

You, you're the man's children, my own sisters!
Try, at least, to rouse our father from this,
this rock-bound, impenetrable silence.
So he won't reject me—a suppliant of the god—
won't cut me off, humiliated so,   1445
not a word in answer.

ANTIGONE:
                    Poor brother,
tell him yourself, exactly why you've come.
As the words flow on, they just may touch some joy
or hit some raw nerve, or tenderness and pity,
and somehow lend a voice to stony silence.   *1450*

POLYNICES:
Then I'll speak out—you're right, good advice—
first I call to the god himself as my defender.
From the god's altar the king of the country
raised me up and sent me here to you, empowered
to speak and listen, and go my way unharmed.   *1455*
These are the pledges I was given, strangers.
Keep them, please,
you and my sisters here, and my old father.

Now, father, I must tell you why I've come.
I am an outcast, driven from our fatherland.   *1460*
As your eldest-born, you see, I claimed the right
to sit upon your throne with all your powers.
For that, Eteocles, my younger brother,
up and thrust me from the land—
and he won out, not by force of argument,   *1465*
not by coming to grips in a test of strength,
no, he bribed the people to his side. And this,
I'm certain, must be the work of a Fury, your Fury,
the curse upon your house—all I've heard
from the seers has borne me out.

                        Well then,   1470
when I made my way to Argos, the old Doric city,
I took Adrastus' daughter for my wife
and bound to me by oath that country's best—
all the lords who had won their fame in combat—
so I might raise a great army, seven spears   1475
forged together, trained on Thebes,
and die for the justice of my cause
or drive out those who drove me from the land.

Yes, but why do I come before you now?
To kneel at your feet, my father! Bearing prayers, 1480
my own, and the prayers of all my comrades:
seven columns, seven spearheads closing
an iron ring around the plain of Thebes.
Who are the captains? That man of the whirling lance,
Amphiaraus, master of battle, master prophet,   1485
lord of the birds that help us see the future.
Second, Oeneus' son, Tydeus of Aetolia.
Third, Eteoclus, born in Argos. Fourth,
Hippomedon, sent to the wars by his father,
Talaus. The fifth, Capaneus, boasts to the skies   1490
he'll raze the walls of Thebes, blast them down with fire!
And sixth, riding out of Arcadia, Parthenopeus,
named for the virgin girl those years ago,
who married once and brought him into life—
Atalanta's trusty son. And last, myself,   1495
your son . . . or if not your son, surely the child
of a hard fate, and yours at least in name—
I lead the undaunted troops of Argos against Thebes.

We beg you now—by these, your children here,
by your own life, father, we all implore you!   1500
Relent, relent in your crushing rage against me,
as I march on to discipline my brother
who drove me out, robbed me of my fatherland.
If there is any truth at all in the oracles,
the side you join, they said, that side will triumph.   1505

So now by the springs, by all the gods of our race,
I beg you, listen to me, yield! Look at me now,
beggar and exile, an exile just like you:
we both fawn on the world for shelter,
you and I, we share the same fate. But he,   1510
he tyrannizes our house—it mortifies me so—
he lords it now, he mocks us both at once.
But if you stand side-by-side with me
and my resolve, father, with little effort,
little time, I'll fling him to the winds.   1515
And then I'll take you home and reestablish you
in your own house, establish myself as well,
once I've thrown the traitor out by force!

Stand by me and that can be my boast.
Without you I am powerless—I can't survive.   1520

LEADER:
For the sake of Theseus who sent him, Oedipus,
say something, whatever seems right to you,
before you send the man away.

OEDIPUS:
                    Believe me,
my friends, guardians of this country,
if Theseus hadn't sent the man my way, 1525
insisting that he hear some words from me,
he'd never have caught the ring of my response.
But now his wish will be granted before he goes.
Oh yes, he'll hear such words from me . . .
they'll bring his life no joy, 1530
  I tell you, never.

Wheeling on POLYNICES.

               You, degenerate—
you when you held the throne and scepter
your blood brother now holds in Thebes,
you drove me into exile, your own father!
You stripped me of my city, you put on my back 1535
these rags you weep to see, now, only now
you've sunk to the same depths of pain as I.
Well, you can keep your tears—but I,
I must suffer *this* so long as I'm alive:
you are the one I must remember— 1540
you destroyed my life! you made me brother
to this, this misery—you rooted me out—
thanks to you I wander, a vagabond, abandoned,
begging my daily bread from strangers through the world.
And if these two girls had not been born to nurse me, 1545
I'd be good as dead—for all you cared! But now,
look, they save my life, they feed me, tend me,
why, they're men, not women, look, when it comes
to shouldering my burdens. But you, my brace of boys,
you're born of a stranger, you're no sons of mine! 1550

And so the eyes of fate look down upon you now,
but not yet with the lightning that will strike
if those armies are really marching hard on Thebes.
Impossible—you'll never tear that city down. No,
you'll fall first, red with your brother's blood   1555
and he stained with yours—equals, twins in blood.
Such were the curses *I* hurled against you long ago
and now, again, I call them up to fight beside me!
You will learn, at last, to respect your parents—
I'll teach you to heap contempt upon your father   1560
because he's blind and bore such ruthless sons.
These daughters never did such things, but you,
you and your pious supplications and your throne—
my curses have you in their power now,
if that Justice, declared from the first of time,   1565
still shares the throne of Zeus with the everlasting laws.

You—die!
        Die and be damned!
                        I spit on you! Out!—
your father cuts you off! Corruption—scum of the earth!—
out!—and pack these curses I call down upon your head:
never to win your mother-country with your spear,   1570
never return to Argos ringed with hills—
                            Die!
Die by your own blood brother's hand—die!—
killing the very man who drove you out!
So I curse your life out!
I call on the dark depths of Tartarus brimming hate,   1575
where all our fathers lie, to hale you home!
I cry to the great goddesses of this grove!
I cry to the great god War
who planted that terrible hatred in your hearts!
Go!—with all my curses thundering in your ears—   1580
go and herald them out to every man in Thebes
and all your loyal comrades under arms! Cry out
that Oedipus has bequeathed these last rights,
these royal rights of birth to both his sons!

LEADER:
I take no joy in your journeys, Polynices,　　　　　　　　　1585
whatever brought you here.
Now go back, as quickly as you can.

POLYNICES:
Oh the long road, the labor come to nothing,
oh my captains! Look how the marches end,
the road our armies trampled out of Argos . . .　　　　　　1590
there's so much death at journey's end, dear god,
I cannot breathe a word of it to my comrades,
nor can I turn them back—I must go to meet
this doom in silence.
　　　　　　　　　My sisters, you, his daughters!
Now that you've heard our father's iron curses,　　　　　　1595
I implore you in the name of the gods,
if father's curses all come true at last,
and if some way back to Thebes is found for you,
don't neglect me, please, give me burial,
the honored rites of death.　　　　　　　　　　　　　　　1600
And the care that wins you praises now,
for helping this old man, will win you more
for the loving service you perform for me.

ANTIGONE:
Polynices, listen to me, I beg you,
just one thing.

POLYNICES:
                  Dearest, what? Antigone, tell me.   1605

ANTIGONE:
Turn back the armies, back to Argos, quickly!
Don't destroy yourself and Thebes.

POLYNICES:
                              Unthinkable—
how could I ever raise the same force again,
once I flinched in the crisis?

ANTIGONE:
                      Again? Oh dear boy,
why should your anger ever rise again?   1610
What do you stand to gain,
razing your father-city to the roots?

POLYNICES:
Exile is humiliating, and I am the elder
and being mocked so brutally by my brother—

ANTIGONE:
                                Don't you see?
You carry out father's prophecies to the finish!   1615
Didn't he cry aloud you'd kill each other,
fighting hand-to-hand?

POLYNICES:
                    True,
that's his wish—but I, I can't give up.

ANTIGONE:
Oh no . . . but who would dare follow you now,
hearing the oracles the man's delivered?   1620

POLYNICES:
I simply won't report them, not a word.
The good leader repeats the good news,
keeps the worst to himself.

ANTIGONE:
So, my brother, your heart is set on this?

POLYNICES:
Yes—
                        ANTIGONE *embraces him.*
        don't hold me back. The road is waiting—   1625
I must travel down that road, doomed by fate
and the curses of my father, all his swarming Furies.
But the two of you, god bless you on your way
if you carry out my wishes once I'm dead . . .
you cannot help me any more in life.   1630
Now, let me go.
                    Gently slipping free of ANTIGONE.
        Goodbye, dear ones.
You'll never look on me again, alive.

ANTIGONE:
Oh my brother!

POLYNICES:
                No mourning for me now.

ANTIGONE:
Who wouldn't mourn you, Polynices?
Rushing to death with open eyes!   1635

POLYNICES:
Death—if that's my fate.

ANTIGONE:
Please, dear brother, listen!

POLYNICES:
Don't try to dissuade me:
it's my duty.

ANTIGONE:
          It's unbearable . . .
robbed of you I might as well be dead.   1640

POLYNICES:
                           No,
that's in the hands of a dark power, destiny—
whether we live or die, who knows?
But the two of you, at least,
I pray to god you never meet with harm.
The world can see you don't deserve to suffer.   1645

Exit, to the left.

CHORUS:
Look, new agonies now, I see them come
from the blind stranger now,
    such heavy doom for his son
unless, perhaps, it is actually destiny at work.
It is not for me to call the commands of heaven empty, futile—
Time is watching, watching over us always,
   bringing down the lives of some,
raising others the next day
into the light again—

Thunder sounds in the distance.

        Listen,
thunder, the sky—Oh god . . .

OEDIPUS:
                    Children, children,   1655
can someone, anyone go for Theseus?
Bring the great man here!

ANTIGONE:
Why so urgent, father, such commands?

OEDIPUS:
This winged thunder of Zeus will take me down
to Death at any moment—send for him, quickly!   1660

*Thunder again, louder. The elders
cry out singly.*

CHORUS:
—Tremendous! Listen, over and over, the skies are crashing—

—Immense, a marvel, flung by the hand of god!

       —The terror's bristling through my hair,
my heart's racing—the lightning blazing the heavens—again!

—Where will it end? what birth will it let loose?   1665

—Oh it terrifies me—the lightning
never bursts for nothing, never
without some dread, some awesome—

A huge peal of thunder, lightning.

—O great sky—O god!

OEDIPUS:
       Dear children,
the destined end has come upon your father.   1670
I can turn my face from it no more.

ANTIGONE:
How do you know? Are you sure this is the sign?

OEDIPUS:
I know it all too well. Quickly, I beg you—
go, someone, bring the lord of the land.

Thunder and lightning crashing on the spot.

CHORUS:
—There—look, blast on blast, it's all around us, 1675
    shattering, thunderheads exploding!

—Mercy, O great power, mercy!—if you are bringing down
  some strange darkness, down on the earth, our mother—

—Give me mercy, I beg you, kindness, not disaster
  for setting eyes on him, a man accurst! 1680

—Don't curse me too, I cry to you,
  Zeus, Zeus, my king!

OEDIPUS:
                Theseus—is he near?
Will he find me still alive, children,
and master of my mind?

ANTIGONE:
              What do you want?
What do you have in mind? what debt, what pledge? 1685

OEDIPUS:
For all his kindness, all he did for me,
now I would give that gift I promised him.

> *The* CHORUS *closes ranks around*
> OEDIPUS.

CHORUS:
Come, Theseus, come if you're close at hand
    or come from the green depths,
the grove of the Ocean Lord Poseidon, come   1690
from sacrificing the oxen at his altar, oh come now!
In the stranger's eyes you earn his kindness, rightful kindness,
you and your city Athens and your people—blessings,
he will bless you for your kindness.
Theseus, king, come quickly!

> *Enter* THESEUS, *right, with his
> attendants.*

THESEUS:
                    What's this?   1695
Another outcry, ringing from all of you,
as clearly from my people as my guest. Why,
the lightning of Zeus?—the hail, the cloudburst
breaking on our heads? When the gods send such a storm
the wildest dark forebodings are in order—   1700
anything can happen.

OEDIPUS:
            My king, I longed for you
and you stand before my eyes! There must be a god
who grants you this, the fortune of your coming.

THESEUS:
What is it, son of Laius, what now?

OEDIPUS:
My life hangs in the balance.
I must not die in bad faith, failing
the pledge I made to you and Athens.

THESEUS:
What proves your time has come, what signs?

OEDIPUS:
                        The gods!
They are their own heralds—they bring me the word,
never failing the signs decreed so long ago.

THESEUS:
You mean, old man, what makes this clear is—

OEDIPUS:
Thunder, yes! crash on crash, incessant—
the lightning, bolt on bolt, hurled by the hand
that never knows defeat.

THESEUS:
              Oh I believe you.
Time and again I've seen your prophecies come right,
you never lie. Now tell me what to do.

OEDIPUS:
I will reveal it all to you, son of Aegeus,
the power that age cannot destroy,
the heritage stored up for you and Athens.
Soon, soon I will lead you on myself, no hand   1720
to lead my way, to the place where I must die.
Never reveal the spot to mortal man,
not even the region, not where it lies hidden.
Then it will always form a defense for you,
a bulwark stronger than many shields,   1725
stronger than the spear of massed allies.

But these are great mysteries . . .
words must never rouse them from their depths.
You will learn them all for yourself, once
you come to our destination, you alone.   1730
I cannot utter them to your people here,
nor to my own children, love them as I do.
No, you alone must keep them safe forever,
and when you reach the end of your own life,
reveal them only to your eldest, dearest son,   1735
and then let him reveal them to his heir
and so through the generations, on forever.

Then you will keep your city safe from Thebes,
the fighters sprung from the Dragon's teeth.
So many cities ride roughshod over their neighbors—   1740
reckless, even if that neighbor lives in peace—
for the gods are strong but slow to see and strike
when a man has flung all fear of god to the winds
and turned to frenzy. Never risk defeat, Theseus,
never divulge what you will learn.
                                      Well,   1745
you know these things, no need to preach to you.
On now, on to our destination . . . I can feel
the god within me urge me on—onward,
we must hesitate no more.

Suddenly possessed of new strength,
OEDIPUS rises to his feet; the children
attempt to help him, but he begins to
move with slow, majestic steps,
beckoning all to follow his path.

Follow me, O my children,
come this way. I stand revealed at last, look, 1750
a strange new role for me—I am your guide
as you were once your father's. On, onward!
No, don't touch me, let me find that sacred grave myself
where the Fates will bury Oedipus in this land.
This way, come, walk on! This is the way 1755
they lead me on, Hermes the Escort of the Dead,
Persephone, Queen of the Dead.

Moving firmly to the right.

O light of the sun,
no light to me! Once you were mine, I think . . .
now for the last time I feel you warm my flesh,
now I go to hide the last breath of life 1760
in the long house of Death.

To THESEUS.

Dearest friend,
you and your country and your loyal followers,
may you be blessed with greatness,
and in your great day remember me, the dead,
the root of all your greatness, everlasting, ever-new. 1765

Passing from sight, he leads forth his
daughters, THESEUS and attendants to
the right. The CHORUS gathers at the
altar, praying.

CHORUS:
Now if it's not forbidden
now let me adore you with my prayers—
invisible, proud Persephone and you,
king of the dead engulfed in night
iron king of the dead, I pray to you! 1770
   Not in pain, not by a doom
that breaks the heart with mourning,
let our friend go down to the world below
the all-enshrouding infinite fields of the dead
the dark house of Death. Numberless agonies 1775
blind and senseless, came his way in life—
now let some power
   some justice grant him glory!
                           Dark Furies!
   Goddesses of the Earth—and you,
the huge beast unconquered, lodged 1780
at the gates that take in all the world—
snarling from the cavern's jaws
   untameable Watchman of the Dead,
the dread of the oldest legends! Death,
I beg you, son of Earth and the Black Depths, 1785
let Cerberus leave the pathway clear for him, our friend
passing down to the endless meadows of the dead.
God of eternal sleep, I call to you,
   let Oedipus rest forever.

Enter a MESSENGER, *from the right.*

MESSENGER:
        My countrymen,
the quickest way to tell you is this:
Oedipus is gone.
But what took place—it's not short in the telling,
not short in all that really happened there.

LEADER:
He's dead, poor man?

MESSENGER:
       Make no mistake,
he's gone, he's left the world forever.

LEADER:
         How?
Some stroke of the gods and free from pain?

MESSENGER:
Yes—there we come to the marvel of it all.
You know how he left this spot, of course,
you saw him go. No friend to lead the way,
he led us all himself.

                    Now, when he reached   1800
the steep descent, the threshold rooted deep
in the earth by the great brazen steps, he stopped ...
pausing at one of the many branching paths there,
near the bowl scooped out in the smooth stone
where the pact sealed by Theseus and Perithous   1805
is cut in stone forever. He took his stand midway
between that bowl and the Rock of Thoricus,
the hollow wild-pear and the marble tomb,
and sat him down and loosed his filthy rags.
Then he called for his daughters, commanded them   1810
to bring water from some running spring, water
to bathe himself and pour the last libations.
And they climbed the gentle rise, just in sight,
the Hill of Demeter, goddess of new green life,
and soon returned with what their father ordered,   1815
bathed him in holy water, decked his body out
in shining linen, the custom for the dead.

But when he was content that all was done,
and of all he wanted, nothing more was needed,
nothing left to do—all at once   1820
Zeus of the Underworld thundered from the depths,
and the young girls shuddered in horror at the sound,
they fell at their father's knees, choked with tears,
they couldn't stop, beating their breasts, wailing,
endless ... but when he heard their sharp piercing cry,   1825
he flung his arms around them both and said, "My children,
this is the day that ends your father's life.
All that I was on earth is gone:
no longer will you bear the heavy burden
of caring for your father. It was hard, I know,   1830
my children, but one word alone repays you
for the labor of your lives—love, my children.
You had love from me as from no other man alive,
and now you must live without me all your days to come."

It was unbearable. Locked in each other's arms   1835
they heaved and sobbed, all three as one.
But when they'd made an end of grief
and the long wail rose up no more,
a deep silence fell . . . and suddenly,
a voice, someone crying out to him, startling,   1840
terrifying, the hair on our heads bristled—
it was calling for him, over and over,
echoing all around us now—it was some god!
"You, you there, Oedipus—what are we waiting for?
You hold us back too long! We must move on, move on!"   1845

Then, knowing it was the god that called him on,
he asked for Theseus, and when our king came up
beside him, Oedipus spoke out, "Oh dear friend,
give my children the binding pledge of your right hand,
and children, give him yours. And swear that you   1850
will never forsake them, not if you can help it—
you will do all within your power, your kindness,
all that is best for them—now and always."

And Theseus, noble man, not giving way to grief,
swore to carry out the wishes of his friend.   1855
And soon as he made that pledge, Oedipus
reached out at once with his blind hands,
feeling for his children, saying, "Oh my children,
now you must be brave, noble in spirit,
you must leave this place behind,   1860
and never ask to see what law forbids
or hear the secret voices none may hear.
Now go—quickly. Only the appointed one,
Theseus, let him stand beside me:
he must see this mystery,   1865
he must witness what will happen now."

That was the last we heard him say, all of us
clustering there, and as we followed the daughters
sobbing, streaming tears . . . moving away we turned
in a moment, looked back, and Oedipus— 1870
we couldn't see the man—he was gone—nowhere!
And the king, alone, shielding his eyes,
both hands spread out against his face as if—
some terrible wonder flashed before his eyes and he,
he could not bear to look. And then, quickly, 1875
we see him bow and kiss the ground and stretch
his arms to the skies, salute the gods of Olympus
and the powers of the Earth in one great prayer,
binding both together.
              But by what doom
Oedipus died, not a man alive can say, 1880
only Theseus, our king.
No blazing bolt of the god took him off,
no whirlwind sweeping inland off the seas,
not in his last hour. No, it was some escort
sent by the gods or the dark world of the dead, 1885
the lightless depths of Earth bursting open in kindness
to receive him. That man went on his way,
I tell you, not with trains of mourners,
not with suffering or with sickness, no,
if the death of any mortal ever was one, 1890
his departure was a marvel!

Consider my story madness if you will.
I don't want your belief, not if you think I'm mad.

LEADER:
And where are the children, Theseus and his friends?

MESSENGER:
Not far. Listen. You hear the sounds of weeping? 1895
It's clear, they're coming right this way.

Enter a solemn cortege, right, with ANTIGONE *and* ISMENE *in the lead, chanting a dirge as the* CHORUS *gathers around them.*

ANTIGONE:
O the misery,
now it is ours, all ours, and not for the moment now
but all our lives, we wail the death
the curse on the blood our blood
our doom born in us by our father . . .   1900
   O for his sake, as long as he lived
we bore his agony, day after day, and now
at the last a grief beyond imagining, baffling—
all we have seen and suffered, all is ours to tell.

CHORUS:
What happened?

ANTIGONE:
We can only guess, my friends.   1905

CHORUS:
He's really gone?

ANTIGONE:
And just as you would have wanted,
wanted most—how else?—when neither war
nor the crashing waves struck him down
but he was snatched away by the fields unseen
swept away by a strange, swift doom . . .   1910
   and O what pain for us!
A deadly night has fallen on our eyes.
Where, I ask you, where do we wander now?—
what alien land, what heaving salt seas—
where will we find the bitter bread of life?   1915

ISMENE:
Where on earth? Oh god, let murderous Death
join me to my old father in the grave . . . such anguish—
how can I face the life that I must live?

CHORUS:
Best of children, sisters arm-in-arm,
we must bear what the gods give us to bear— 1920
don't fire up your hearts with so much grief.
No reason to blame the pass you've come to now.

ANTIGONE:
                                                So,
you can really yearn for sorrows past to come again!
What wrenched my heart was love, love after all
as long as I held my father in my arms! 1925
Father, O dear father
  now you shroud yourself
in the dark world of the dead forever
yes but not even there, there below the earth—
you'll never lack our love, my sister's love and mine. 1930

CHORUS:
His work is done?

ANTIGONE:
                    And done as he wanted most.

CHORUS:
How, what do you mean?

ANTIGONE:
                    He has died on foreign soil
the soil of his choice . . . he has his bed forever
covered deep in the shadows of the dead and
left behind him mourning warm with tears.   1935
My eyes are streaming for you, father,
    you see? I grieve, I mourn you—
cannot quench my grief, can't wipe from sight
the blinding tears of sorrow. O you wanted to die
on foreign soil, but so alone, so desolate—   1940
why not in my arms?

ISMENE:
                    It breaks my heart!
What awaits us now, dear sister, what new fate?
We're destitute, robbed of father.

CHORUS:
                    But look,
he's free, he's ended his life with blessings—
children, end your grief. No one alive   1945
is free and clear of pain.

ANTIGONE:
                    Back, dear,
let's hurry back!

ISMENE:
              Why, to do what?

ANTIGONE:
I'm mad with longing—

ISMENE:
                  What?

ANTIGONE:
To see that last home in the earth—

ISMENE:
Whose?

ANTIGONE:
       Father's! Oh god help me— 1950

ISMENE:
How can we? It's forbidden,
can't you see—?

ANTIGONE:
          Why rail against me so?

ISMENE:
And don't you remember too—?

ANTIGONE:
              What else, what more?

ISMENE:
He's gone without a tomb, and no one saw him go.

ANTIGONE:
Take me there, take me, kill me too!

ISMENE:
               So desperate . . . 1955
what's left for me? So deserted, lost—
how can I go on living?

CHORUS:
       Children,
dear ones have no fear.

ANTIGONE:
>   But where to go, to escape?

CHORUS:
You escaped before.

ANTIGONE:
>   Escaped what?

CHORUS:
Ruin, disaster—both of you.

ANTIGONE:
>   Oh yes,   1960
well I know—

CHORUS:
>   Then what do you have in mind?

ANTIGONE:
How can we travel home to Thebes?
I see no way.

CHORUS:
>   Don't go home, don't even try!

ANTIGONE:
But we're in such straits.

CHORUS:
>   You were before!

ANTIGONE:
Bad enough then, but now it's so much worse!   1965

CHORUS:
True, true, a terrible sea of troubles
overwhelms you both.

ANTIGONE:
     Oh god, where do we turn?
What last hope? Where will the great power,
destiny, drive us now?

       Enter THESEUS *and his guard from the right.*

THESEUS:
  Stop, my children, weep no more. Here   1970
  where the dark forces store up kindness
  both for living and the dead,
  there is no room for grieving here—
  it might bring down the anger of the gods.

ANTIGONE:
  Oh Theseus, we beg you on our knees.   1975

THESEUS:
  What do you want, children? Why so urgent?

ANTIGONE:
  We long to see our father's tomb with our own eyes!

THESEUS:
  Impossible. It's forbidden: you must not go.

ANTIGONE:
  Why not? Majesty, king of Athens!

THESEUS:
> Your father
> forbade it, children. He commanded me
> that no one may go near that place,
> not a living voice invade that grave:
> it's sacred, it's his everlasting rest.
> And he said that if I kept my pledge
> I'd keep my country free of harm forever.
> I swore it, and the powers heard my vows,
> and Zeus's son above all,
> the guardian of our oaths who sees all things.

ANTIGONE:
> So be it. If this is father's will,
> we will be content—we must.
> But send us back to Thebes, I beg you,
> home to our old ancestral house.
> Somehow we must stop the slaughter
> marching against our brothers!

THESEUS:
> That I will do, and whatever else I can
> to benefit your lives and please the dead,
> the great dead, swept from sight just now.
> That is my part—I must never fail.

CHORUS:
> Come, my children, weep no more,
> raise the dirge no longer. All rests
> in the hands of a mighty power.

Exit ANTIGONE *and* ISMENE,
*accompanied by escorts, to the left,
the direction of Thebes;* THESEUS
and the CHORUS *to the right,
toward Athens.*

A NOTE ON THE TEXT OF SOPHOCLES

THIS BOOK contains an English translation, by Robert Fagles, of three plays which were first performed, before a Greek-speaking audience, in the fifth century B.C. The reader who consults the notes on pages 395–419 will soon become aware that in many passages, some of them important for overall interpretation, there is scholarly disagreement about the words of the original Greek. This translation, though it follows in the main the text of A. C. Pearson, sometimes adopts a different reading—that of Sir Richard Jebb, for example, or the most recent editor, Roger Dawe. The text is not the only matter in dispute; lines are often assigned to different speakers, and stage directions (even such vital matters as exits and entrances) vary from one edition or translation to another. These problems stem from the extraordinary nature of the process by which the words of Sophocles have been preserved for over two thousand years.

He was not, in the modern sense, a "writer"; the official inscription commemorating the winner of the dramatic competition for the year 447 B.C., for example, says: "Sophocles was the teacher." He taught his chorus their songs and his actors their lines; like Shakespeare, he was a playwright—not a "writer" but a "maker" of plays: author, composer, choreographer and director all in one. But he must have worked from a written version, and these manuscripts of his are the most likely source of the book texts we know were in circulation in late fifth-century Athens. These texts are the origin of the long, handwritten tradition which saved seven of his plays from oblivion so that they were available for Aldo Manuzio of Venice, who issued the first printed edition in 1502.

About the books which were produced, circulated privately and also bought and sold in fifth-century Athens we know very little more than the fact that manuscripts were circulated among friends and copies made for private use; copies were also made for sale by booksellers' employees (probably slaves). In any such hand-copied tradition errors abound and tend to be perpetuated; in addition, the format used for recording dramatic texts was one which invited involuntary error on a large scale. We have no such manuscripts from Sophocles' time, but fragments of papyrus books from Ptolemaic Egypt, the earliest dating from the third century B.C., give us an idea of what they must have been like. The lines of dialogue are arranged in columns, to be read from left to right and top to bottom. Words are not divided, and punctuation is almost nonexistent. Speakers are identified only at rare intervals; after such identification only change of speaker is marked—by a short dash under the first letters of the line where it occurs (if there is a space or a colon later in the line, the speaker changes there and not at the beginning).

Quite apart from the compounded errors and the deliberate omissions and interpolations which might occur in the book text, there was undoubtedly much distortion in the versions staged by the traveling theatrical companies which, in the fourth century, took the classics of Attic drama to every corner of the Greek world. Theatrical producers, as we know from the bizarre versions of Shakespeare's plays performed in the seventeenth and eighteenth centuries, have no qualms when it comes to cutting or adding to suit the fashion of the time. By the second half of the fourth century such tampering with the classic texts seems to have become a matter of public concern in Athens, for in 330 B.C. the leading Athenian statesman, Lycurgus, proposed legislation designed to ensure that in Athens, if not elsewhere, the plays of Aeschylus, Sophocles and Euripides would be staged in correct versions. The actors had to read over, with a city magistrate, the official text; no departures from it would be permitted. But we do not know what this official text was like; it may have contained interpolations and alterations that came into the text early and remained undetected.

What the situation obviously called for was editorial work on the part of scholars, but this was to take place not in the Athens of Lycurgus but in the following century and at Alexandria, the new city founded by Alexander in Egypt. Under the Macedonian dynasty which ruled Egypt after Alexander's death, the great collections of the Alexandrian library were assembled, and the scholars and poets attached to it began the long task of comparing manuscripts and making commentaries. (King Ptolemy III, we are told, managed to acquire for the library the "official" Athenian copy of the tragic poets.) It is from these Alexandrian editions that our text derives; but they were based on a textual tradition which could easily have suffered major corruption, addition and omission in the years between the death of Sophocles in 406 and the law of Lycurgus in 330. It is this blank page in the history of the text which allows modern scholars to make a case, to take one famous example, for omitting lines 904-5 through 920 (993-1012 in this translation) in Antigone's last speech.

The Alexandrian editions set a standard that helped to protect the dramatic texts from major interpolation and corruption. Meanwhile the danger of contamination from reckless theatrical adaptation lessened as performance of what were now ancient classics became a rare phenomenon. As with the passing of the years those classics became more ancient still, their words more difficult to understand, their content more alien to the religious and philosophical ideas of the times, demand for copies ceased; in the last centuries of the Roman Empire the bulk of the great legacy of Attic drama vanished forever as the last papyrus rolls disintegrated. A selection, however, was preserved, probably for use in schools: seven plays of Aeschylus, seven of Sophocles and—a reflection of his greater popularity in later ages—ten of Euripides. In the fifth century A.D., as the old Roman civilization collapsed in the West, knowledge of Greek was extinguished; Dante, who placed Homer in the limbo of the pagan poets in his great poem, could not have read the text of Homer even if he had seen a copy of it. But in the East, in the Greek-speaking empire of Byzantium, the selected tragic texts continued to be copied for school use, and papyrus was replaced by more durable parchment. By the tenth century A.D. the copyists had abandoned the ancient capital letters for the smaller cursive script of their own time, which observed word division and so improved legibility. The editors also replaced the old confusing signs for change of speakers with the modern system—an abbreviation of the character's name before each new speech. In the late centuries of the Byzantine Empire there was a revival of scholarly interest in the ancient texts (it was at this time that an old manuscript containing nine more plays of Euripides was discovered). Scholarly editors produced editions of the extant remains of Greek tragedy in which the text was surrounded on all sides by selections from commentaries ancient and modern.

Meanwhile in Western Europe, especially in Italy, interest in ancient Greek literature was on the rise. Boccaccio, in the generation after Dante, studied the language under a native Greek teacher, and, as demand increased, manuscripts of the Greek classics were brought across the Adriatic in increasing number. As the Turkish armies approached the capital of Byzantium, scholars fled to the West to interpret and teach. When at last the city fell to the Turks in 1453, manuscripts of almost all the Greek literature we now possess were already circulating in handwritten copies in the West; in the course of the sixteenth century the first printed editions appeared. Since the publication of those first editions, which, for the most part, simply reproduced the particular manuscript the printer had at his disposal, thousands of scholars have worked to clear the text of the errors and corruptions that are the inevitable product of two thousand years of handwritten transmission. Determination of the dates and relationships of the more than two hundred manuscripts which survive, comparison of variant readings, careful study of the prevalent types of error to be found in the work of Byzantine copyists, a constantly refined understanding of the grammar, syntax and characteristic idioms of fifth-century Greek, and an exact analysis of the subtle and complicated metric patterns of the choral odes—all these scholarly disciplines have combined to produce a Greek text of which we can say with some confidence, that even though many disputed (and some desperately corrupt) passages remain, it is closer to the text of the Sophoclean original than anything that has been available since the first five centuries before the birth of Christ.

TEXTUAL VARIANTS

Listed below are the readings adopted wherever the translation represents a text other than that of A. C. Pearson (Oxford: Oxford University Press, 1924; reprinted with corrections, 1928). In most of these cases the text preferred is that of Sir Richard Jebb (Cambridge: Cambridge University Press, *Antigone*, 3rd edition, 1900; *Oedipus Tyrannus*, 2nd edition, 1887; *Oedipus at Colonus*, 3rd edition, 1900) or Roger Dawe (Leipzig: Teubner, *Oedipus Tyrannus*, 1975; *Antigone, Oedipus at Colonus*, 1979). The line numbers refer to the Greek original.

ANTIGONE

24	chrêsei—J	576	XO.—J
108	oxytoroî—D	606	pant' agreuôn—J
110	hos . . . Polyneikous—J	628	tês mellogamou nymphês—Mss.
130	hyperopliais—J	674	symmachou—J
196	ephagnisai—J	687	chaterôi—J
213	pou g'—J	782	ktêmasi—J
241	stochazei—J	859	oikton—J
351	ochmazetai—J	966	Kyanean pelagei—J
368	pareirôn—Mss.	1293	EX.—D
551	gelô g'—J	1301	hêd' oxythêktôi bômia peri xiphei—J
572	IS.—Mss.	1303	kleinon lachos—J
574	IS.—Mss.		

OEDIPUS TYRANNUS

194	epouron—J	971	paronta—J
425	ha s' exisôsei—J	1035	deinon—J
525	toupos—J	1091	se ge . . . Oidipoun—J
685	proponoumenas—J	1101	g' eunateira tis—J
742	melas—D	1108	helikôpidôn—D
891	thixetai—J	1280	kaka—Mss.
894	euxetai—J	1350	elys'—J
943–44	Polybus; / AG. ei de mê—Mss.	1513	eai zên, tou biou—J

OEDIPUS AT COLONUS

79 soi—J
154 prosthêsei—J
198 hêsychaiai / OI. iô moi moi. / AN. basei—J
243 toumou [UU] antomai—D
278 môrous—D
321 monês tod' esti, dêlon—D
369 loigôi—D
458 prostatisi—J
547 an, hous ephoneus', em' apôlesan—J
716 hali cherson—D
861–62 legois an. KR. touto nyn pepraxetai, / ên mê m'—D
882 [Zeus moi xynistô.]—J
954–55 to follow 959—D
1061 eis nomon—J
1068 katheis'—J
1069 [stomiôn]—J
1076 antasein—J
1083–84 anôth' . . . eôrêsasa—D
1118 hou kasti . . . toumon hôd'—J
1164 elthein monon—J
1176 toud'—J
1231 plaga—J
1250–53 in Mss. order—J
1348 dêmouchoi—J
1359 kakôn—J
1435–36 sphô d' euodoiê Zeus, tad' ei thanonti moi / teleit', epei ou moi zônti g'—J
1453–54 taut' aei chronos, strephôn—J
1492 akra / peri gual'—J
1560–61 lissomai / apona mêd'—J
1632 horkian—J
1694 pherein chrê—Mss.
1702 oude g' enerth'—J
1715 authis hôd'—J
1733 epenarixon—J
1752 xyn'—J

NOTES ON THE TRANSLATION

ANTIGONE

4 *The two of us:* the intimate bond between the two sisters (and the two brothers) is emphasized in the original Greek by an untranslatable linguistic usage—the dual, a set of endings for verbs, nouns and adjectives that is used only when two subjects are concerned (there is a different set of endings—the plural—for more than two). Significantly, Antigone no longer uses these forms to speak of herself and her sister after Ismene refuses to help her bury their brother.

6 *Our lives are pain:* the translation here is dictated rather by the logic of the passage than the actual Greek words. The phrase in Greek to which these words correspond is clearly corrupt (it seems to interrupt a culminating series of negatives with a positive), and no satisfactory emendation or explanation has ever been offered.

12 *The doom reserved for enemies:* this seems to refer to the fact that Creon had also exposed the corpses of the other six (non-Theban) attackers of the city; they are foreign "enemies," whereas Polynices, for Antigone, is still a "friend," since he was a blood relative. The exposure of the other bodies was part of the legend as we find it elsewhere (in Euripides' play *The Suppliants,* for example) and is referred to in Tiresias' speech to Creon later in our play (1202–5). Some scholars interpret the Greek differently, to mean "evils planned by enemies," i.e., by Creon.

43 *Stoning to death:* a penalty which involves the community in the execution; it is therefore particularly appropriate in cases of treason, where the criminal has acted against the whole citizen body. It depends, of course, on the willingness of the citizens to carry it out, and it is noticeable that though Creon later refuses to accept Haemon's assertion that public opinion favors Antigone (776–82), he changes his mind about the penalty and substitutes one which does not require citizen participation.

52 *Will you lift up his body . . . ?* If she is to bury the body (and she speaks of "lifting" it), Antigone obviously needs Ismene's help; without it all she can do is perform a symbolic ritual—sprinkling the corpse with dust and pouring libations.

88 *An outrage sacred to the gods:* literally, "committing a holy crime." What is criminal in the eyes of Creon is holy in the eyes of the gods Antigone champions.

113 EXIT ANTIGONE. There is of course no stage direction in our text (see pp. 389–90). We suggest that Antigone leaves the stage here not only because after her speech she obviously has nothing more to say to Ismene, but also because the effect of her harsh dismissal of her sister would be weakened if she then stood silent while Ismene had the last word. We suggest that she starts out toward the side exit and Ismene speaks to her retreating figure before she herself goes off stage, but through the door into the palace.

117–79 The *parodos* (literally, "the way past") is the name of the space between the end of the stage building and the end of the spectators' benches (see Introduction, pp. 19, 258). Through these two passageways the chorus made its entrance, proceeding to the *orchêstra*, the circular dancing-floor in front of the stage building. The word *parodos* is also used to denote the first choral song, the lines which the chorus chants as it marches in.

This song is a victory ode, a celebration of the city's escape from capture, sack and destruction. The chorus imagines the enemy running in panic before the rising sun; their shields are white (122) perhaps because the name Argos suggests the adjective *argos*, which means "shining." The enemy assault of the previous day they compare to an eagle descending on its prey, but it was met and routed by a dragon (138); the Thebans believed that they were descended from dragons' teeth, which, sown in the soil by Cadmus, their first king, turned into armored men. Of all the seven chieftains who attacked the gates, Capaneus was the most violent and boastful; high on a scaling ladder he reached the top of the wall but was struck down by a lightning bolt of Zeus (147). The defeat of the other attackers is the work of Ares (154), the war god, who is also one of the patron deities of Thebes. The seven chieftains were all killed; all seven were stripped of their armor, which was then arranged on wooden frames in the likeness of a warrior. This is what the Greeks called a *tropaion* (our word "trophy"); the Greek word suggests "turning point," and in fact the trophy was set up at the point where the losing side first turned and ran. The god who engineered such reversals was Zeus *Tropaios*—"god of the breaking rout of battle" (159). In the last stanza the dancers address Victory, who is always represented in Greek art as a winged female figure; they look forward to the joys of peace, the revelry associated with the god Dionysus, born of a Theban mother.

188 *Their children:* i.e., the children of Oedipus and Jocasta.

213 *Truer than blood itself:* this is an attempt to bring out in English the double meaning of the word translated "friendships"; the Greek word *philous* means both "friends" and "close relations."

215 *Closely akin:* the Greek word means literally "brother to." But Creon is in fact disregarding the claims of kinship.

278 *Someone's just buried it:* this is a token burial (see n. 52); it is defined in the lines that follow (289–92). The sprinkling of dust and the pouring of a libation were considered the equivalent of burial where nothing more could be done and so were a direct defiance of Creon's order (see 346).

300–1 *Red-hot iron . . . go through fire:* traditional (and hyperbolic) assertions of truthfulness; the reference is to some form of trial by ordeal in which only the liar would get burned.

376–416 The chorus entered the *orchêstra* to the strains of the *parodos;* it now, with the stage area empty of actors, sings the first *stasimon*. The word means something like "stationary"; it distinguishes the songs the chorus sings once it has reached the *orchêstra* (where it will, normally, remain until the end of the play) from the *parodos,* which it sings while marching in. But of course the chorus is not actually stationary; its members dance in formation as they sing.

This famous hymn to the inventiveness and creativeness of man has important thematic significance for the play, in which a ruler, in the name of man's creation, the state, defies age-old laws: the ode ends with a warning that man's energy and resourcefulness may lead him to destruction as well as greatness. But choral odes, though one of their important functions is to suggest and discuss the wider implications of the action, usually have an immediate dramatic relevance as well. In this case the chorus must be thinking of the daring and ingenuity of the person who gave Polynices' body symbolic burial. This does not mean that they are expressing approval of the action; the wonders of the world, of which man is the foremost, are "terrible wonders."

The ode's vision of human history as progress from helplessness to near mastery of the environment reappears in other fifth-century dramatic texts, notably in the *Prometheus Bound* and the Euripidean *Suppli-*

ants. It is likely that all these accounts are based on a book (now lost) by the sophist Protagoras called *The State of Things in the Beginning.*

385 *The breed of stallions:* mules, then, as now, the work animal of a Greek farm.

409 *Weaves in:* this is a literal translation of the reading found in all the manuscripts, *pareirôn.* Though the word occurs elsewhere in fifth-century tragedy, editors have thought the metaphor too violent here; most editors take it as a copyist's mistake for *gerairôn,* which would give the meaning "honors," "reveres."

424 *Act of mad defiance:* the chorus here and later (677, "fury at the heart") can explain Antigone's defiance of power only as mental aberration; Creon speaks in similar terms of the two sisters when Ismene wishes to join her sister in death ("They're both mad, I tell you . . ." 632).

480 *Three . . . libations:* drink-offerings to the dead; they might be of honey, wine, olive oil, or water.

590 The verbs used in this famous line, *synechthein* and *symphilein,* appear nowhere else in Greek literature and may have been expressly coined by Sophocles to express the distinction Antigone is making: that she is incapable of taking sides in her brothers' political hatred for each other but shares in the blood relationship which, she believes, unites them in love in the world below.

645–49 ISMENE. *Dearest Haemon . . .* All the manuscripts give this line to Ismene. But manuscript attributions are very often wrong (see pp. 389–90) and many editors give the line to Antigone. (The phrase in Creon's line that follows, translated "your talk of marriage," could equally well mean "your marriage" and so refer to Antigone, who has not been talking about marriage, instead of Ismene, who has.) If the line is Ismene's, however, Sophocles has given us an Antigone who never mentions Haemon, though we learn later that he loves her more than his own life. But there is a technical reason (apart from any question of interpretation) against giving the line to Antigone: Ismene must have the next reply to Creon (647, "Creon—you're really going to rob your son of Antigone?"), and this would present us with a phenomenon for which we have no parallel—a long exchange of single lines between two actors interrupted for one line by a third. Dawe has recently proposed a solution to this difficulty: to give all three lines (including line 649, the one here assigned to the leader) to Antigone. This is linguistically unassailable (line 647 would then mean: "Creon—you're really going to rob your son of *me*?"); her next

NOTES: ANTIGONE

line would mean: "It's decided then? I'm going to die?"; and Creon's reply would mean: "Decided, yes. By you and me." This reading has its very attractive aspects but gives us an Antigone whose second line sounds a completely uncharacteristic note of self-pity and is in effect a plea for her life—also uncharacteristic. We have assigned 645 and 647 to Ismene, 649 to the leader of the chorus.

656–700 The chorus sees an explanation for the death which now threatens the two last remaining members of the house of Oedipus: it is the working of a hereditary doom. The reason for it is not given (though legends known to some of the audience traced it back to the wrongdoing of Laius, father of Oedipus) but it is thought of as the work of the gods. In the opening speech of the play Antigone spoke in similar terms and attributed the sorrows of her line to Zeus. And in the second unit of this *stasimon* the chorus sings of the power of Zeus and man's inability to override it. So far, clearly, they have been meditating on the fate of Antigone, but their reflections proceed along a line which does not seem relevant to her case. The law of Zeus is that

> *no towering form of greatness*
> *enters into the lives of mortals*
> *free and clear of ruin.* (687–89)

As they develop this theme along lines thoroughly familiar to the audience, which shared this instinctive feeling that greatness is dangerous, it must have become clear that their words express anxiety not for Antigone, the helpless and condemned, but for Creon, the man who holds and wields supreme power in the state.

667–69 *Sorrows of the house . . . piling on the sorrows of the dead.* This could be read as "sorrows of the dead . . . fall on the sorrows of the living." Both interpretations come to much the same thing.

676 *Bloody knife: kopis* is the Greek word. The manuscripts all read *konis*, which means "dust." It is true that the dust she has thrown on Polynices' corpse has brought her to her death, but the metaphor seems too violent and most editors print *kopis*, a conjecture made by Jortin, an English scholar of the eighteenth century.

711–12 *Than you, / whatever good direction . . .* The Greek is ambiguous and could mean "than your good leadership" or "than you, if you give proper leadership."

736 *Zeus . . . kindred blood:* Zeus *Homaimos* (see Glossary).

794 *Spread them . . . empty.* A metaphor from writing tablets, two slats of wood covered with wax, on which the message was inscribed. It would be delivered closed and sealed; the recipient would open it and read—in this case to find the tablet blank.

872-73 *Short rations . . . piety demands . . .* The city would be kept "free of defilement" not only because (contrary to Creon's first decision) the citizens would not be involved in stoning Antigone to death but also because, if Antigone were to starve to death (or commit suicide), there would literally be no blood on anyone's hands. Greek superstitious belief thought of responsibility for killing in terms of pollution by the blood of the victim, which called for blood in return. We know of no parallels to Creon's sentence, except the similar punishment inflicted in Rome on Vestal Virgins who broke their vows of chastity.

879-94 *Love . . .* The Greek world *erôs* has a narrower field of meaning than its English equivalent; it denotes the passionate aspect of sexual attraction, an irresistible force which brings its victims close to madness. The immediate occasion of this hymn to Eros is of course the chorus' fear that Haemon, infuriated by the prospect of losing Antigone, may "do something violent" (862). But the song also reminds the audience that Creon has now offended not only the gods who preside over the lower world and those who sustain the bonds of family friendship, but also Eros and Aphrodite who, as the concluding lines of the ode emphasize, are great powers in the universe—"Throned in power, side-by-side with the mighty laws!" (892).

889 *This kindred strife:* the Greek adjective *xynaimon* (literally, "common-blood") recalls Haemon's name.

895-969 The first half of the scene which follows the choral ode is a lyric dialogue known as a *kommos:* actor and chorus sing in responsion. At first the chorus addresses Antigone in a march-type rhythm (anapests) that was probably chanted rather than sung; she replies in song, in fully lyric meters. At line 943, as emotion rises to a high pitch, the chorus, too, breaks into full song. Creon's harsh intervention (969) is couched in iambic spoken verse, and Antigone uses the same medium for her farewell speech (978-1021). But the scene ends in the chanted rhythm of marching anapests as Antigone is led off to her tomb (1027-34).

909 *Not crowned with glory . . .* The usual version of this line is: "crowned with glory . . ." The Greek word *oukoun* can be negative or positive, depending on the accent, which determines the pronunciation; since these written accents were not yet in use in Sophocles' time, no one will ever know for sure which meaning he intended. We take the view that the chorus is expressing pity for Antigone's ignominious and abnormal death; she has no funeral at which her fame and praise are recited, she will not die by either of the usual causes—violence or disease—but by a living death. It is, as they say, her own choice; she is "a law to [herself]" (912).

915 *Niobe* boasted that her children were more beautiful than Apollo and Artemis, the children of Leto by Zeus. Apollo and Artemis killed Niobe's twelve (or fourteen) children with bow and arrow; Niobe herself, inconsolably weeping, turned to stone. On Mount Sipylus, in Asia Minor, there was a cliff face which from a distance looked like a weeping woman; it was identified with Niobe.

925 *But she was a god . . .* The chorus reproves Antigone for comparing her own death to that of Niobe, who was not strictly a god, but moved on terms of equality with the gods. The chorus' condescending tone accounts for Antigone's indignant outburst in the next few lines.

944 *Smashing against the high throne of Justice!* The text is very disturbed here. Different readings would add the detail "with your foot" (or "feet") and a radically different sense: "falling in supplication before the high throne . . ."

957 *Your marriage murders mine:* Polynices had married the daughter of Adrastus of Argos, to seal the alliance which enabled him to march against Thebes.

977 The Greek word translated "stranger's rights," *metoikias*, had a precise technical sense in Athens; it described the status of a resident alien who was not a full citizen. Creon speaks as if Antigone had already forfeited her citizenship by her action and become a *metoikos*, a resident alien; he will now deprive her of even that status, by burying her alive. Similarly at lines 940 and 956 Antigone speaks of herself as an alien, *metoikos*, both in the world of the living and that of the dead.

988 *My loving brother, Eteocles . . .* The name Eteocles does not appear in the Greek but has been added by the translator to remove a possible ambiguity.

989 *When you died . . .* Antigone's speech has been judged adversely by many critics, who suspect its authenticity; some would go so far as to suppress the whole passage from this point on; others content themselves with removing lines 993 to 1012 (904–5 through 920 in the Greek). We believe the whole of the speech is genuine; for a defense of this position, see the Introduction, pp. 45–50.

1028 *First gods of the race:* the Theban royal house was descended from Cadmus, whose wife Harmonia was the daughter of Aphrodite and Ares. Dionysus was the son of Zeus and Semele, a daughter of Cadmus. See the Genealogy, p. 425.

1035-90 *Danaë, Danaë* . . . The dramatic relevance of the mythological material exploited in this choral ode is not as clear to us as it must have been to the original audience; the second half of the ode, in particular, alludes to stories of which we have only fragmentary, late and conflicting accounts.

The chorus, which reprimanded Antigone for comparing herself to Niobe, now tries to find some satisfactory parallels. Acrisius, king of Argos, was told by an oracle that his grandson would be the cause of his death. He had only one child, Danaë, and, to prevent her from bearing a child, he shut her up in a bronze prison (a tower in some accounts, or, as here, a sort of underground vault). But Zeus, in the form of golden sunlight, reached her and she gave birth to the hero Perseus, who, many years later, after killing the Gorgon Medusa and rescuing the princess Andromeda from the sea monster, accidentally killed his grandfather Acrisius at an athletic contest. The point of comparison with Antigone is clearly the imprisonment in an underground room, and the fact that the room was for Danaë a place to which a forbidden bridegroom forced an entrance will not be lost on the audience when, later on, it hears of Haemon's entry into the tomb of Antigone, and its tragic sequel. But, the parallel once established, the chorus goes on to sing of the power of fate, which no human power (wealth, military strength, fortifications, fleets—the powers of the state) can defy. Acrisius could not escape what was predicted; but what has this to do with Antigone? The resources of power are Creon's, not hers, and he, like Acrisius, tried to prevent the consummation of a marriage. In these lines the chorus is made to express, even if it may not, as a character, understand fully the implication of its own words, its fear for Creon, the beginning of its disenchantment with his course of action.

The next parallel with Antigone, Lycurgus, king of the barbarous Thracians, also has imprisonment as its base. Lycurgus (like Pentheus in Euripides' *Bacchae*) attempted to suppress the worship of Dionysus; he pursued the wild women devotees on the hills, laid hands on the god, mocked and insulted him. Dionysus confined him in a rock—a rocky cave or a miraculous stone envelope—and he went mad. (In one version of the legend, not hinted at here but probably known to the audience, he killed his son in his mad fit.) Here imprisonment, the connection with Antigone, is overshadowed by the ominous resemblances to Creon: he is the one who uses force against a woman, against the gods of the underworld; his is the angry, taunting voice, the frenzied rage. And he will be responsible in the end for the death of his son.

For the last two stanzas of the ode there is no sure line of interpretation. The myth to which it refers (but so cryptically that only two of the people involved are named in the text) told the story of Cleopatra, daughter of an Athenian princess and Boreas, the North Wind. She was married to the Thracian king Phineus, by whom she had two sons. They were blinded by Phineus' second wife; in some versions Cleopatra was already dead, in others she was imprisoned by the new wife and later released. (In some versions, the sons were imprisoned too—like Antigone, in a tomb.) Sophocles could rely on the audience's familiarity with this material (he wrote two plays dealing with Phineus) but we are left to grasp at straws. The last lines of the ode, an address to Antigone which echoes the chorus' similar address at the beginning ("my child," 1042 and 1090) suggests strongly that Antigone is compared to Cleopatra here, as she is to Danaë in the opening lines. In that case Sophocles is almost certainly referring to a version (perhaps that of one of his own plays) in which Cleopatra, like Danaë and Antigone, was imprisoned. We have therefore taken the liberty, in order to produce a translation which makes some kind of sense, of putting this crucial detail into the text. But the reader is warned that lines 1080–81—"their mother doomed to chains, / walled off in a tomb of stone"—have no equivalent in the Greek text.

1096 *Never wavered from your advice before:* this may be just an acknowledgment of the omnipresence of Tiresias in Theban affairs over many generations. On the other hand it may refer to a legend that Tiresias advised Creon, during the attack by the Seven, that Thebes could only be saved by the sacrifice of his son Megareus (who did in fact give his life for his fellow-citizens). Anyone in the audience who remembered this might see bitter irony in Creon's line (1098) "I owe you a great deal, I swear to that." The death of Megareus will later (1428–31) be blamed on Creon by his wife Eurydice.

1102 *Warnings of my craft:* in this speech Tiresias describes the results of two different techniques of foretelling the future: interpretation, first, of the movements and voices of birds; next, of the behavior of the animal flesh burnt in sacrifice to the gods. The birds, as Tiresias tells us later (1125–26), have been eating the flesh of the corpse exposed by Creon's order; their voices, normally intelligible to the prophet, now convey nothing but their fury as they fight each other. Tiresias turns to the other method of divination, but the fire will not blaze up; it is quenched by the abnormal ooze from the long thighbones. These are all signs that the gods are "deaf to our prayers," as the prophet soon tells Creon (1127).

1150 *Silver-gold of Sardis:* electrum, a natural mixture of silver and gold ("white gold") found in the river near Sardis in Asia Minor.

1192–93 *Violence / you have forced upon the heavens:* by leaving a corpse exposed Creon has not only deprived the lower gods of their rights, he has also polluted with death the province of the Olympian gods of the upper air. The Furies, avenging spirits of both lower and upper gods, lie in wait for him now.

1200 *Cries for men and women break / throughout your halls:* Tiresias prophesies the deaths of Haemon and Eurydice.

1201–2 *Great hatred . . . cities in tumult:* Creon was eventually forced to bury the bodies of the other champions, so Athenian legend ran, by an Athenian army under the leadership of Theseus (this is the theme of Euripides' *Suppliants*). But in the next generation, the sons of the Seven, the *Epigonoi*, attacked Thebes again and this time succeeded in taking the city.

1239–72 *God of a hundred names! . . .* The tone of this choral song is one of exultation; the old men rejoice that Creon has seen the error of his ways and call on the Theban god Dionysus to appear, to come dancing, and as a healer to lead the joyous celebration. The hopes expressed in the song are quickly belied by the tragic events announced by the messenger; a similar ironic sequence is to be found in *Oedipus the King* (1195–1310). The hymn to Dionysus is constructed along the lines of real religious hymns: first the invocation of the god under his (or her) many titles, then a reference to the god's place of origin (Thebes), an enumeration of the most important places of his worship (Delphi, Nysa), an appeal to the god to come to the aid of the worshiper, and finally an invocation of the god by new names and titles.

1243 *King of Eleusis:* Iacchus (1271), the young god associated with Demeter and Persephone in the mystery religion centered at Eleusis in Attica, was often identified with Dionysus (*Bakchos*). Dionysus was supposed to be present, in the winter season, at Apollo's site, Delphi on Mount Parnassus, where the "twin peaks" of the cliffs (1250) towered above the sanctuary and the Castalian spring flowed below

(1253). *Nysa* (1254) is a name given to many mountains in the ancient world, but the reference here is probably to the one on the long island of Euboea, opposite Theban territory, and separated from it by the Euripus ("the moaning straits," 1265).

1321 *Hecate of the Crossroads:* a goddess associated with burial grounds and the darkness of the night; offerings to her were left at crossroads. Here she is thought of as associated with Pluto (another name of Hades), as one whose privileges have been curtailed by Creon's action.

1341 *The tomb's very mouth:* Sophocles evidently imagined Antigone's prison on the model of the great domed Mycenaean tombs, built of stone and then covered with earth. Haemon has prised loose some of the stones to effect an entrance; once inside this, Creon's men go along a passage to the "mouth" (i.e., the doorway) of the main chamber.

1346-47 *We found her . . . / hanged by the neck . . .* The details are not clear. These words seem to mean that the speaker saw Antigone still hanging. At the end of his speech he describes Haemon as embracing Antigone—"there he lies, body enfolding body" (1369)—in terms which clearly imply that her body has been lowered to the ground. Sophocles does not tell us how or when this happened, but we probably are meant to imagine that Haemon cut the rope with his sword—which would be the normal, instinctive reaction to the sight of a hanging body.

OEDIPUS THE KING

3 *Branches wound in wool:* the priests come as suppliants, people who have lost all hope of salvation except through divine intervention. Such suppliants carried branches of olive or laurel, which had tufts of wool tied around them. The branches were laid on the altar of the god or gods to whom supplication was made and they were left there until the worshipers' prayer was granted. It is significant that though the altar in the *orchêstra* represents an altar of Apollo (as we learn later, 1007), the priest, addressing Oedipus, speaks of "your altars" (18); when Oedipus promises to find the murderer of Laius he tells the priests to take up the branches (161). He acts, and is seen by his fellow-citizens, as almost divine.

5 *The Healer: Paian,* a title of Apollo. We know from the beginning of Homer's *Iliad* that Apollo could send plague as well as cure it. There is no overt suggestion in this play that Apollo has caused the plague to come to Thebes (in fact the chorus later associates him with other gods as a rescuer, 184, 231–34), but the original prophecy was made by Apollo and his hand is felt to be mysteriously at work in its fulfillment and the revelation, prompted by the onset of the plague, that it has been fulfilled.

26–27 *River-shrine where the embers glow and die . . .* An oracular shrine of Apollo by the Theban river, the Ismenus, where the future was foretold by priests who interpreted as prophetic signs any unusual behavior of the burnt offerings on the fire. The translation is an explanatory expansion of the original, which reads simply—"at the prophetic ash of Ismenus." Compare Tiresias' speech in *Antigone* 1111–21.

54 *What do you know?* The Greek phrase *oistha pou*, with its resemblance to the name *Oidipous* (the Greek form), is the first of a series of such punning references to the name of the man who seems to know everything but does not in fact even know who he is.

80 *One cure:* the first of a series of images of Oedipus as physician, which ends in the revelation (and his realization) that he is not the physician but the disease (see 1529).

89 *The god makes clear:* ambiguous in the original. Apollo will make clear his demands; he will also, in the end, make clear the truth.

99–100 *Even the hardest things to bear . . .* Creon is vague and ambiguous; he wants to deliver his message to Oedipus in private.

109 *Corruption:* the Greek word is *miasma*, which is literally a stain. The blood of the murdered man is thought of as something which pollutes not only the killer but all those who come in contact with him.

139–40 *Thieves . . . A thief:* Oedipus, a leader of men himself, thinks of the leader, not the gang; he takes it for granted that this brigand chieftain must have been backed by conspirators in Thebes. (His suspicion will later fasten on Tiresias and Creon.) It is an ironic twist that though here he speaks of one attacker rather than many, he will later (931–34) base his hopes that he is innocent on the reports that Laius was killed not by one man but by many. These reports (789–90) stem from the story told by the one survivor of the encounter at the crossroads. The shepherd's motive for reporting that Laius was killed by a band of attackers is never made clear; perhaps we are to assume that he exaggerated the number of the attackers so that he would not be asked why he and the wagon driver did not succeed in defending their king.

168–244 *Zeus! . . .* The *parodos* (see *Antigone* n. 117–79). The chorus, older citizens of Thebes, have not heard the news which Creon brought from Delphi; they know only that the emissaries sent to Delphi have returned. They sing, in sorrow and terror, of the plague and its ravages; the song is a hymn of supplication to the gods, calling for salvation. They open with a prayer to Athena, Artemis and Apollo and at the conclusion of the hymn invoke the supreme god Zeus, Apollo and Artemis and lastly Dionysus, the god born of a Theban mother.

169 *Welcome voice of Zeus:* Apollo was the prophetic god at Delphi but he spoke for and in the name of his father, Zeus.

173 *Healer of Delos:* Apollo was supposed to have been born on Delos, a very small island in the Cyclades. It was a famous center of his worship.

175 *Some new sacrifice? some ancient rite from the past . . . ?* Cities which consulted the Delphic oracle in time of plague or other calamity were often ordered to make ritual expiation by sacrifice or some other means. In 426–25 B.C., for example, the Athenians followed the instructions of an oracle (we do not know if it was Delphi) to "purify" the island of Delos by removing all the bones from the graves and forbidding future burials in sacred territory; this seems to be connected in some way with the plague that afflicted Athens from 430–25.

201 *Winging west:* the west, the region of the setting sun, is thought of as the location of the underworld.

216 *Golden daughter of god:* Athena.

219 *Raging god of war:* Ares (named in the Greek). He is not elsewhere associated with plague; possibly this unusual identification is a reflection of the situation in Athens during the early years of the war (430–25)—plague inside the city and Spartan invasion outside.

239 *Your name and ours are one:* Dionysus, son of Zeus, was born of a Theban mother, and Thebes was traditionally the first Greek city which celebrated his rites.

250–51 *There would have been no mystery . . .* The interpretation of these lines is disputed; the translation follows the explanation offered by Dawe, *Studies in the Text of Sophocles,* Vol. 1 (Leiden: Brill, 1973), pp. 217–19.

271 *Never shelter him:* since his identity is unknown this may sound like a singularly ineffectual measure. Yet exactly such a proclamation, against an unidentified murderer, is recommended in Plato's *Laws,* and there are indications that it was standard practice in fifth-century Athens.

296 *Wife who shares our seed:* the Greek word *homosporon* is ambiguous; it can also mean "blood relation," as it clearly does when Tiresias uses it to describe Oedipus' relationship to Laius (522–23).

304–6 *Son of Labdacus descended of Polydorus* . . . Oedipus, an outsider who has not inherited but won the throne of Thebes, recites the full royal genealogy as if he were its legitimate successor, almost as if he were trying to include himself in the long procession of Theban kings. As he will soon learn to his sorrow, he is in fact the true heir to the throne. To underscore this point (which would not have been lost on Sophocles' audience) the translator has added the words—"their power and mine are one" (306).

385 *The one you live with*: in the Greek the veiled reference to Jocasta is more forceful, since the word translated "the one" has a feminine ending (agreeing with the feminine noun *orgê*—"temper").

428–30 *Not your fate / to fall at my hands. Apollo is quite enough* . . . This translates a text printed by all editors but which has no manuscript authority. The manuscript reading would give us:

> *True, it is not my fate*
> *to fall at your hands. Apollo is quite enough,*
> *and he will take some pains to work that out.*

This meaning is not ruled out by the preceding speech of Oedipus, since his lines (427–28), because of an ambiguity inherent in Greek syntax, could perfectly well mean: "Neither I nor anyone else who sees the light would ever raise a hand against you." What tells against the manuscript reading is the idea that Tiresias would fall at the hands of his divine patron Apollo. These words could, however, be taken in a general sense: "You could not harm me; if anything is to happen to me, it will be Apollo's work." But since all editors accept the lines as emended (with only minor changes) by the German scholar Brunck in 1786, we have thought it best to present that version in the translation.

458 *Witch-hunt*: the Greek word means literally "driving out the pollution, the accursed object." This was a familiar idea in fifth-century Athens. In the diplomatic maneuvers that preceded the outbreak of the Peloponnesian War in 431 B.C. the Spartans sent envoys to tell the Athenians to "drive out the accursed object"—they meant Pericles, whose remote ancestors had once committed a sacrilegious act. Pericles replied in kind: the Spartans, too, had past offenses against the gods to atone for.

507 TURNING HIS BACK ON TIRESIAS, MOVING TOWARD THE PALACE. There is of course no manuscript authority for this stage direction. But it seems to us that the logic of the situation demands it. The king has dismissed the prophet with contempt; why should he now listen to a long speech from him? And if he does stand still, listening to this long and terrifying prophecy, why does he make no reply? Why does he ask no questions? (He did before.) Worse still, how can the audience believe that he does not connect what Tiresias says with the prophecy that Apollo made to him at Delphi? Two scenes later he tells Jocasta about this prophecy (868-75) but speaks as if he has not heard what Tiresias said.

All these difficulties are resolved if he does not hear the crucial portion of Tiresias' speech (520-23) and by the time these lines are delivered he is almost through the doors. Tiresias, then, is delivering his tirade to an actor who goes off stage without hearing him; this is in fact a recognized convention of the Greek stage, where menacing or mocking remarks, which in the dramatic situation must not be heard by their target, are often directed to the back of an actor on his way out. Tiresias is blind, but this need not mean that he does not know Oedipus is leaving; he can hear him—the acoustics of the Greek stage are extraordinary, as any visitor to Epidaurus knows. For a full defense of this stage direction see "Sophocles, *Oedipus Tyrannos* 446: Exit Oedipus?" in *Greek, Roman and Byzantine Studies* 21.4 (1980): 321-32.

526-72 *Who is the man . . . ?* The chorus, in its first *stasimon*, imagines the unidentified murderer of Laius as an outcast in the wilds, pursued by Apollo and the Furies, the avengers of blood. He will not escape "the dread voices of Delphi . . . the doom that never dies" (546-49); they mean the recent Apolline proclamation, but the audience thinks also of the prophecies made long ago to Oedipus. In the second half of their song they dismiss Tiresias' repeated statements that the murderer is Oedipus himself. For one thing, they can think of no motive—no "blood feud between / Laius' house and the son of Polybus" (554-55)—for they think of Oedipus as the son of Polybus, king of Corinth. There seems to be no evidence which links a king whose "fame . . . rings throughout Thebes" (558) and the murderer whose presence in Thebes is the cause of the plague. They are not rejecting divine foreknowledge and prophecy—"Zeus and Apollo know" (561)—only the fallible visions of a human prophet. This was a respectable position in fifth-century Athens, where there were many professional prophets, some of them exploiters of public credulity for their own profit. The chorus will not abandon Oedipus without proof; he was their savior from "the she-hawk" (569), the Sphinx.

653-90 *Look at it this way first . . .* Creon's speech, which sounds so reasonable to modern ears, may have made a different impression on the original audience. It is an argument from probability, from lack of motive, and this was a well-known fifth-century technique of argument, taught by professional rhetoricians, the sophists, as a defense to be used when evidence was lacking. So it may have sounded slightly glib and shopworn to Sophocles' contemporaries. (Oedipus, of course, has no evidence or witnesses either; he is acting on mere suspicion.)

699 *Just to show how ugly a grudge can* . . . The translation follows Pearson's text. Other editors, finding stylistic difficulties in the lines, rearrange them or assume that a line—or more than one—has been lost. We take *phthonein* not in the sense of "envy" (one reason for assigning this line to Oedipus rather than to Creon) but as meaning "bear a grudge," "show malice, hatred." We also follow Pearson's suggestion that Creon is interrupted by Oedipus; he does not finish the sentence.

725-67 THE CHORUS . . . BEGINS TO CHANT. From here to line 733 the chorus and Oedipus converse in sung lyric meters; at 735 the chorus sings until Oedipus at 741, in spoken iambic verse, resumes the dialogue with Creon. After Creon's exit (750) the chorus and Jocasta are singing; Oedipus has two spoken lines at 760 and the chorus concludes the *kommos* (see *Antigone* n. 895-969) with a final lyric stanza (761-67). The recourse to song and to more emotional meters emphasizes the dramatic tension of the scene; it is only the impassioned appeal by the chorus which saves Creon from immediate execution.

736 *By the blazing sun:* since the sun, in his daily journey from east to west, saw everything that happened on earth, he was an appropriate god by whom to swear one's innocence.

754 *Loose, ignorant talk:* the chorus is reluctant to speak clearly. They feel uneasily that something has gone wrong and wish to "end the trouble here, just where they [Oedipus and Creon] left it" (759).

792 *Fastened his ankles:* Jocasta, as we learn later (1133-34), is not telling the full truth—the scars on Oedipus' feet must have come from some sort of metal fastening which pierced the flesh.

954-97 *Destiny guide me always* . . . In the first *stasimon* (554-72) the chorus dismissed the accusations leveled at Oedipus by Tiresias, questioned the validity of pronouncements made by mere human prophets and expressed their firm belief in the innocence of their ruler, as well as confidence in his leadership. Since then, however, that belief and

NOTES: OEDIPUS THE KING

that confidence have been undermined. The chorus has seen Oedipus condemn Creon to death without any real evidence of wrongdoing on his part—an action more characteristic of a dictator, a "tyrant," than of a king; they have heard of events which make it seem probable that Oedipus is indeed the killer of Laius, as he himself fears may be the case; they have just heard Jocasta dismiss with contempt a prophecy, not of Tiresias, but of Apollo himself. This second *stasimon* reflects their profound anxiety, as they seek to distance themselves from the king who may turn out to be the polluted killer, the cause of the plague, and the queen whose impious rejection of Apollo's prophecy fills them with fear. As they pray that their own lives may be lived in reverence and purity, they invoke the great laws which lay down the norms of human action and which are the creation not of men but of the gods (957-62).

In the second stanza the chorus poses against the laws the figure of the tyrant, an all-powerful ruler on whose action there are no human curbs and who, scaling the heights of power and arrogance, crashes to his fall. But then, as if they wished to qualify this grim parable (which in the dramatic context can hardly refer to anyone but Oedipus), they single out for praise the vigorous action, the competitive energy "which makes the city strong" (969: again the reference to Oedipus, this time as the savior of the city, is inescapable).

But in the third stanza the emphasis is once more placed on the figure of the great transgressor, and this time his offenses are not so much political as religious: he shows no reverence for the gods, "laying hands on the holy things untouchable" (980). This last phrase is probably intended as a general image of impiety, but to the audience it suggests Oedipus' incestuous marriage. As the song develops, it becomes clear that these images of pride and violence are provoked by Jocasta's rejection of divine prophecy (a rejection which Oedipus condones). For the elders go on to call for the fulfillment of the prophecies, terrible though they are; if the "oracles sent to Laius" are not fulfilled (994), there is no reason to worship the gods, to go any more to the oracles at Delphi, Abae and Olympia, to "join the sacred dance" (984).

1012-14 *Lead us . . . Oedipus . . . you know where he is?* In the original Greek these three lines rhyme: *mathoim' hopou, Oidipou, katisth' hopou.* Rhyme is not a feature of Greek verse and such final assonances are extremely rare. That they are not accidental here is clear from the fact that the ending of the first line means "learn where" and of the third 'know where"—both unmistakable reminders that part of *Oidipous*, *Oidi*, is almost identical with the verb "I know," *oida*.

1046 *Your father is no more—Polybus—he's dead!* The Greek suggests an ambiguity which has ironic force; until the final word "dead" is heard the sentence could mean: "come to tell you your father is not Polybus any more..."

1188–89 *Chance, / the great goddess:* that Chance which Jocasta had named as the ruling principle of unpredictable chaos (1069–70) has become, for Oedipus, a patron deity which by a series of strange coincidences has brought him to the highest pinnacle of human prosperity. His illusion will not last long.

1195–1214 *Yes—if I am a true prophet...* In this short (third) *stasimon* the chorus, fear and disapproval both momentarily forgotten as they are inspired by Oedipus' heroic confidence and infected by his enthusiasm, speculates about the nature of the revelation to come. Clearly Oedipus will be proved not a foreigner but a citizen of Thebes; the Theban mountain Cithaeron is his "nurse, his mountain-mother" (1200). They go further still. Oedipus called himself the son of Chance, but the chorus, remembering the mythical tales of foundlings who turned out to be sons of gods, thinks of a higher birth: he may be the son of Pan, of Apollo himself, of Hermes or of Dionysus.

1206 *Nymphs who seem to live forever:* nymphs were not mortal creatures but, though they lived much longer than human beings, they were not, like the gods, immortal.

1248 *Three whole seasons, six months at a stretch:* the two men were following a migratory pattern still followed by shepherds in the north of Greece: in the summer months they move with their flocks from the plains to the high mountain pastures. Cithaeron is the highest mountain area (1,409 meters) between Corinthian territory to the south and Thebes to the north.

1249 *The rising of Arcturus:* Arcturus (the name means "Bear-watcher") is the principal star in the constellation Boötes, which circles round the Bear (the constellation we call the Big Dipper). Its "rising" is its reappearance in the night sky just before dawn, in mid-September. To the ancient Greeks this was the sign that summer was over: it was time to gather the grapes, drive the flocks to winter pasture and beach the ships.

1307 *O light—now let me look my last on you!* At this stage (as we learn from the messenger's speech later, 1387) Oedipus wished to kill himself, but the phrase is darkly prophetic of his self-blinding.

1311–50 *O the generations of men . . .* The fourth *stasimon* is a somber and magnificent lament for the fall of Oedipus and, since he is a "great example" (1318, the Greek word is *paradeigma*, paradigm), for the fragility of all human prosperity and achievement. The language of the play has presented Oedipus as a calculator and the chorus now states the result of the great calculation: "adding the total / of all your lives I find they come to nothing . . ." (1312–13). This is not the play's last word on the human condition, however; the chorus is overly pessimistic now, just as it was overly optimistic in the previous *stasimon*.

1357 *The Nile:* the original names the Phasis, an eastern river flowing into the Black Sea. We have substituted an eastern river more familiar to the English reader.

1407–8 *The ones you never should have seen:* Laius as his victim and Jocasta as his wife. *The ones you longed to see, to know:* Laius and Jocasta as his father and mother.

1432–96 *O the terror*—Oedipus and the chorus engage in a dialogue which is mostly sung—a *kommos*. The emotional medium of song is appropriate for the blinded hero's lamentations and self-accusations; as his passion exhausts itself he returns to the iambic meter of speech. It is clear from the words that the actor, coming out of the stage door, imitates the movements of a newly blind man, wandering aimlessly; the dramatic impact was heightened by the new mask he had put on for this entrance, one representing the blood streaming down from the eye sockets.

1671 *I try to say what I mean; it's my habit.* It is not clear, however, exactly what he does mean. His previous line (1670), "You'll get your wish at once," could mean either: "Yes, I will drive you out of Thebes" or "Yes, the gods will tell me to drive you out," i.e., he will consult the oracle, as he had decided earlier (1573–82). Sophocles leaves the matter ambiguous here: in *Oedipus at Colonus* we are told that Creon kept Oedipus in Thebes, but expelled him much later, when he had become content to stay.

1678–84 *People of Thebes, my countrymen . . .* This concluding speech of the chorus has been condemned by some editors (including the most recent, Dawe) as a later addition. It presents some serious textual difficulties, and the first two lines also appear in a speech of Oedipus at the end of Euripides' play *The Phoenician Women*. It was, however, normal Sophoclean practice to end a play with a short choral speech, and if this one is not genuine it probably replaced something similar.

OEDIPUS AT COLONUS

SCENE . . . This opening stage direction is based on indications in the text. The grove is mentioned in lines 17–19, the statue of the hero Colonus in lines 70–71, the rocky ledge in line 22, and the large outcropping of rock in lines 211–12.

64 *Hallowed ground:* in the lines which follow, Sophocles credits his birthplace, Colonus, with a wealth of divine and heroic presences. The Greek word *kolônos* means "hill" and the hill in question was called Horse Hill (*kolônos hippios*) to distinguish it from another hill a mile or so away inside the city of Athens called Agora Hill (*kolônos agoraios*). The hero *Colonus* (70) was a "horseman" and the god *Poseidon* (65) was also connected with horses (though his main sphere of dominion was the sea). Athenian legend told of the contest between Poseidon and Athena for possession of Attica; Zeus decreed that it would go to the one who produced the gift most useful to man. Poseidon created the horse, and Athena (who won), the olive tree. This legend is the background of the great ode in praise of Athens which the chorus sings later in the play (761–817). The *Titans* (66) were the older generation of gods, overthrown by Zeus and the Olympians. *Prometheus* (67) defied Zeus and gave fire to mankind; from the shrine of the hero Academus, hard by Colonus, torch-bearers ran a ceremonial race into Athens. *The Brazen Threshold* (68) seems to have been the name for a cave or chasm which was thought to lead to the lower world; it is "brazen" because Homer so describes the entrance to Hades. Its designation as *the bulwark of Athens* (69) is puzzling; perhaps its connection with the underworld makes it a barrier against attack (it is mentioned in a prophecy of a Theban penetration into Attic territory).

73 *All his people carry on his name:* Colonus was one of the demes, the regional units of Attica, and an Athenian's official name included that of his deme (Sophocles' name was: Sophocles, son of Sophillus, from Colonus).

122 *We who drink no wine:* libations poured to the Eumenides might be of water, milk and honey, but never wine (540). Oedipus drinks no wine simply because a destitute beggar would get none and would have to be content with water.

142–268 *Look for the man* . . . The entry song of the chorus, the *parodos*, is set in agitated, lyric rhythms appropriate for their excitement, as they search the stage for the trespasser on holy ground. Almost immediately, with the first words of Oedipus (160), the *parodos* becomes a long *kommos*, a lyric dialogue between actor and chorus, which continues as far as line 268. The grove is forbidden ground, reserved for those presences which are both terrible and kindly—Furies, queens of terror, daughters of darkness but also Eumenides, "Kindly Ones." The people of Colonus go by the grove with eyes averted in silent prayer; the news that a foreign vagrant, a blind beggar, has entered the grove fills them with fear and indignation.

278 *The only city on earth to save the ruined stranger:* this image of Athens as the savior and protector of the oppressed and unfortunate reappears time and again in Attic tragedy. Athens was supposed to have sheltered the children of Heracles, persecuted by the tyrant Eurystheus, to have welcomed Heracles after he killed his whole family in a fit of madness, to have forced Thebes to bury the corpses of the Seven. It is to that great reputation (how far it was in fact deserved we do not know) that Oedipus here appeals.

339 *Sleek colt:* the original identifies it as a colt from Etna, in Sicily—a prized breed in the Greek world.

340 *Broad brim of her hat:* the original specifies a hat from Thessaly; it was a wide-brimmed felt hat, well adapted for travel under the fierce Greek sun.

366–71 *Just like Egyptians . . .* In the *Histories* of Sophocles' friend Herodotus we read: "the Egyptians . . . in their manners and customs seem to have reversed the ordinary practices of mankind. The women go to market to buy and sell while the men stay at home and work the loom . . ." (2.35). Herodotus goes on to list many more such "reversals" of "normal practice."

477 *Drummed off native ground:* at the end of *Oedipus the King* (see n. 1671) it is not clear what is going to happen to Oedipus; he begs Creon to drive him into exile, as the oracle demanded, but Creon seems hesitant to do so. Here, as in other places, Sophocles has the earlier play in mind and establishes continuity between the two.

483 *That first day . . . when all my rage was seething:* compare *Oedipus the King* 1571–72.

524 *Appease those Spirits:* the elaborate ritual instructions which follow will guide Oedipus as he conciliates the Furies in whose forbidden precinct he took refuge. But they also create a mysterious religious atmosphere which will surround Oedipus from now on as he moves toward his transformation.

576–616 *A terrible thing, my friend . . .* At the end of the scene, as Ismene goes off stage, the audience must have expected a *stasimon*, at last.

Instead they hear another *kommos*, as agitated and emotionally disturbed as the first. The chorus relentlessly presses Oedipus for the details of his horrendous past.

616 *I came to this:* i.e., the killing of his father. The text is corrupt at this point; we have followed Jebb (Mekler).

632–33 *I too . . . was reared in exile . . .* Theseus was the son of Aegeus, king of Athens, but was brought up in Troezen in ignorance of his father's identity. When he grew up his mother gave him proofs of his paternity and sent him to Athens.

635 *Grappled dangers pressing for my life:* on the way Theseus fought with and killed many monsters and brigands.

683 *Thebes is doomed to be struck down in this land.* The prophecy of Apollo, as reported by Ismene (425–57) said that the Thebans would suffer from the wrath of Oedipus "that day they take their stand upon your tomb" (457). It is left to Oedipus to decide where that Theban defeat will take place; this is his gift to Athens.

717 *He is our ally:* this phrase, as well as the words "mutual rights" (718), seems to refer simply to the traditional courtesies exchanged between members of royal houses (not to a political alliance between Thebes and Athens).

761–817 *Here, stranger . . .* For a discussion of the major themes of this great choral ode, see the Introduction, pp. 267–69; for details, see the Glossary and n. 64.

762 *Horses are a glory:* not only because Poseidon created the horse as a gift to Athens but also because the local hero Colonus is a horseman (and is so represented on stage).

770 *Sacred wood of god:* Dionysus, with whom the ivy and the wine (see 769) are closely associated.

779 *Mother and Daughter:* Demeter and Persephone; the two goddesses of the Eleusinian mysteries, which promised their initiates a blessed existence beyond the grave.

783 *Cephisus:* a river of Attica, famous for the abundance of its waters (most Attic rivers run dry in the summer).

788 *Charioteer:* Aphrodite was often represented driving a chariot drawn by sparrows, doves or swans; the chariot had golden reins.

792 *Pelops' broad Dorian island:* the peninsula still known as the Peloponnese—literally, "Pelops' island" (*nêsos*).

800 *Guardian Zeus:* literally, Zeus *Morios*. Certain olive groves were considered the property of the city, placed under the protection of Zeus *Morios;* it was a serious offense to cut down trees on such protected sites.

NOTES: OEDIPUS AT COLONUS

814–17 *And your ship* . . . The Greek text of the final lines is disputed. We have followed the version printed by Dawe. The lines as printed by Jebb and Pearson could be rendered as follows:

> and your long flashing oar, honed to the hand
> whips the seas with wonder
> mounting the white manes of the sea
> racing the sea-nymphs dancing past the prow!

869 *Where I would suffer most:* not only would his wish to reward Athens be frustrated, he knows too that Creon will not bury him in Theban soil.

954–1008 *O Athens!* . . . Lines 954 to 963 are, in the original, the first section of a short *kommos* (the corresponding second section, 999–1008, comes immediately before the entry of Theseus). In both, the lyric meters and swift changes of speaker give formal expression to the excited emotion and action: in the first Antigone is dragged away by Creon's guards and in the second Creon is about to seize Oedipus too, but is prevented by the arrival of Theseus.

975 *Indulging your rage despite the pleas of loved ones:* see *Oedipus the King* 722–50.

983–84 *Unless, perhaps, / the king of the country blocks my way!* Creon can afford to be sarcastic; so far he has been opposed only by the ineffectual chorus of old men. Some editors, however, change the pronoun and give this line to the chorus: "unless, perhaps, the king of the country blocks your way."

1027 *Where the two highways meet:* a road junction on the way to Thebes where the main Theban force is waiting for Creon to rejoin them.

1063 *A resident alien:* the word is *metoikos* (see *Antigone* n. 977). Theseus is speaking ironically; he means "prisoner."

1170 *Others will ride them down:* the cavalry dispatched by Theseus at 1024–31.

1193–1239 *Oh god, to be there!* . . . In this second *stasimon* the chorus wishes it could be present at the victory it foresees for the Athenian cavalry.

1197 *Apollo guards the pass:* there was a temple at the pass of Daphni, where a road from Athens goes through the Aegalean hills to the sea, to join the coastal road, which leads to Eleusis, site of the Eleusinian mysteries.

1201 *Golden key of silence:* initiates in the mysteries were sworn never to reveal the nature of the rites and in fact no one ever did; we do not know more than a few details.

1207 *Or soon they'll clash* . . . The chorus is thinking of a different route to the coast road, one running round the northern end of the Aegalean range. In that case the cavalry, after rounding the hills, will turn west through a plain to the coast.

1264 *The journey I've been through:* Oedipus means his mental agony while he waited, alone and blind, for news of his kidnapped daughters.

1378–1410 *Show me a man* . . . For some remarks on the tone of this third *stasimon* see the Introduction, p. 273.

1444 *Suppliant of the god:* Poseidon (1314).

1460 *I am an outcast:* for the mythical background of what follows see the Introduction, pp. 28–29.

1467 *Bribed the people:* the Greek word Polynices uses, *peisas,* means literally "persuade" but often has the sense of "bribe." Here it seems necessary to assume that meaning, since Polynices has already said that Eteocles won out "not by force of argument."

1468 *The work of . . . your Fury:* Polynices, with typical insensitivity, puts the blame for the quarrel between the brothers on his father's dreadful destiny.

1482–98 *Seven columns, seven spearheads:* the Seven against Thebes. See the Glossary.

1490 *Capaneus:* compare *Antigone* 147–51.

1527 *Ring of my response:* Oedipus describes his own voice with a word (*omphê*) which is often used of divine oracles.

1646–95 *Look, new agonies now* . . . Another *kommos*. The choral songs are distributed over the ensuing scene in short units: lines 1646 to 1655 correspond metrically to lines 1661 to 1669, and at line 1675 a second unit begins, echoed metrically by lines 1688–95. In between the short bursts of choral song Oedipus and Antigone speak in regular iambic meter.

1712 *Thunder:* this was one of the signs specified in the original prophecy (116); it heralds Oedipus' death and transfiguration.

1739 *Sprung from the Dragon's teeth:* see *Antigone* n. 117–79.

1766–89 *Now, if it's not forbidden* . . . The fourth *stasimon* is a prayer to the dread gods of the underworld. The chorus prays that Oedipus' death will be swift and painless.

1780 *The huge beast:* the three-headed dog, Cerberus, who guarded the entrance to Hades.

1802 *Great brazen steps:* see n. 64.

1805–8 *Pact sealed by Theseus and Perithous* . . . these local details, which were familiar to Sophocles' audience, are very puzzling to us.

NOTES: OEDIPUS AT COLONUS

Theseus and Perithous went down to Hades to carry off Persephone; failing in the attempt, they were imprisoned there (and rescued later by Heracles). What the "pact" was, we do not know (perhaps just an oath to stand by each other in their mad enterprise); as for what was "cut in stone" (1806), it is generally thought that there must have been some unintelligible marks cut on the rock which were popularly believed to be the "pact." As for other details, Jebb has the appropriate words. "The power and beauty of this passage are in no way lessened for us because we know nothing of the basin [bowl] or the stone, the tree or the tomb. . . . Their significance is essentially local. . . . They show us how the blind man, who had never been at Colonus before, placed himself at precisely the due point in the midst of its complex sanctities."

1814 *Hill of Demeter:* a nearby hill with a shrine of Demeter *Euchloös,* a name which identifies her as the protectress of the wheat in its first, green, stage.

1865 *See this mystery:* the Greek does in fact use a technical phrase associated with the mysteries of Eleusis. These rites have been alluded to constantly throughout the play; the language Sophocles uses in this passage confers on the passing of Oedipus a sacramental character.

1896–1969 *O the misery . . .* This line is the beginning of a *kommos* which continues until line 1969. The first part of it (1896–1943) is a funeral lament for Oedipus, sung by his daughters. This would normally be sung over the grave, in the presence of the corpse; hence Antigone's passionate determination (1946–55) to go back and find Oedipus' last resting place.

1959 *You escaped before:* i.e., when Theseus took you and your father in.

1988 *Guardian of our oaths:* the Greek for oath is *horkos* and the oath personified, *Horkos,* is a being who sees to it that sworn oaths are kept. He is associated with Zeus, who is the supreme guarantor of oaths.

SELECT BIBLIOGRAPHY
OF MODERN BOOKS IN ENGLISH

I. *The following list includes only books of general interest which are devoted exclusively to Sophocles, or those which have specific chapters that involve the Theban Plays.*

Adams, S. M. *Sophocles the Playwright*. Toronto: University of Toronto Press, 1957.
Ahl, Frederick. *Sophocles' Oedipus: Evidence and Self-Conviction*. Ithaca and London: Cornell University Press, 1991.
Blundell, Mary Whitlock. *Helping Friends and Harming Enemies: A Study in Sophocles and Greek Ethics*. Cambridge: Cambridge University Press, 1989.
Bowra, Sir Maurice. *Sophoclean Tragedy*. Oxford: Clarendon Press, 1944.
Budelmann, Felix. *The Language of Sophocles: Communality, Communication, and Involvement*. Cambridge: Cambridge University Press, 2000.
Bushnell, Rebecca W. *Prophesying Tragedy: Sign and Voice in Sophocles' Theban Plays*. Ithaca: Cornell University Press, 1988.
Cameron, Alister. *The Identity of Oedipus the King: Five Essays on the Oedipus Tyrannus*. New York: New York University Press; London: University of London Press, 1968.
Edmunds, Lowell. *Oedipus: The Ancient Legend and Its Later Analogues*. Baltimore and London: The Johns Hopkins University Press, 1985.
Fergusson, Francis. *The Idea of a Theater: A Study of Ten Plays, The Art of Drama in Changing Perspective* (Chapter 1). Princeton: Princeton University Press; London: Oxford University Press, 1949; reprinted, New York: Doubleday, 1953.
Gellie, G. H. *Sophocles: A Reading*. Carlton, Victoria: Melbourne University Press, 1972.
Goheen, R. F. *The Imagery of Sophocles' Antigone: A Study of Poetic Language and Structure*. Princeton: Princeton University Press, 1951.

Goldhill, Simon. *Reading Greek Tragedy*. Cambridge, 1986.

Griffin, Jasper, ed. *Sophocles Revisited: Essays Presented to Sir Hugh Lloyd-Jones*. Oxford: Oxford University Press, 1999.

Jones, John. *On Aristotle and Greek Tragedy* (Section 3, Chapters 5 and 6). New York: Oxford University Press; London: Chatto and Windus, 1962; reprinted, New York: Oxford University Press, 1968.

Kirkwood, G. M. *A Study of Sophoclean Drama*. Ithaca: Cornell University Press, 1958.

Kitto, H. D. F. *Form and Meaning in Drama: A Study of Six Greek Plays and of Hamlet* (Chapter 5). 2nd ed. London: Methuen, 1964; New York: Barnes and Noble, 1968.

———. *Greek Tragedy: A Literary Study*. 2nd ed. New York: Doubleday, 1964; 3rd ed. London: Methuen, 1966.

———. *Sophocles, Dramatist and Philosopher*. London: Oxford University Press, 1958.

Knox, B. M. W. *The Heroic Temper: Studies in Sophoclean Tragedy*. Sather Classical Lectures, Vol. 35. Berkeley and Los Angeles: University of California Press, 1964.

———. *Oedipus at Thebes: Sophocles' Tragic Hero and His Time*. New Haven: Yale University Press, 1957; 2nd ed., 1966; reissued 1998.

Lattimore, Richmond. *The Poetry of Greek Tragedy* (Chapter 4). Baltimore: The Johns Hopkins University Press, 1958; reprinted, New York: Harper and Row, 1966.

Lloyd-Jones, Sir Hugh. *The Justice of Zeus* (Chapter 5). Sather Classical Lectures, Vol. 41. Berkeley and Los Angeles: University of California Press, 1971.

Mueller, Martin. *Children of Oedipus and Other Essays on the Imitation of Greek Tragedy, 1550-1800* (Chapter 4). Toronto, Buffalo, London: University of Toronto Press, 1980.

Nussbaum, Martha. *The Fragility of Goodness: Luck and Ethics in Greek Tragedy and Philosophy* (Chapter 3). Cambridge, England, and New York: Cambridge University Press, 1986.

O'Brien, M. J., ed. *Twentieth-Century Interpretations of Oedipus Rex*. Englewood Cliffs, N.J.: Prentice-Hall, 1968.

Pucci, Pietro. *Oedipus and the Fabrication of the Father: Oedipus Tyrannus in Modern Criticism and Philosophy*. Baltimore and London: The Johns Hopkins University Press, 1992.

Reinhardt, Karl. *Sophokles*. Frankfurt: Klostermann, 1933; English trs. D. and H. Harvey, New York: Barnes and Noble, 1978.

Scodel, Ruth. *Sophocles*. Cambridge, Mass.: Harvard University Press, 1984.

Scott, William C. *Musical Design in Sophoclean Theater*. Hanover, N.H.: University Press of New England for Dartmouth College, 1996.
Seale, David. *Vision and Stagecraft in Sophocles*. Chicago: University of Chicago Press, 1982.
Segal, Charles. *Oedipus Tyrannus: Tragic Heroism and the Limits of Knowledge*. New York: Twayne Publishers, 1993.
_____. *Sophocles' Tragic World: Divinity, Nature, Society*. Cambridge: Harvard University Press, 1995.
_____. *Tragedy and Civilization: An Interpretation of Sophocles*. Martin Classical Lectures, Vol. 26. Cambridge: Harvard University Press, 1981.
Stanford, W. B. *Ambiguity in Greek Literature: Studies in Theory and Practice* (Chapter 11). Oxford: Basil Blackwell, 1939; reprinted, New York: Johnson Reprint, 1972.
Steiner, George. *Antigones*. New York and Oxford: Oxford University Press, 1984.
Vernant, Jean-Pierre, and Pierre Vidal-Naquet. *Myth and Tragedy in Ancient Greece*, trs. Janet Lloyd. New York, 1988.
Waldock, A. J. A. *Sophocles the Dramatist*. Cambridge: Cambridge University Press, 1951.
Webster, T. B. L. *An Introduction to Sophocles*. Oxford: Clarendon Press, 1936; 2nd ed., London: Methuen, 1969.
Whitman, C. H. *Sophocles: A Study of Heroic Humanism*. Cambridge: Harvard University Press, 1951.
Wilkins, John, and Matthew Macleod. *Sophocles: Antigone & Oedipus the King—A Companion to the Penguin Translation of Robert Fagles*. London: Bristol Classical Press, 1987.
Winnington-Ingram, R. P. *Sophocles: An Interpretation*. Cambridge and New York: Cambridge University Press, 1980.
Woodard, T. M., ed. *Sophocles: A Collection of Critical Essays*. Englewood Cliffs, N.J.: Prentice-Hall, 1966.

II. *Selected general treatments of Greek tragedy.*

Easterling, P. E., ed. *The Cambridge Companion to Greek Tragedy*. Cambridge: Cambridge University Press, 1997.
Else, Gerald F. *The Origin and Early Form of Greek Tragedy*. Martin Classical Lectures, Vol. 20. Cambridge: Harvard University Press, 1965.
Knox, B. M. W. *Word and Action: Essays on the Ancient Theater*. Baltimore and London: The Johns Hopkins University Press, 1979.

Kott, Jan. *The Eating of the Gods: An Interpretation of Greek Tragedy*. New York: Random House, 1973.

Rehm, Rush. *Greek Tragic Theatre*. London and New York: Routledge, 1992.

Steiner, George. *The Death of Tragedy*. New York: Alfred A. Knopf; London: Faber and Faber, 1961.

Taplin, Oliver. *Greek Tragedy in Action*. Berkeley and Los Angeles: University of California Press; London: Methuen, 1978.

Vickers, Brian. *Towards Greek Tragedy: Drama, Myth, Society*. London: Longman, 1973.

Walcot, Peter. *Greek Drama in Its Theatrical and Social Context*. Cardiff: University of Wales Press, 1976.

Winkler, John J., and Froma Zeitlin, eds. *Nothing to Do with Dionysus? Athenian Drama in Its Social Context*. Princeton: Princeton University Press, 1990.

THE GENEALOGY OF OEDIPUS
ACCORDING TO SOPHOCLES

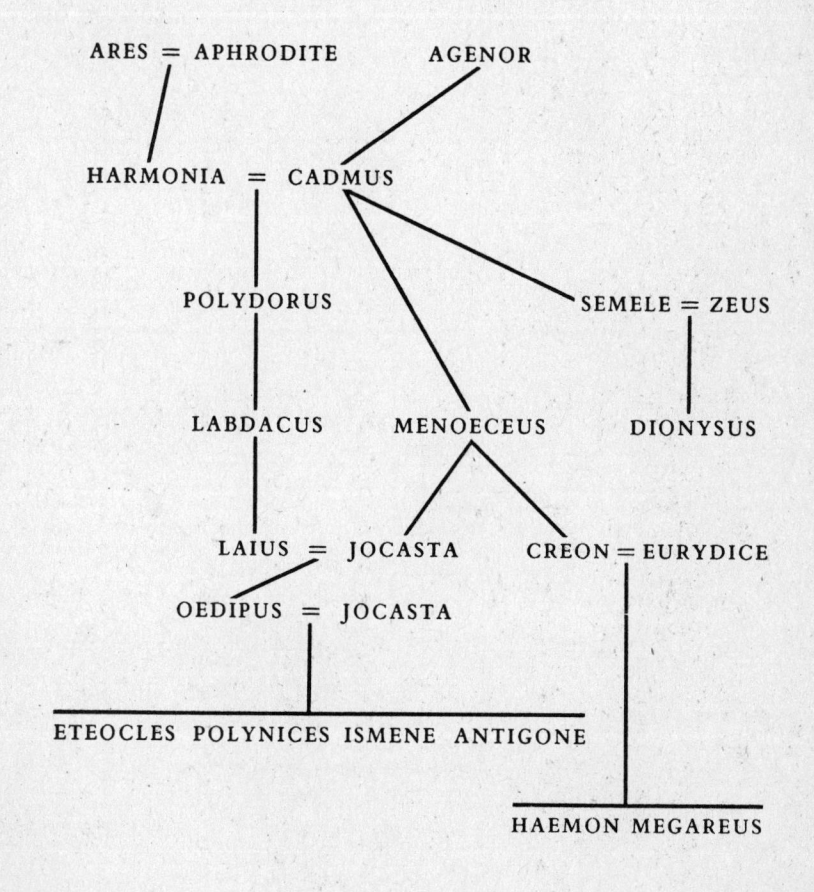

```
ARES = APHRODITE        AGENOR
         |                 \
         |                  \
HARMONIA  =  CADMUS
             |    \
             |     \
         POLYDORUS  \
             |       SEMELE = ZEUS
             |                  |
         LABDACUS   MENOECEUS   DIONYSUS
             |         / \
             |        /   \
          LAIUS = JOCASTA  CREON = EURYDICE
             |                       |
         OEDIPUS = JOCASTA           |
                |                    |
   ─────────────────────────        |
   ETEOCLES POLYNICES ISMENE ANTIGONE
                                     |
                              ──────────────
                              HAEMON MEGAREUS
```

GLOSSARY

ABAE: site of an oracle of Apollo, located north of Thebes.
ACHERON: one of the rivers of the lower world.
AEGEUS: king of Athens, father of Theseus.
AGENOR: father of Cadmus, who founded Thebes.
ANTIGONE: daughter of Oedipus and Jocasta.
APHRODITE: the love goddess, daughter of Zeus.
APOLLO: son of Zeus, he is a prophet (Delphi the most important of his oracular sites), a healer (in this capacity he is sometimes addressed as *Paian*) and a patron of the arts (especially poetry and music).
ARCTURUS: the brightest star in the constellation Boötes, its reappearance in the autumn sky marked the beginning of the winter season for the Greeks.
ARES: the war god, he is particularly associated with Thrace, the barbarous territory to the north of Greece; he is also a patron deity of Thebes.
ARGOS: a powerful city of the Peloponnese, it sent the Seven Champions against Thebes.
ARTEMIS: daughter of Zeus, virgin goddess and protector of wild animals.
ATHENA (sometimes known as Pallas): virgin daughter of Zeus, she is the patron of the domestic arts and comes to be thought of as the embodiment of wisdom and moderation. She is the protecting divinity of Athens.
BACCHUS: another name of Dionysus.
CADMUS: founder of Thebes, son of Agenor.
CASTALIA: the sacred spring at Delphi.
CEPHISUS: a river of Attica.
CERBERUS: the three-headed dog that guarded the entrance to Hades.
CITHAERON: the mountain range between Thebes and Corinth on which the baby Oedipus was exposed.
COLONUS: a village to the north of Athens to which the blind Oedipus came in his old age (and where Sophocles was born).

CORINTH: a prosperous seaport on the Gulf of Corinth; home of Polybus and Merope, who brought Oedipus up in ignorance of his real identity.

CREON: brother of Jocasta, he succeeded Oedipus as ruler of Thebes.

DANAË: daughter of Acrisius and mother, by Zeus, of the hero Perseus.

DAULIA: a district north of the road from Thebes to Delphi.

DELOS: a very small island in the center of the Cyclades in the Aegean Sea. Birthplace of Apollo and Artemis, it was sacred to Apollo.

DELPHI: on the north shore of the Corinthian Gulf, site of the most famous oracle of Apollo.

DEMETER: goddess of the grain crops. Together with her daughter Persephone, she was the presiding deity of the Eleusinian mysteries.

DIONYSUS: son of Zeus by Semele, a Theban princess. Dionysus is the god of ecstatic release, especially associated with wine.

DIRCE: a river of Thebes.

ELEUSIS: a city of Attica, site of the celebration of the Eleusinian mysteries.

EROS: son of Aphrodite, the personification of passionate sexual love.

ETEOCLES: son of Oedipus, brother of Antigone.

EUMENIDES: "Kindly Ones," a title given to the Furies at Athens, where they were protective as well as punishing spirits.

EURYDICE: wife of Creon.

FURIES (Erinyes): avenging spirits whose task it is to exact blood for blood when no human avenger is left alive. They are particularly concerned with injuries done by one member of a family to another.

GREAT GODDESSES: the two presiding deities of the Eleusinian mysteries, Demeter and Persephone.

HADES: brother of Zeus and Poseidon, he is the ruler of the underworld, the land of the dead.

HAEMON: son of Creon, betrothed to Antigone.

HECATE: a goddess associated with ghosts and witchcraft. Since crossroads were thought to be haunted places, offerings to her were often placed there.

HERMES: the messenger of the gods. One of his functions is to escort the souls of the dead to the lower world.

IACCHUS: a deity associated with the ritual of the Eleusinian mysteries but often identified with Dionysus.

ISMENE: daughter of Oedipus, sister of Antigone.

ISMENUS: a river of Thebes.

JOCASTA: wife and mother of Oedipus.

GLOSSARY

LABDACUS: father of Laius, grandfather of Oedipus.

LAIUS: father of Oedipus.

LYCURGUS: a king of Thrace who tried to repress the worship of Dionysus and was imprisoned as punishment.

MEGAREUS: son of Creon and Eurydice, killed during the siege of Thebes by the Seven.

MEROPE: queen of Corinth, foster mother of Oedipus.

MOUNT OF ARES (Areopagus): a hill at Athens which was the seat of the first court of law.

NIOBE: a queen of Phrygia in Asia Minor, who boasted that her children were more beautiful than Apollo and Artemis. The two gods killed them all and Niobe wasted away in mourning. A rock in Phrygia which had water running down it was supposed to be Niobe, turned to stone.

NYMPHS: female spirits, long-lived but not immortal, who represent the divine powers of mountains, woods and rivers.

NYSA: a mountain on the island of Euboea, which stretches along the Attic and Boeotian coastlines.

OEDIPUS: son of Laius and Jocasta.

OLYMPIA: a major religious center in the Peloponnese, site of an oracle and temple of Zeus.

OLYMPUS: a mountain mass in northern Greece, where the Olympian gods were supposed to live.

PAN: a god of the uncultivated upland country.

PARNASSUS: a mountain on the north side of the Gulf of Corinth; the oracle at Delphi was situated on its southern slope.

PELOPS: a king who gave his name to the Peloponnese.

PERITHOUS: a hero who accompanied Theseus on his descent to the lower world in an attempt to kidnap Persephone.

PERSEPHONE: daughter of Demeter, queen of the lower world and one of the two divinities of the Eleusinian mysteries.

PHOCIS: the district in central Greece in which Delphi is situated.

PLUTO: one of the names of Hades, the king of the world of the dead.

POLYBUS: king of Corinth, foster father of Oedipus.

POLYDORUS: son of Agenor, great-grandfather of Oedipus.

POLYNICES: son of Oedipus and Jocasta, brother of Antigone.

POSEIDON: brother of Zeus, ruling god of the sea.

SARDIS: capital of the Lydian kingdom, on the coast of Asia Minor, famous for its precious metals.

SEMELE: a Theban princess, the mother of Dionysus by Zeus.

THE SEVEN AGAINST THEBES: a collective title for the Seven Champions, who, led by Polynices, made the unsuccessful assault on the city. The list sometimes varies from one account to another but in the Theban Plays of Sophocles it remains constant. The six warriors who followed Polynices were: AMPHIARAUS, a prophet who foresaw his own death; TYDEUS, son of Oeneus, from the western district of Aetolia; ETEOCLUS (not to be confused with Eteocles); HIPPOMEDON, son of Talaus; CAPANEUS, the fiercest of the Seven—his storming of the walls and destruction by the thunderbolt of Zeus is alluded to in *Antigone* 141–52; PARTHENOPEUS, from Arcadia, son of Atalanta.

SPHINX: a winged monster with a human, female face, which devoured young men who failed to answer her riddle.

TANTALUS: king of Phrygia, father of Pelops.

TARTARUS: the lower depths of the house of Hades, the kingdom of the dead.

THEBES: the principal city of the Boeotian plain.

THESEUS: king of Athens, he welcomes Oedipus to Colonus.

THRACE: the area to the north of Greece, inhabited by uncivilized tribes.

TIRESIAS: a blind Theban prophet.

ZEUS: supreme ruler of the gods and father of many of them. He is referred to under many different titles. As *Chthonios*, he is an underworld divinity; as *Herkeios*, the protector of the hearth and the family; as *Homaimos*, the god of blood relationships; as *Morios*, the protector of the olive trees of Attica; and as *Tropaios*, the god who presides over the decisive moment in battle when one side turns to flee.

FOR THE BEST IN PAPERBACKS, LOOK FOR THE 🐧

In every corner of the world, on every subject under the sun, Penguin represents quality and variety—the very best in publishing today.

For complete information about books available from Penguin—including Penguin Classics, Penguin Compass, and Puffins—and how to order them, write to us at the appropriate address below. Please note that for copyright reasons the selection of books varies from country to country.

In the United States: Please write to *Penguin Group (USA), P.O. Box 12289 Dept. B, Newark, New Jersey 07101-5289* or call 1-800-788-6262.

In the United Kingdom: Please write to *Dept. EP, Penguin Books Ltd, Bath Road, Harmondsworth, West Drayton, Middlesex UB7 0DA.*

In Canada: Please write to *Penguin Books Canada Ltd, 10 Alcorn Avenue, Suite 300, Toronto, Ontario M4V 3B2.*

In Australia: Please write to *Penguin Books Australia Ltd, P.O. Box 257, Ringwood, Victoria 3134.*

In New Zealand: Please write to *Penguin Books (NZ) Ltd, Private Bag 102902, North Shore Mail Centre, Auckland 10.*

In India: Please write to *Penguin Books India Pvt Ltd, 11 Panchsheel Shopping Centre, Panchsheel Park, New Delhi 110 017.*

In the Netherlands: Please write to *Penguin Books Netherlands bv, Postbus 3507, NL-1001 AH Amsterdam.*

In Germany: Please write to *Penguin Books Deutschland GmbH, Metzlerstrasse 26, 60594 Frankfurt am Main.*

In Spain: Please write to *Penguin Books S. A., Bravo Murillo 19, 1° B, 28015 Madrid.*

In Italy: Please write to *Penguin Italia s.r.l., Via Benedetto Croce 2, 20094 Corsico, Milano.*

In France: Please write to *Penguin France, Le Carré Wilson, 62 rue Benjamin Baillaud, 31500 Toulouse.*

In Japan: Please write to *Penguin Books Japan Ltd, Kaneko Building, 2-3-25 Koraku, Bunkyo-Ku, Tokyo 112.*

In South Africa: Please write to *Penguin Books South Africa (Pty) Ltd, Private Bag X14, Parkview, 2122 Johannesburg.*